A Man and his Horse

Xie Wenwei

Published by
ACA Publishing Ltd.
University House
11-13 Lower Grosvenor Place
London SW1W 0EX, UK
Tel: +44 (0)20 7834 7676
Fax: +44 (0)20 7973 0076
Email: info@alaincharlesasia.com
Web:www.alaincharlesasia.com
Beijing Office
Tel: +86(0)10 8472 1250
Fax: +86(0)10 5885 0639

Author: Xie Wenwei
Translator: Wang Chiying
Editor: David Lammie
Cover art: Daniel Li

Published by ACA Publishing Ltd in association
with the New World Press

ISBN 978-1-910760-44-4

A catalogue record for *A Man and His Horse* is available from the National
Bibliographic Service of the British Library.

Contents

Preface

I spent the whole of 2014, the year of the horse according to the Chinese zodiac, writing the story of me and Little Black. Of course, it brought back memories of my life at the Inner Mongolia Production and Construction Corps, including my first love. Four decades have passed since I left the Corps, but Little Black has never left my heart. My memories of the horse forced me to travel to Inner Mongolia a decade ago just to look for her. In the vast prairie, however, it was hard to find any vestige of Little Black, which gave me ample cause for melancholy and pain.

The year of the horse made me miss her all the more. The moment I closed my eyes, the image of Little Black dashing in the wilderness would appear. I could see her shiny black hair, a lithe and robust figure with an agile and free gait. During the hardest period of my life, Little Black gave me courage and strength. She befriended me and loved me, and enabled me to keep going even during the most depressing times. When I was walking in the valley of the shadow of death, she empowered me to break through confusion and bewilderment, and persevere with a positive attitude. In those days of injustice, she carried me from darkness to light and from setbacks to glory.

My wife best understands my special feelings for Little Black. Before the start of the year of the horse, she bought a precious gift for my sixty-fifth birthday. It came in a huge box. She spent half a day just assembling the contents before placing the gift at the turn of the staircase. When I returned home from work at the hospital and saw it for the first time, the lovely surprise touched me to the quick. The little black horse of the grassland was now right here in my home. I could see her every time I went up or down the stairs and I would routinely greet her in an endearing tone of voice. Hence, the year of the horse became a year of many thoughts, a year that brought me back to that special era – those tender, unforgettable days as an 'educated youth'. As I strived to place myself back in time, memories flooded back as the scenes of my younger days loomed larger and larger. I kept typing day and night and words began gushing out like an endless stream.

Chapter 1

Years of Innocence

I was born in 1949, the year the People's Republic of China was founded, on the eve of the lunar new year. In my younger days I used to brag about that fact, thinking that only great men could be born on such a special day. Only decades later did I realise my birthday rather faded into insignificance because of the annual Chinese new year's eve dinner. I hardly had any birthday celebrations at all. And, because I was born at the end of the lunar year, it was hard to determine whether I was an ox or a rat according to the Chinese zodiac. When relatives joked about me being 'a hair on the tip of a rat's tail', my dad would come to the rescue, claiming that because spring had started when I was born, local custom determined that I was in fact an ox, though in all good conscience I felt that did not make sense. The subject remained a mystery until I met with a fortune-teller. Depending on the specific time of birth of the year, he said, the ox and the rat actually experienced utterly different fortunes.

The seemingly knowledgeable fortune-teller sized me up with his eyes half closed and asked: "Have you ever sprained your ankle?"

I tilted my head to one side to consider, and then nodded emphatically – yes, as a sports fanatic I was prone to spraining my ankle. The fortune-teller immediately concluded I was born in the year of the ox.

As if to substantiate that conclusion, my mum said that my due date fell within the year of the ox. On the day I was born, she said, she had exhausted herself helping Dad sort and shelve books. By evening, while playing cards with friends, she began to feel spasms of abdominal pain and was rushed to hospital. I was born premature by about one month, she said. I got the pet name 'Xiaoxiao' (meaning 'small') because I weighed just two kilograms.

This narrative actually serves little purpose but to clarify one thing: it took a miracle for me to survive because I was born before being fully developed in the womb. Congenital deficiency meant that I was going to be a weakling. If born during a major war or catastrophe, I could have died prematurely or ended up being abandoned. Even in times of peace, I would not be immune from falling victim to bullies. Assuming I worked really hard and had the backing of powerful friends along the way, I stood a slim chance of having a moderately successful career after going through many trials and tribulations.

I have only a few vague memories of my early childhood. My impression was that I lived in a large building in Shanghai with a big gallery connected with several doors that led to a bedroom, study, balcony, bathroom and kitchen. Besides a couch used for receiving guests, the gallery was furnished with a long dinner table laid with British-made cutlery. Through a back door, the gallery was connected to a large balcony that could be used to spend time with guests or to stay cool in summer. The balcony had windows on all sides. A side door served as an exit to a spiral staircase that stretched out into the garden. Mum later told me the building was none other than Merryfield Mansion. I dimly recall walking from the gallery into a small room, inside which stood a large bamboo basket filled with all kinds of toys. I would typically throw one toy into the basket and then pick up another before staggering out of the room.

This may well be the only thing I can remember about our apartment in Shanghai. Thereafter, I went to Beijing with my parents and two nannies, Ah San and Dan Bao, who were from Nanxun, Zhejiang province. Hiring nannies from Nanxun might have been a family tradition, due to the fact that my ancestors were rich and powerful people from that area.

My parents never discussed that part of my family history, and they seemed intent on keeping it that way. Being brought up by nannies was nothing honourable in the first few years of the new republic. It created nothing but jealousy from neighbouring children – so much so that I dared not even go out on the streets alone. The wilder kids would pelt me with rocks and clods of mud as they yelled out my nickname 'Little Master', which meant something similar to 'local tyrant and evil gentry'. On the other hand, congenital deficiency and physical infirmity made me a recipient of excessive care and pampering. The two nannies took turns taking care of me all day long, something that had a lasting influence on me. For example, the Shanghai dialect I speak today is mixed with a Nanxun accent. At bedtime, they patted me gently as they sang melodious Jiangnan lullabies. One of the lullabies had a simple line that I still remember today: "This sweetheart will soon fall asleep..."

I led a privileged and spoiled life as a child but began to feel my limitations as I started mixing in society. At six, I was sent to a reputable kindergarten where I spent most of my time playing alone in a corner. I was reticent and soft-spoken. I knew I had to guard myself against bullies, but never imagined I could be bullied by girls. At the kindergarten there was one particular boy who wore spectacles, and he had a brawny sister. The brother looked frail and skinny, while the sister was a tomboy who often wrestled and messed around with boys without any concern for the differences of gender.

This boy regarded me as something of a younger brother, which explains why I enjoyed playing with him. But one day, the girl suddenly jumped in front of me and gave me a dirty look, blaming me for picking on her brother. Not knowing how to argue my case, I lost my nerve and ran straight out of the kindergarten into the primary school. Following close behind, she was on the point of catching me when I abruptly turned into the boys' toilet. Instead of giving up, she waited patiently outside until all of the bigger boys had left and I was the only one there. She then stormed in, grabbed me by the collar and dragged me out into a quiet corner where she slapped my face more than a dozen times. She then strode off singing and hopping. I was mortified as I tried to soothe the pain of my reddened face.

That was the first time I had experienced such an affront. Being timid and shy, I dared not tell my teachers or parents about what I was going through but quietly suffered my grievances. This eventually led to a permanent spiritual trauma. According to Sigmund Freud, the grandfather of psychology, psychological trauma sustained during childhood can subconsciously affect a person for life. This was definitely the case for me.

From then on, I began to fear girls, especially termagants. And without knowing why, this fear later turned into reverence. After completing kindergarten, I went to Huiwen primary school, where several girl classmates came from privileged families. I lived in a bungalow with a courtyard of its own, while two of my female classmates whom I adored lived in tall mansions. One of them lived in a mansion right next to the *hutong* where I lived. She had a fair and healthy complexion and learned how to play the piano at a very young age. We often went to school and back together. Quiet and serious, often knitting her eyebrows, she seemed to have a frail personality like mine. Therefore, just as identical charges repel each other, we did not quite gel, and her beauty did not appeal to me. If we hung out together, we would both end up being bullied. I was in no position to protect her. Because of my prenatal deficiency and frailty, I instinctively sought friendships with girls who were more robust. I was drawn to the strong and had a particular desire for Amazonian types.

Another girl whom I had a crush on lived in a western-style mansion near Chongwenmen in the southeastern part of central Beijing. I was infatuated with her during my last two years of primary school. Though she wasn't exactly beautiful, she had a pair of shining and delightfully eloquent eyes. My heart would skip a beat when our eyes met, and I would bow my head out of bashfulness. She was an 'A' student and outstanding in sports. Healthy, strong and agile, she won all the sprint races on sports day. I seldom saw her practise at all. Her running prowess seemed to be innate. I enjoyed seeing her run and I watched her avidly in all of her races. My heart would leap with joy every time she reached the finish line, and I would replay those scenes in my mind for many days to come. She was an unparalleled goddess in my heart.

Cowardice prevented me from revealing my feelings for her. A popular approach in those days was to hand out a note, but I dared not even do that. Instead, I would follow her on my way home and watch her walk into that small mansion before I would continue on to my own house. I did that on numerous occasions.

I had only one face-to-face encounter with her, on the day of graduation from primary school. I was moving on to the No. 2 Boys' Junior High School while she was going to attend the No. 12 Girls' Junior High School. Sensing the impending separation, all students in my class suddenly ignored the gender barrier and started fooling around in the classroom, thus leading to physical contact between classmates of the opposite sex. I got caught up in this too, and dumbly reached out to grab at my idol, but ended up brushing her eyes, causing her to blink. She was not badly hurt but she moved to sit on a desk and buried her head in her arms.

I panicked and was at a loss what to do next. I stood stupefied in front of her, without uttering a word of comfort or apology. I had no way of knowing whether she was aware of my crush on her and the fact that I had followed her home. Nor did I know whether she was waiting for me to take some action. After all, how was a twelve-year-old boy supposed to understand a girl's heart? My hesitance finally got to her and led her to do something that shocked everyone. She threw herself in front of me and slapped me twice on the face before picking up her schoolbag and vanishing. She was gone, and I was never to see her again. In future, there would be a distance of only a couple of bus stops between the two schools and I deliberately walked past her school on countless occasions in the hope of seeing her and expressing my overdue apology. But Providence never granted me such an opportunity.

I was just an inconspicuous boy, while my idol was the class beauty. I was among the last batch of students to become communist young pioneers, in fourth grade. We were the most 'backward' and mischievous elements. I did not belong to either of these categories, since I was shy and retiring, and often hung my head and whispered like a mosquito when answering the teachers' questions. Therefore I was easily ignored and neglected by my teachers. My frail physique and lack of talent made me look like a doormat that even girls could trample on. Fortunately, my male classmates often stepped in to protect me instead of bullying me.

During this time, I was putting on more height than weight, which made me look even more lean and fragile. This factor, combined with my apparently simple and honest personality, meant I could hardly avoid being hounded by some of the bullies. In a small alley near my house lived a wild kid known as 'Silly Bald', who had bulging biceps and absolutely no hair on his head. Though still a child, he had a deep voice and pronounced vertical wrinkles on his face. Each encounter with Silly Bald was a misfortune for me. He would always pick a fight or bully me one way or another. Timid by nature, I simply absorbed whatever came my way, without telling any adult about it.

One day, on my way back home after buying rice from a store, I bumped into Silly Bald. I was already struggling to carry the ten kilogram bag. He came over with a cynical grin on his face and a vicious look in his eyes. He pushed me up against a wall, pulled a needle out of his pocket and brandished it before my eyes. He was trying to stab me in the face, or at least scare me, and he seemed to enjoy seeing me squirm before him.

Fortunately, my neighbour Madam Chen saw it all, stopped Silly Bald and told my mum about it. Mum put on her army uniform and went straight to Silly Bald's house, where she found out he was living with his grandma because his parents worked far away from home. He had fallen into hooliganism after being expelled from school for brawling. But Mum formed a good impression of him and believed him when he bowed deeply to her and pledged never to bully me again.

But he was actually lying and went back to his bullying ways until I was about to graduate from primary school. On the morning of my last day at primary school, I met Silly Bald on my way to school again. He slapped me hard on the face, leaving a clear impression of five fingers. My classmates were outraged and wanted to settle the matter with him. Several of the bolder ones walked in front of me as I pointed out Silly Bald to them. My classmates then went forward to block his path while I hid behind a tree. But no fight ensued because sneaky Silly Bald told them they were looking for the wrong person. Taking him at his word, my credulous classmates let go of him and left me vulnerable to future trouble.

In the days to come, I no longer had the protection of my male classmates as Silly Bald sought revenge. Every time I saw him in the distance I would go into hiding like a frightened fowl before a hunter. The No. 2 Boys' Junior High School was just a few blocks from my home and I travelled there by bike. One day, straight after I got on the bike, I felt a hand grabbing the bike's rear rack. It was Silly Bald. I tried to move on but couldn't get going. So I had to stop and get back on again. But each time I was ready to pedal, he would grab my bike again to halt my progress. Worried about being late for school, I felt cornered and incensed. I could tolerate him no more. In an unprecedented burst of anger, I channelled years of abuse and humiliation into an unexpected compulsion to fight back. I threw my bike and schoolbag to the roadside, thrust myself in front of him, and started punching him like crazy. Silly Bald was taken aback by my sudden resistance. He used one hand to block my *wangba quan* (turtle fist) and the other to hit me on the chin with a hook. By then I had grown taller than Silly Bald and my arms were long enough to overwhelm him even though I was only using my irregular turtle fists to deal with him. His fists barely reached me at all as my hands kept flying in front of his eyes. He started retreating as I advanced step by step and finally hit him in the face – once, twice, three times. Years of suppressed anger had found a release. The scuffle did not end until several women on the street began screaming.

After that, Silly Bald never bothered me again, not even daring to look me in my eyes. Sometime later, he seemed to disappear altogether and I never got to see him again. Still later, I got word that he was sent to a youth detention centre. Nevertheless, my first act of resistance demonstrated my capacity for courage. When pressed to the extreme, my dormant masculinity would burst out. Although I remained fearful of strong-minded girls, I could now easily stand up to male bullies. Whom would I fear now that I knew I could subdue even a hooligan such as Silly Bald?

My path from cowardice to courage was probably a consequence of my secure home life, which was infused with a gentle and kind atmosphere from the beginning. After moving from Shanghai to Beijing, we lived in a detached but dilapidated courtyard my dad had rented near Beijing railway station. Despite its large area with a forecourt, backyard, kitchen and eight other rooms of various size, the house always seemed to be in need of repair.

The landlord was a sole proprietor who charged a monthly rent of forty-two yuan. Actually, the initial rent was forty yuan. In 1959, the year of the 'natural disaster', a scruffy and skinny middle-aged man came pestering my dad for a rent increase. My dad disagreed, arguing that it was already on the high side. I reckoned that the landlord probably wanted to add just a couple of more yuan and I was right. My dad agreed to the deal immediately.

Having lived there for over twenty years, I can still picture that courtyard whenever I close my eyes. On summer nights, we used to stay out for the cool and enjoy the sweetness of the flowers carried over by the gentle breeze. Between five and six I would sit on a stool to hear my dad tell stories from *Outlaws of the Marsh* and *Three Kingdoms*. Among southerners, Dad could be regarded as tall. He had good looks, bright and intelligent eyes, and a fair complexion. He spoke loudly and vividly like a born storyteller, and he often switched between Mandarin and Shanghai dialect. I was enraptured by his graphic descriptions coupled with rich facial expressions and different postures. With no television and few other forms of entertainment, my greatest fun was to hear Dad tell stories. Every day after dinner, I would sit on the stool and wait eagerly for him to begin. The moment he opened his mouth I would be completely rapt, and my eyes would gleam with excitement. The end of a chapter was usually the most disappointing part since it typically meant time for bed. It was like seeing a huge plate of delicious food removed when I was still in the middle of enjoying it. I would then beseech him for an extra story, which would be granted only if it was a Saturday and when he was in a good mood.

A political campaign came in the summer of 1955, when Dad was done with *Outlaws of the Marsh* and had finished several chapters of *Three Kingdoms*. From then on, he stopped story-telling altogether, not because he had no time, but because he had become an utterly different person, with anguish and melancholy written on his face. Sometime later, he was no longer around and I waited anxiously for him to show up and continue with stories from *Three Kingdoms*. I kept asking those around me where he had been and when he would return. The answers were all vague and uncertain. My mum's face was clouded over with worry, and her eyes were wet with tears. The elderly nurse Ah San, who had raised Dad, was deeply attached to him. She sighed and groaned deeply, and kept praying for him in secret. All these signs made me realise the serious nature of his case.

Then, one day, Dad's employer sent an amiable man to our house to give us Dad's salary for three months and to tell us the good news of his imminent return. This dispersed all feelings of nervousness and fear in the home. The following day, Dad came back as expected, and I saw his usual self again, even though three months' isolated investigation made him quieter and more cautious and sensitive about political topics. He rarely visited anyone and chose to stay home reading and listening to classical music. However, as an intellectual, he needed a channel to express his thoughts.

Over the next ten years, Dad got used to being confined to home. Several of his old friends would still come to visit and they enjoyed hearing him analyse current affairs at home and abroad, and appreciated his views on politics. On such occasions, he would open up and chat to his heart's content. In his happier moments, he would stand up like a great man with one hand in his pocket, and the other gesturing. Carried away by his own eloquence, he would talk and talk and give no opportunity for other people to cut in. As a keen and faithful listener, I witnessed how his resourceful mind was able to generate unstoppable currents of thought and express them clearly and precisely.

My dad's intellect must have been outstanding, even though it had never been measured. Skipping grades from primary school to high school, he remained a top student right up to his years at St John's University in Shanghai during the 1930s. He had a photographic memory. He could easily decipher books that I failed to comprehend, and while retelling stories, he could present details in a way that was no less compelling than a film director. In his most captivating moments, he would go out of his way to recite a Tang dynasty (618-907) poem. The cadence of his Shanghai dialect was so absorbing that I often felt as if I were enjoying a local opera.

When I had a question, Dad did not stop to give me the perfect answer but would patiently explain the complexities of the subject. On seeing the confused expression on my face, Mum would smile and say in Shanghai dialect: "That's enough. He won't get it all."

With the advent of various political movements, Dad keenly felt that thorough analysis of social issues posed a risk to us children and could even bring disaster to the family as a whole. So he repeatedly told me to stay away from politics, to lie low and play dumb in all political activities. In my father's eyes, developing a work skill mattered more than anything else. So he asked me to learn different areas of expertise, retain as much knowledge as possible and get a professional skill.

As I grew older, political campaigns came along in succession, each larger in scale than the previous one. At the age of seventeen, I encountered the country's largest and most soul-stirring political movement that involved each and every individual. During the first few months, I felt happy and excited about it because I could get out of the classroom, enjoy free train rides and visit other parts of the country. The most fun part of it was the liberty I experienced in using a writing brush to write large-character posters and putting them up in public forums. In the later stages of the campaign, however, when we got less busy, we would have difficulty finding books to read because anything of interest was likely burned during the 'Fight against the Four Olds' (Old Customs, Old Culture, Old Habits and Old Ideas). I began to feel a sense of panic as my yearning for knowledge grew. What worried me most was a hunch that I would shortly leave school and be sent for hard manual labour in a new and unknown place.

Chapter 2

Aged Twenty

If the memories of my age of innocence were vague and piecemeal, those of life after the age of twenty were crystal clear. All those who went through that era had painful experiences of their own. The kind of physical and spiritual trauma that they went through was most likely deep-rooted and long-lasting. My own experience was not particularly bloody or tragic, thanks to my dad's advice to avoid political storms and live humbly in places as far away from politics as possible. So I was indeed fortunate compared with many of my peers, though I did suffer poverty and spiritual buffeting as I whiled away my time with a horse on a grassy, salty land during the prime of my life, when all this time I should have been gaining knowledge in the classroom.

The year 1969 marked the peak of a revolution that involved China's entire population of 600 million. I was twenty years old, an age when I should have been in college, but all the schools across the country had been closed. All those of my age and with good family origins, known as the 'five red categories', chose to play an active role in that movement. The 'five red', including revolutionary officials, revolutionary soldiers, workers, and poor and lower-middle peasants, served as its backbone. Those whose family origins belonged to the 'five black categories', namely, landlords, rich peasants, counter-revolutionaries, rightists and capitalists, were barred from saying or doing anything without approval because they were targets of the revolution.

At first, I filled out 'office clerk' in the family origin column of my background forms so that I would be regarded as being worthy of joining the revolutionary ranks and thereby avoid being targeted. I was actually doing my dad's bidding because I knew he wanted the best for all our family. I was also aware of the fact that my dad never had any permanent job before 1949 because my grandfather was a prominent capitalist who owned Shanghai's first knitting factory. However, Dad's interests lay in books and social issues rather than business. He had published a number of articles in some underground publications that criticised social evils. Grandpa would never force Dad into doing anything. To provide Dad with a decent monthly income, Grandpa simply gave him the nominal title of general manager in a family-owned pharmaceutical factory. Since he was never directly involved in the daily operations of the factory, and nor did he own any shares in the business, Dad felt that he could reasonably be regarded as a clerk rather than a capitalist. So it was not unreasonable for him to suggest we enter 'clerk' in the family background columns in various forms.

By the third year of the political movement, however, officials from my father's employer suddenly descended on my family. They came in a big truck and began swarming in as soon as they arrived at our house. Looking furious and combative, they set about putting Dad and Grandma in one room and us kids in another. A few of them lectured the whole family while others busied themselves rummaging through the chests, cabinets and drawers for valuables, some of which they wrapped in parcels of various sizes and threw onto the truck. Precious gems such as diamond rings and emeralds that belonged to Grandma were bagged and packed into a leather briefcase and then taken away. Less valuable things such as items of daily use were placed in boxes before being sealed. As if to add to our hurt, they put up a huge poster on our doorpost that read, 'Down with capitalist XX!', with 'XX' standing for Dad's name. The poster was reminiscent of the scarlet tattoos carved in the faces of criminals in ancient times. From then on, the whole family had to live like second-class citizens. Since there was no toilet in our house, we had to relieve ourselves in the public facility opposite. Each time we went outdoors we would see that prominent poster and face the hateful and contemptuous looks of our neighbours. So we had to lower our heads, go to the toilet quietly and then return as fast as we could. Later, I would even try to refrain from going to the toilet during the daytime. The poster was giving me so much trouble that I discouraged my classmates from visiting our home, for fear that they might raise the issue of my family background.

Over time, the upper part of the poster began to peel off. So I purposely decided to go to the toilet late at night. When nobody was around, I gently lifted the top part of the poster so that it began to sag down a little more as the days went by. Finally, one day, a strong gust of wind blew the poster away. A heavy load that had been weighing on my mind was finally lifted.

Thereafter, I had to write 'capitalist' instead of 'clerk' in the family background columns in various work forms, effectively labelling myself a member of the 'black five'. By official decree, we high school students were forced to 'graduate' and seek job placements even though we had just finished first year. All jobs back then were assigned on the basis of on an applicant's family background. The first batch of 'red fives' all joined the army. Dressed in green uniforms and decked in red flowers, they were the ones who would march out of campus proudly singing the military anthem *March of the PLA*. I was filled with envy, but I could not even dream of joining the army. My mum had been an army woman but she was in detention at the time. The second batch of my classmates got hired by factories in Beijing. All 'red fives' were qualified for factory jobs. Even clerks or small business owners who were 'redeemable' would get opportunities. In other words, I was beyond all hope now that I was a 'black five'.

I thought I would most likely be assigned to the Inner Mongolia Production and Construction Corps because it was open to students from every family background except 'class enemy'. And it was my heart's desire to go there too. But I was naïve in ignoring the fact that my parents were still locked up as enemies of the people. My name did not show up on the approved list even though I was the first in my class to sign up for the Corps. I could only see a bleak future ahead of me.

If I couldn't go to Inner Mongolia, my next alternative would be the Yunnan Corps, which was even farther away from Beijing. I didn't want to go there because it would take days and nights of travel even by train. Other alternatives would be to settle down in a production brigade in rural Inner Mongolia or northern Shaanxi province and make a living as a farmer. However, that would provide no guarantee of sustenance because, if I got caught up in a famine, I might starve to death. After much deliberation, I decided that the Inner Mongolia Corps was the best option because it offered a collective, military lifestyle and a partial rations supply system through which my daily needs would be met. The drawback of my plan was a lack of official approval.

Grandma and we three kids were then living on a stipend of twenty yuan a month in a *hutong* near Beijing railway station. So we had to tighten our belts and eat only carbohydrates. All our personal belongings having been confiscated, each of us was left with a single set of patched clothes that had faded due to frequent washing. Sometimes, when acquaintances unfamiliar with our situation came to visit, they would find out what we were going through just by seeing our living conditions. After exchanging a few words with us, they would then take off immediately to avoid becoming involved in any trouble.

In those days, staying home was no different from being locked up in jail. My only distraction was to take a walk alone in and around the railway station after dinner, and my way of escape from contemptuous looks around me was to hang around streams of strangers who had no way of knowing anything about my family background.

I saw travellers eating simple meals in crowded roadside restaurants. Fifteen-cent 'ants on a tree' (minced meat sautéed with vermicelli), a two-cent bowl of rice and a three-cent bowl of soup with chopped spring onions and soy sauce would have been a banquet for me, but I could not afford such dishes for a long time to come. After swallowing a mouthful of saliva, I walked around the station before finally deciding to enter. I paced back and forth in the crowded station hall, walked around the passageway surrounded with circular handrails on the second floor, and kept ruminating on the paths of my life. I could see no future and no way out for myself in an isolated world where I had no one to talk to. Like a headless chicken, I was wandering in circles in the big waiting hall of Beijing railway station.

Ever since my father was labelled a capitalist in the posted slogan at our door, I began to confine myself to the house so as to avoid interacting with people. Every time a high school classmate came to see me, I would retreat to an inner room and shove my sister out to tell them I wasn't home. For a long time, I seldom went to school. And even when I did, I would just show up to find out what was going on and then head straight back home. I had become a loner. At a key moment in my destiny, however, I felt the need to consult my classmates and seek their help. I thought of two of my junior high school friends who used to be my deskmates. One was called Chen Hua and the other Li Qin. I went to junior high school during the preliminary stage of the political campaign, when no factions had been formed to fight against one another. I always thought friendships built while studying and living together would be pure, sincere and true. This was especially the case at the No.2 Boys' Junior High School, which had a great learning environment. I would think of those friends whenever I felt isolated and helpless. Maybe due to my withdrawn personality, I did not have many friends back then. Few teachers or students knew me. Only those who had shared a desk managed to develop a deep and close relationship with me. Chen and Li were definitely my closest friends.

Chen and I shared the same desk during the second year of junior high. Warm-hearted and well-organised, Chen was in charge of physical education in the class. He was a good-looking young man with bushy eyebrows and thick lips. By contrast, I had a poor physique and often looked frail and sickly. My sinuses would get infected whenever I got the flu. To treat the condition, I had to visit the Army Hospital (predecessor of the General Hospital of Beijing military region) for physical therapy, even though it wasn't very effective. Chen suggested regular exercise and I chose to go running in the morning. My sinuses got better after I had been running consistently for just one month. From then on, I became addicted to long-distance running, but due to my physical problems I was only able to achieve mediocre results. At sports events during the second and third years of junior high, I came sixth in the 400 metres, but I often fell seriously ill afterwards.

Chen had a passion for literature at school. He practised fiction writing by imitating established writers. I found his compositions absorbing. His wartime stories had an appealing uniqueness though they were not exactly faithful to the topic given to us by our Chinese teacher. However, the writings that Chen were proudest of did not impress the teacher. He got no more than a 'C' grade, which made him very depressed. Since then, he stopped writing fiction and began regular compositions that earned him one 'A' after another.

During the 'unprecedented' political campaign, Chen frequently rode his bike to see me. As a student at the school affiliated to Tsinghua University, he had access to lots of information. I was interested in hearing him talk about various things that were happening on campus. Sometimes we would cycle to the university to read 'big character posters' early in the morning, have lunch there at noon and then cycle back home by dusk.

With a strong build and large eyes under thick eyebrows, Li Qin looked impressively masculine. We were deskmates during the last term of third grade in junior high school. I saw him a lot even during the idle period of the political campaign. When it was time to apply for admission to senior high school, I thought he would choose No.2 Senior High School because his father was a history teacher there. To my surprise, he refused to use that connection, but chose an even better school and got enrolled. So I deeply admired him for his drive and independence.

I went to seek Chen's advice at his house in Dongdan, but his mother told me he had already settled down in rural Shaanxi province. And then I found out from Li's mum that Li had settled down in Yan'an, also in Shaanxi province, which was quite shocking to me because I would never have thought of doing that myself. Li's mum and I talked for a good two hours. Sensing that I was much more vulnerable than her son, she felt sorry for me because of the difficult personal circumstances my family faced. So she gave me his address in Yan'an and told me to go to him for shelter if I needed somewhere to stay. I felt encouraged and strengthened, and ready to venture into the world alone now that I had something to hang onto.

The night after the visit there was a thunderstorm. I again went wandering in the hall of Beijing railway station. Emboldened by having Li Qin's address, I now had the urge to plan something big and brave, which was quite unusual for a coward like me. I knew my only option was to sneak onto the train and mix among new recruits of the Corps bound for Inner Mongolia. Once I got there, I would pester the authorities for acceptance. They would at least give me food to eat, I thought, and even if I got sent back, I would have evaded the 'tidal waves' that were about to engulf me since the school's next step would be to talk me into joining the Yunnan Corps in the far south. So I made up my mind and stopped prevaricating. I learned that two of the trains carrying recruits to Inner Mongolia had already left and there was only one more remaining, the one that would depart in two days. That would be my last chance.

Chapter 3

Farewell, Mum!

The moment I made up my mind to sneak onto the train to Inner Mongolia, I knew I would have to part with my loved ones. By then, Dad was already at the May Seventh cadre school, a de facto labour camp in Chaling, Hunan province, while Mum remained in custody in a 'cowshed' where victims of the Cultural Revolution were kept. After saying goodbye to my seventy-odd-year-old grandma and my two sisters, I took a bag of Mum's clothes with me and walked from my home near Beijing railway station to the General Hospital of Beijing military region located in Dongsi's Sixth Alleyway where Mum was detained. It would only cost seven cents by bus to get there. But I decided to spend an hour or two walking the road that I had walked countless times in the past. Before leaving for the countryside, I wanted to take one last look at those familiar trees, houses and shops. I wanted to remind myself of the urban environment I grew up in. I began to miss my incarcerated mum as I walked along the pavement. Because she was born into a wealthy family in Shanghai, she was labelled a 'bourgeois lady' in one of the large-character posters targeting her. She graduated from the French-run Aurora University in Shanghai and learned to speak both English and French there. She was an effervescent 'campus belle', and she frequently represented her class to address mass gatherings.

After graduation from college, Mum could have gone to France to work as a registered dietitian, but she chose instead to be a clinical nutritionist in Shanghai's Guangci Hospital. In a large basement ward, she saw gaunt elderly people, ill-nourished children, burns victims and patients in need of surgical wound care. They were all in urgent need of nutrition and care from dieticians, but the hospital only provided such services to wealthy patients in the first-class wards. So she left her job at the hospital. Later on, she took some temporary tutoring and painting work to make some money. In an era of turmoil, she gave up her career and became a full-time homemaker. In that role she assisted Dad in working for the Communist Party. They ran a bookstore that sold progressive underground publications and tried to win over national bourgeoisie to the Communists' side.

After 1949, Mum accompanied Dad to Beijing. The Korean war was causing thousands of casualties, many of whom were sent back to the capital for treatment. The Army Hospital was in desperate need of a nutritionist to help the People's Volunteer Army provide patients with an improved and balanced diet. Mum was able to take on that role. She was energetic, motivated, efficient and creatively effective. She earned the trust and praise from her supervisors and was honoured as an Advanced Worker of Beijing city for three consecutive years. Mum was not part of the army during her first few years of employment in the hospital. It was a time when the People's Liberation Army (PLA) enjoyed high prestige in the minds of the people because of its victories over the Chinese Nationalist government and over US-led UN forces. I myself was a PLA supporter because I had seen so many war films. During my first year in primary school, I had a classmate whose father was a young lieutenant. Wearing an army uniform, he came to school to see his son on a weekly basis. I was filled with envy as I gazed at his uniform. While in second grade, I contracted pneumonia and was admitted to the army hospital. After befriending some other child patients in the same ward, I came to know that their parents were all members of the PLA. How I wished Mum would join too! On the day of my release from hospital, Mum came over to pick me up. The moment I woke up from a siesta, I saw a brand-new army uniform and belt on my bed. She had joined the army! When I checked out the uniform, I saw a bar and three stars on the shoulders. She had been made a captain! I couldn't have been more excited.

Just like the swell of the sea, Mum's career had its fair share of ups and downs. In a sudden turn of events, an unprecedented political storm soon plunged her into a deep valley – she was transformed from a multi-award-winner to the pariah status of a downtrodden 'reactionary academic'. And that was not the end of her misfortune. During the later stage of the campaign, I was sent to work in an orchard in Nanyuan, Beijing. Meanwhile, a group of officers and soldiers from Mum's hospital came in a big truck and broke into our house in the dead of night and confiscated all kinds of valuables before taking Mum away and jailing her in a 'cowshed'. Although the ransacking of homes usually occurred during the drive to 'abolish the Four Olds' in an earlier stage of the campaign, the two raids on our home took place in a later period known as 'purging of the class rank'. I had to start my career at a time when my family fortunes were at their lowest point, so my prospects were doomed.

Admittedly, my own actions during a low ebb of the movement did play an important part in the family's downfall, so guilt and remorse welled up in my heart.

It happened at a time when I was stricken with acute viral myocarditis and had to be hospitalised. Internal Medicine Ward No. 5 of the General Hospital of Beijing military region was originally used for high-ranking officials but was converted to common use during a campaign to fight against privilege. Luckily, I was admitted to a two-bed ward with a toilet and bathroom that only VIPs would have been entitled to in the past. My roommate was the bodyguard of a regional commander with whom I soon became friends. During my first two weeks in hospital, the doctor ordered me to stay in bed. Mum came to see me twice a day and cooked whatever food I would ask for. At that time the movement in military hospitals had just begun, and Mum had only been slightly affected for being a 'liberal' academic. She was still working and in active service. So she could care for me when I was sick.

Two weeks later, my pulse had returned to normal and I began to move around. I paced along the long corridor plastered with large-character posters written by officials, soldiers, medical professionals and, most especially, nursing students. There was a debate going on among these people, and I gradually figured out their divergent views. It was basically a numbers game in which the majority suppressed the minority. The majority consisted of officials, soldiers, lower- and medium-level healthcare professionals and most of the nursing students. The minority comprised a small number of nursing students and they actually had the sympathy of the great majority of workers and senior intellectuals (including Mum), except that they dared not speak out. In that twisted age, it was very hard to tell which faction, whether they were in the majority or not, was right or wrong because the entire society from top to bottom was radicalised. Even such a debate held today would be difficult to judge. Either out of sympathy for the weak or as a result of my subconscious stand on issues, I developed some thoughts on the status of the movement at the hospital that I wanted to express. So I scribbled them down on a yellowing piece of paper that I had picked up somewhere. Contrary to my dad's advice, I jumped into politics head on instead of staying away from it. I can barely remember what I actually wrote, but I know it was an objective, short but in-depth article written in a literary style. My pen name was Wen Bo, a patient of Internal Medicine Ward No. 5.

I put up the small-character poster in a corner of the corridor. As a middle school student, I was curious to know how people would react. I enjoyed the way people read that tiny piece of paper with their eyes wide open and I was eager to hear their comments. To my great surprise, my seemingly mischievous act caused quite a stir at the hospital, and I became well-known overnight. However, Mum paid a huge price for my stupid act and suffered considerably.

The following day, people swarmed around the small poster to copy what I had written. Someone even converted it into a large-character poster and put it up in a prominent spot. In just a few days, more than a dozen large-character posters were created in support of me.

Because they didn't know how old I was, some of the attackers compared me to an old fox hiding in a dark corner. Judged by my writing style, they most likely took me for some crafty big shot. Had they known from the outset I was merely a high school student, they might not have made such a fuss about it. Eventually, most of the hospital staff knew my identity, and a nurse who had been working under Mum put up a banner that labelled me a filial son of the bourgeoisie. But a greater number of people simply admired me for what I did.

The huge effect generated by my small-character poster was entirely determined by the special circumstances of the time. The General Hospital of Beijing military region was in the middle of a kind of tug-of-war, with one faction trying to overpower the other. Because the hospital was affected late on in the movement, my poster stirred up a lot of thinking and served to create waves. In less than a month, the minority faction turned into the majority, and still later, the two factions were locked in a stalemate that lasted for more than a year. Eventually, my mum's opponents won, and she had to suffer the consequences of defeat.

While recalling past events, I subconsciously made my way to the hospital and stopped before an array of bungalows that were used as makeshift cells to jail 'reactionary academic authorities' who were also referred to as 'spirits of evil'. Mum was one of them.

I told the workers' publicity team why I was there. They bid me to sit down on a bench and wait for Mum. The hospital as a whole was filled with an atmosphere of terror and the 'cowshed' was particularly horrifying. I felt it was no different from a regular prison as I sat trembling on the bench. Finally, Mum came out with a sad look in her dull, deep-set eyes. She was not yet fifty, but her hair had turned completely grey.

"How are the rest of the family?" Mum asked in a low voice.

"Fine," I said. "We are all waiting for you to come back home."

I spoke emphatically and slowly, reminding her to hold on and not to give up hope. When I told her that I would be heading for the Inner Mongolia Corps the very next day, she gave a faint smile, probably assuming I had been officially approved. In order not to raise her concerns, I omitted telling her all the details. I handed her the bag of clothes I had brought and touched her hands as a way of saying goodbye. If I had given her a straightforward handshake, the workers' publicity team might have accused me of failing to make a clean break with a 'class enemy'. I saw a twinkling in her eyes the moment I touched her, and I realised she knew I was saying goodbye. And the pain and sorrow in my heart was quelled. Mum was soon told to go, and our conversation had to end.

I now sat face to face with a leader of the workers' publicity team. He was a tall and imposing man with an oblong face and small eyes that resembled a thin line when closed but cast a ray of cruel light when open. His rich and exaggerated facial expressions seemed to indicate he had something to disclose to me, maybe some heinous 'criminal acts' committed by Mum that necessitated my having a clean break with her. The official before me used to be a grassroots cadre from a nearby factory. Now that he was in control of the General Hospital of Beijing military region (a position that would have been beyond him in the past) and able to wield power over 'evil spirits' who were formerly departmental chiefs and scholars, he had every reason to hold his head overbearingly high. Faced with a young man who was here to visit an inmate and now seated timidly before him, he would not miss the opportunity to show off his authority. He lit a cigarette, took a puff and blew out a wisp of smoke. He then lowered his head and blew twice over his freshly brewed cup of tea before picking it up to take a sip.

Finally, he raised his head, took a glance at me and said in a solemn tone: "Before liberation, your mother was quite a character!"

To emphasise what he was saying and to get my attention, he raised his voice and added: "She was quite a big shot."

I fretted, concerned that he would label Mum a spy dispatched by the Kuomintang into the Communist Party. If a Communist Party member like her had been found to have done something inconsistent with her identity, especially under previous regimes, she would have been done for. Once categorised as a class enemy, she would probably never return home again, and my future would be imperilled. So I held my breath and anxiously waited to hear what he would say next.

He took another puff on his cigarette, and then took a sip of tea, as if deliberately withholding what he was trying to say. After glancing at me and clearing his throat, he finally spoke with due cadence and rhythm.

"Your mother used to be quite romantic."

So Mum was not a spy, and therefore not a class enemy! But what did he mean by "romantic" and "big shot"? What kind of person was she anyway? Could she have been a social butterfly, good at building relations with the elite? I held my breath and waited very humbly and patiently for the official to declare his verdict. This overweening man took another puff on his cigarette and blew out a number of smoke rings before taking another big gulp of tea. He held his breath, opened his eyes wide and stared straight at me, reminiscent of Dzerzhinsky in the Russian film *Lenin in 1918*. I became scared again, worried that he might give Mum an even more demeaning label. He cleared his throat and started yelling in an apparent attempt to shock me while maintaining the rhythm of his speech.

"Your mother was a 'college campus belle' before liberation!"

I heaved a deep sigh of relief, as all my anxiety disappeared. Now that Mum wasn't a 'class enemy', she would be released from the 'cowshed' sooner or later. So my mind was set on sneaking onto a train bound for Inner Mongolia to join the Production and Construction Corps. In fact, the crucial issue with Mum was not her 'campus belle' status, but her foreign brothers – one in the US, the other in Canada. While staying at my maternal grandma's house, I had seen a colour photo of the family that one of my uncles had sent from Boston. The colourfully dressed family with two puppies were standing by a car in front of a villa. The lifestyle displayed in the picture would be no big deal in China nowadays, but in the 1970s it was considered bourgeoisie and decadent, and the picture could have been used as proof of treason.

In those days, family history and overseas relations were two heavy loads weighing on my heart. They were like dark clouds that I had no power to dispel. Knowing that I would soon leave school and step into the outside world, and that my journey would be bumpy and full of discrimination and repression, I decided to follow my dad's advice by going to remote areas and learning to live humbly and keep a low profile. Therefore, after saying goodbye to Mum, I made up my mind to sneak onto the train to Inner Mongolia.

Chapter 4

Saying Goodbye to Grandma

My grandma was a native of Suzhou, and she lived both there and in Beijing. Because Dad was her only child, she tended to stay in Beijing more. I noticed something unusual about Grandma and always felt she was special when I was still only small, although I knew little of her life. Not until many years after her death did I find out she was the second 'princess' at the Humble Administrator's Garden (Zhuozhengyuan) in Suzhou.

The east chamber, a separate single room in the family courtyard house, was where Grandma used to live. In my young mind, it was a room of mystery because the door was always shut. If Grandma went to Suzhou, the door would naturally be locked; the queer thing about it was that it remained closed even when she was there. Sometimes when I walked past her chamber, saw the door ajar and looked through the crevice, I would be greeted by nothing but darkness because the windows were covered in thick, heavy curtains. Rarely would I get a chance to enter Grandma's chamber, except on one or two occasions where I saw a bed and a desk and nothing else but large suitcases, which were stacked up from floor to ceiling. There was no other space to spare.

Grandma's daily routine was quite different to that of the average person. A couple of times at night when I got up to go to the toilet, I saw the lights on in Grandma's room, even at three in the morning. She usually got up around noon. She was very hygienic and took good care of herself, spending almost an hour a day just combing her hair and another good hour washing her feet. She had a very nice dresser, complete with a bronze mirror and all manner of fancy wooden combs that she would use ritualistically to comb her hair until it shone.

Grandma had had her feet bound since childhood. After balancing a basin of water in front of her, she would carefully untie her bound feet and gradually reveal their warped shape and the five toes that seemed a lot longer than normal but were all folded up and twisted. She would then insert the deformed feet in the water, soak them through and rub them. Next, she would gently rub each of her toes with a pumice stone. She did this very slowly, sometimes with her eyes closed, as if in meditation. Knowing that her feet were tightly wrapped all day long, and only now had temporary relief, I could feel just how gratifying the whole process must have been for her, just like how a prisoner might feel on being given a ten-minute outdoor break. My heart would go out to her every time I witnessed this ritual.

And yet Grandma seemed to take all this for granted. Once she had had her feet wrapped up again, she would gingerly go out in small steps to empty the water. After lunch each day, it was her habit to take one or two items out of a suitcase and sell them at a store in Dongdan and then go shopping and eating at Dong'an market on Wangfujing Street. By dinner time, she would return in a tricycle and take out boxes of delicacies from her bag for us to enjoy.

But Grandma's suitcases were not inexhaustible treasure troves. The number of items inside dwindled over time, and the money in her purse could run short. One day, Dad and I accompanied her to a shop in Dongdan to sell a roll of fabric. The shop made an offer of 2.5 yuan per *chi* (about one third of a metre), but Grandma kept asking for more by telling them how good the fabric was. In the end, the shop owner agreed to pay 2.8 yuan per *chi*. I thought it was a good price and wished Grandma would agree to it and sell straightaway. To my surprise, she kept asking for three yuan per *chi*. As a last resort, the buyer moved to try the cloth. He gave it a gentle pull and it came apart. It turned out that, after sitting in Grandma's suitcase for decades, the cloth had become damp and fragile. This caused the buyer to reduce the price to two yuan per *chi*. So grandma had to start another round of haggling and finally agreed a compromised deal of 2.2 yuan per *chi*. The very fact that this former wealthy lady from the Humble Administrator's Garden would now stoop to haggle over such trivialities was a telling indication that her financial status was in decline.

And yet there were harder days to come. In times of famine, we had to tighten our belts in order to survive. Under a monthly food rationing system, we could only receive limited quotas of food, cooking oil and meat. As growing children, we all experienced varying degrees of malnutrition. Grandma hopped along streets and lanes on her small feet to pick up discarded Chinese cabbage roots, had them cleaned, cut and boiled for hours until they turned soft. Next, maybe following a Zhuozhengyuan recipe, she cooked some milk so that it turned into cream and mixed it with the boiled cabbage roots. It was so delicious that the flavour has remained in my memory forever.

It gave us some relief that Grandma had been living in Suzhou prior to the Cultural Revolution. Compared with tumultuous Beijing, Suzhou was more of a safe haven. However, one day during the third year of the political campaign, Dad received a telegram from Grandma saying that she was coming to the capital. The Grandma who arrived at the train station was a quiet woman with a wrinkled face and a pair of puzzled, gloomy and somewhat fearful eyes below tightly knit eyebrows. She looked quite composed though, as if it was just a normal visit. Only decades later did I find out she had been driven out of Suzhou where, as the descendant of a former bourgeoisie family, she could hardly escape the attention and criticism of the 'revolutionary masses'. Fully aware of the difficulties the family faced, she did not breathe a word about her own situation.

The last period of Grandma's life was a time when the family as a whole was falling apart. Dad was sent to the May Seventh cadre school, while Mum ended up jailed in a 'cowshed'. When I made up my mind to head for Inner Mongolia by sneaking onto a train, I had no one to see me off on the day of departure. With luggage in hand, I walked out of the house and headed for the lane exit all alone, when Grandma ran up to me and grabbed me by the collar. She dug into her pocket and produced a handful of change that she thrust into my hands. I knew she had nothing else to give me. A family living allowance of twenty yuan a month could hardly keep the pot boiling. She wanted to give me everything, but how could I possibly take it all? In order not to disappoint her, I agreed to take twenty cents.

I put the rest of the money back into Grandma's pocket, gave her a hug and told her to take care of herself. My eyes turned wet, but I tried not to let it show. When I grabbed her wizened hands and went about saying goodbye,

I saw clearly the tears of sorrow flowing from her eyes and trickling down her hoary face. I waved to her as I walked away, until I came to the exit of the lane. It wasn't a normal farewell, there was something fatalistic about it. Only three years later did I realise I was never going to see her again.

I beat back my tears, waved decisively to Grandma, and like a warrior called to die in battle, strode straight off to Beijing railway station. When passing by the roadside restaurant close to the station, I sat down and ordered a plate of 'ants on a tree', a bowl of soy sauce soup dotted with shredded spring onion and a large bowl of rice. I polished off this much-coveted meal, leaving not a single grain of rice in the bowl. The meal satisfied me, enlivened me and strengthened me. I got up and marched towards the train station, as a famous quote from Lu Xun sprung to my mind:

> Hope can neither be said to exist, nor not to exist. It's just like the roads across the earth. The earth had no roads in the beginning. A road is made as numerous people walk the same path.

Chapter 5

En Route to Inner Mongolia

When I pushed through the crowd into Beijing railway station, I saw a train transporting educated youths about to leave for Inner Mongolia. Hundreds of students and their parents gathered at the station. The train was decked with some red streamers written with the following words:

> Cultivate and garrison the border area.
> Answer Chairman Mao's call by settling down in the countryside.
> Go wherever the country needs us most!
> Go wherever the greatest hardships exist!

Songs of *Chairman Mao's Quotations* blasted from the loudspeakers:

> It is crucial that educated youths should go to rural areas and receive re-education from poor and lower-middle peasants...

I surreptitiously looked all around: the train was pulling about a dozen carriages. Almost all students recruited to the Inner Mongolia Production and Construction Corps had boarded, so the carriages were filled up with future 'soldiers'. Because no uniforms had been distributed, they were still wearing school uniforms of different hues. I was wearing a light grey jacket and a pair of faded army trousers, which I had urged my mum to get in exchange for a pair of new trousers. Now it was the perfect occasion for me to wear them. All the carriage windows were thrown open, beneath which stood parents and students saying goodbye to one another – some hugging, others weeping together. All entrances to the carriages were carefully guarded by workers' publicity team members and military personnel to prevent illegal boarding.

A man who looked like an officer was giving instructions to his subordinates: "Many people are trying to sneak onto the train today. Guard the doors well, or we'll run into a lot of trouble."

I knew it was hard to get into the carriages in the conventional manner because PLA soldiers were keeping a close eye on the doors and were constantly head counting. Mingling among some students who were saying goodbye to their loved ones, I had with me a bag that contained a set of toiletries, a notebook, a pen and the then compulsory *Chairman Mao's Quotations*. I began looking for an opportunity to sneak through a window, but it wouldn't have been possible without someone's help. I looked around and saw below a window a small group of people with no parents around. Several youths in army trousers looked as if they were children of the army or government officials. So I went up to them to initiate a conversation.

"Friends! Are you going to the Inner Mongolia Corps?"

When they saw me wearing old army trousers, they took me for one of their own and said: "We're not going. We're here to say goodbye to a friend. Which compound do you live in?"

"The General Hospital of Beijing military region compound. Can I ask you to do me a favour? Give me a push when the train starts so I may get on board, OK?"

The one I was talking with was wearing an army cap askew, below which showed a domineering face, a wide forehead, a high-bridged nose and small moustache. His tall, burly figure gave me the impression that he would be good in a brawl. Seeing him hesitate, I instantly removed a large Chairman Mao badge I was wearing, the largest one I owned, and put it in his pocket. He then nodded his consent.

The train finally roared into life and the station started reverberating with cries of sorrow. The songs of *Chairman Mao's Quotations* that came from the loudspeaker blasted at top volume, in an attempt to muffle the weeping. Hands were thrust from the windows to clutch those of relatives on the platform. Parents were busy giving final instructions to their children, while classmates and friends exchanged parting words of blessing. The man I had 'bribed' with the badge held me up as some of his friends pushed me through the window just before the train rolled off. The way in which I smuggled myself into Inner Mongolia was something I would never forget. Perhaps today's young people would not understand my motive, but I had no other choice. The Corps was probably my only way out.

The educated youths who occupied the seats on the train were still immersed in the emotion of parting from their relatives. In an attempt to enliven the atmosphere, the military guards tried to start a sing-song, but few joined in. Worried about their future lives and careers, the youths looked perplexed. Some were crying by themselves, others were looking out of the window with their chins resting on their hands, still others fell into deep contemplation, their eyes looking dull and vacant.

I began to search for a safe hiding place immediately after entering one of the carriages. The train had a total of twelve carriages – six for boys and six for girls. I naturally chose to mix with the boys first, but the military guards kept showing up in the boys' carriages to conduct a head count in order to screen out unwanted passengers. So I had to inch along one car after another before coming to a stop at the connection between the boys' and girls' carriages. One step more would mean entering the female zone, which would make me strikingly conspicuous and put me in danger of eviction. I saw several military guards coming nearer so I decided to flee to the toilet and lock myself in. About twenty minutes later, I heard someone knock on the door. Fearing that it might be a military guard, I held my breath and stayed put, until I heard a female voice whisper: "It's clear now. The military guards are all gone. Come out quick. We need to use the toilet."

As I opened the door softly and peered out, I saw a tall, slim girl standing right there in front of me. Either on account of her striking beauty or my own lack of contact with young women, a quick glance at her radiant face made my own face flush. I instinctively made way for her and almost tripped as I walked down the aisle. She smiled before entering the toilet and shutting the door.

Between the two connecting carriages lay lots of flax sacks. I checked both directions and it seemed to be a safe spot for the time being. I leant on the sacks and wondered whether I could spend the night there. Soon, the toilet door opened, and the girl came out and gingerly approached me. I held my breath and my heart pounded. I subconsciously adjusted my pose.

"Did you sneak in?"

I nodded.

"Why did you not get approval?"

Her sweet, tender and melodious voice was like honey. However, beset with many worries, I was extremely sensitive to everything around me and didn't want to attract attention. So I responded in a somewhat nonchalant and absent-minded manner. Instead of answering her questions directly, I just raised my head a little and stole another look at her. I saw a pair of shining eyes below her then fashionable short, dark hair, a slightly large and ruddy face, and a tall and straight nose and deep laugh lines. Her cherry lips, so eloquently expressive of love, reminded me of a fairy typically depicted in traditional Chinese paintings. My face turned crimson, my heart raced and my palms became clammy.

The girl saw my timidity and worried look as she pursed her lips and tried not to laugh out loud. She obviously liked me and felt some compassion for me, so she very considerately left me alone for the time being.

"See me if you need any help," she whispered, before taking off to her seat. "My name is Zhang Yue. It means 'jade moon'."

Only now did I dare raise my head and gaze at her departing figure. She saw my enamoured eyes as she looked back from her seat. She gave me a sweet smile that made me duck my head in shame, but my heart was filled with delight, and my strained nerves saw slight, temporary relief.

The old train shook violently, producing a deafening sound as it rumbled along the tracks. Leaning on the flax sacks, I soon started dozing off in the rhythm of the rickety carriage. By evening, the sound of people serving and eating food wakened me and I started to feel hungry. Fortunately, I had eaten a big lunch that could sustain me through the next day. In order to save energy, I chose to continue sleeping. By around 8 or 9pm, however, I grew so hungry that I began to feel dizzy. Right then, I sensed someone walking past, very gingerly, like a floating fairy. Just then, a paper bag was thrown into my hands.

Inside the bag was a bread roll, an egg and an apple. I looked back. Sure enough, it was Zhang Yue on her way back to her seat. I felt another blast of excitement pass through me as I started devouring the food, each bite reminding me of Yue's lovely face and sweet voice. I was immersed in indescribable happiness.

The train rumbled on. By midnight, nearly all the passengers had fallen asleep while I stayed wide awake. What had just happened was all new to me, especially my encounter with Zhang Yue. She was much more mature than me even though she looked a few years younger. She had the build of an Amazon, with broad shoulders and a height of close to 1.7 metres. I felt she was a unique girl sent by the Divine to rescue me from adversity. I had no idea what had caused her to show me compassion and give me help. Was it my melancholy, shyness or anxiety, or a combination of all three? Could she have been driven by a special feeling for me or was she just simply curious? In any case, she was a very kind-hearted person. Amid the noisy rumble of the train, my thoughts raced in all directions for most of that night until I finally fell into a sweet sleep.

By daybreak, the educated youths started to wake up one after another. Weighed down with a myriad of sorrowful thoughts, they yawned as they went about washing and grooming themselves before returning to their seats to look through the window at the barren scenes outside. Just then, there was an uproar as some young people on the run were caught by the chasing military guards. They were singled out during an all-train head count and would eventually be escorted back to Beijing after being forced off the train at Baotou station.

While sleeping on a flax sack, I had already caught the attention of two military guards and I had sensed them walking past me at midnight. One of them said to the other: "The guy lying on the sack must be an illegal passenger. Keep an eye on him tomorrow morning."

However, I was too exhausted to do anything. I just thought they were unlikely to take any action until daybreak, and simply let myself drift back to sleep again. Obviously, they had started their rounding-up campaign sooner than I expected.

I sprang to my feet and looked around. The search and seizure campaign had just begun in the boys' carriage furthest from me. I could not run into any of the female students' carriages. So I turned back and squeezed towards the boys' carriages near where the military guards were and noticed that several students had already been seized and escorted to a dining section where they were under close watch that made escape impossible. I had to turn back again. Just then, a military guard in the distance seemed to have noticed me and began to advance. I moved quickly to another carriage and set off like a thief, but my legs failed me, and I was twice close to tripping over. Eventually, having failed to find a hiding place, I had to run back to my original spot. Right then, another young man got caught. Panic-stricken and desperate, and not knowing where to turn for help, I was prepared for the worst, but instinctively fled towards the girls' carriage.

When I got to the divide between the boys' and girls' carriages, there seemed to be only one last hideout left – the toilet. However, at that time of morning, many were now queueing for the toilet, so I literally had to fight my way in. Seizing the moment when a girl had just exited and another was about to enter, I said "Wait" and thrust myself forward. To my astonishment, the girl at the door was none other than Zhang Yue. I was thrilled, believing I had met salvation. In fact, Zhang Yue had seen how I was being hounded and had been waiting at the toilet door to help me out. She pushed me straight into the toilet and whispered: "Be sure to shut the door and come out when I knock three times."

The military guard who was chasing me got hold of another young man, sent him away and turned back. As he walked past the toilet, he pointed to it and asked Zhang Yue: "Did you see someone go in there?"

"He turned back," said Zhang Yue. "This toilet is for girls, and there is a girl in there now."

The military guard seemed suspicious, but because there were so many girls around him, he felt it inappropriate to linger. So he left me alone for the time being. The train slowly pulled into Baotou station. I hid in the toilet like a thief, with one hand grabbing the door knob and the other pressed on the bolt. I could hear two military guards talking.

"I've checked all the front cars and found no sign. He is the only one missing. He must be in the toilet. Come on! Have someone open the door."

Quite soon, a conductor came to open the door with a set of keys. I was so scared that I used both hands to hold the door handle. The key failed to turn and was withdrawn.

"The key's got stuck. There must be someone inside."

"Is there any other way to get it open?"

"No. At least not now."

By now the train had come to a halt at Baotou station. The military guard and the conductor had to leave. Through the toilet window, I saw more than half a dozen people escorted off the train and delivered to two military men. I secretly celebrated my lucky escape and felt truly grateful for what Zhang Yue had done for me and revered her as a saviour.

The train pulled out of Baotou station and peace returned to the carriage I was hiding in. I exulted on hearing the expected three knocks on the door. Zhang Yue was telling me it was now safe to come out. But I still worried about being caught. On the other hand, I knew I could not possibly stay in the toilet and deny its proper use to the female passengers. So I timidly stepped out, after checking both sides. Zhang Yue laughed when she saw how shocked I was looking. The sound of her laughter drove away all of my anxiety.

"Why do you look so scared? The train won't stop again before it reaches the final destination of Urat Front banner. There is no incentive for them to catch you anymore." She had a sweet and penetrating voice that reached the bottom of my heart.

I must have blushed again as I raised my head to look at her with a sense of relief. As an introvert, I had always been shy of looking at girls, especially beauties like Zhang Yue. She had a ruddy face, a slim frame, prominent breasts and stylishly cropped hair. Her whole being emanated the galvanising vigour of youth. Her irresistible allure eclipsed that of a famous movie star that I used to admire.

"Thanks for helping me out in my hour of need. My name is Wen Bo," I said, defying my timidity.

"You deserve my help because we are revolutionary comrades-in- arms! Your name's easy to remember. Does it mean 'gentle and learned'?"

I nodded as Zhang Yue laughed again.

"Your name makes me think you are a scholar. It's probably hard on you when you are driven to acting like a thief. Had it not been for me, you would have been captured a long time ago. Your clumsiness impelled me to help, and I did, didn't I? Are you grateful?"

Zhang talked rapidly, like a machine gun. I could hardly catch up with her. My face reddened again as I stammered out what I wanted to say from the bottom of my heart: "You saved me. I will never forget you."

Touched by my words, Zhang Yue's face crimsoned as she spontaneously put a hand on my arm. I felt a surge of heat down my spine. It was the first time I had ever been touched by a young woman. I must have overreacted. Seeing how excited I was, Zhang Yue withdrew her hand quickly and began chatting. The rumble of the train made it hard for us to hear each other, so we moved closer. I could smell her and feel the warmth of her body. The secretion of hormones in my body and the release of enkephalin in my brain must have accelerated because I was so willing and happy to answer her questions. I felt like I was ready to reveal the recesses of my heart and the deep secrets and thoughts in my mind.

"Why did they bar you from the Corps?"

"Because of my family background. My mum used to be a PLA surgeon. She has been placed under isolated investigation as a spy suspect just because she has brothers who live overseas."

Until then, I had never talked so much or so openly to a girl. My thinking was that, by opening up to her, I would receive more sympathy and, possibly, greater help.

"So what? My mum was jailed by the Kuomintang for her involvement in a student movement before liberation. She is also under investigation and her case is continuing."

Zhang Yue was evidently trying to comfort me by sharing her family secrets. Our hearts drew closer to each other than ever before.

"Which hospital did your mother work at? In which department?"

"She was a nutritionist in the VIP ward of the General Hospital of Beijing military region."

Zhang Yue looked surprised. "Really?" she said. "I must have seen her when my dad was hospitalised in the VIP ward. She looked beautiful and elegant, and she made nutritious recipes for my dad. I actually saw her as recently as the day before yesterday, when I was saying goodbye to my dad at the hospital. She was sweeping the corridor."

Initially, these words gave hope, but as she continued talking they felt like a needle stabbed into my heart. I bowed my head and fell silent. Realising she had said something out of place, Zhang Yue tried to comfort me, but she couldn't find the right words. As a smart girl, she knew what I most wanted to hear.

"Do you really want to join the Corps?" she whispered.

I nodded as I looked up at her beautiful face, which was by now almost touching me.

"I know Chief of Staff Wang at the Corps headquarters. He used to work for my dad. I will talk to him about your case later."

Her words were like a glass of mellow wine. 'Saviour' Zhang Yue was now the sun of my heart. She had not only helped me flee the military guards, she may even be able to help me stay in the Production Corps. And in future...

My face betrayed these thoughts to Zhang Yue. She smiled at me before running back to her seat and joining her lively group of friends. From the train came the strident Chairman Mao songs. I must have looked silly standing there, but I did see a glimmer of hope through which I could pluck up courage, seek a way out and find a good future.

Chapter 6

The Carters' Inn

The clinic of the Twelfth Regiment of the Inner Mongolia Production and Construction Corps' Second Division was located in the town of Xin'an in Urat Front banner. A town with a population of thousands was thought of as large in those days. So Xin'an was a town of considerable size, and it had a bridge spanning a river that ran through it. Along the banks were a number of stout, aged trees. A few kilometres east of the centre was an old inn for carters built during the reign of Emperor Guangxu (1875-1908) in the Qing dynasty (1644-1911). Initially a postal station, the building contained wooden beams that were inscribed with dragons and phoenixes. Further down from the inn was the more prosperous part of Xin'an, where there were a number of rural courtyards inhabited by people of considerable standing, mostly officials, technicians and artisans. Several more kilometres further north was the centre of town and the headquarters of the Twelfth Regiment, lined with rows and rows of brick bungalows. They included two rows of neatly-connected bungalows that were used as the regiment's clinic. Though not recently constructed, they were the most presentable buildings in the entire town.

On arriving at Xin'an, each of the educated youths from Beijing was provided with a military uniform without a collar lapel or cap insignia. I was the only person who didn't get one. Compared with the valiant-looking soldiers of the Corps, I appeared quite drab and countrified in my own grey uniform. This sapped my self-confidence and I sought refuge in an inconspicuous corner where I could observe the female soldiers in the distance. Among them, Zhang Yue was the most prominent and visible. Wearing a new uniform, she stood out among her peers because of her

38

height and shining beauty. My own dispirited demeanour and shabby garments were in sharp contrast.

Though the educated youths of Beijing had to leave the capital for the frontier region of Inner Mongolia, they were relatively lucky because they were provided with the basic means of sustenance. On their very first day, each of them got an army uniform, a set of bedding, a towel and an enamel porcelain cup printed with the words '*tun ken shu bian*' ('Using troops to exploit the virgin land of the border region'). They were all busy cleaning their rooms and making their beds. So I, the only one who managed to sneak into their ranks, was completely ignored and isolated.

I strolled aimlessly on the dirt roads of Xin'an. I did not know where to go, or what to do next. I wondered if I should talk directly to the military guards, who were actually regimental staff officers or people in charge, but I felt powerless to persuade them. It would be like walking into a trap, and then being escorted back to Beijing. If I did nothing, however, without a penny to my name, I wouldn't even be able to obtain basic food and lodging. I wandered listlessly in Xin'an all day. At dusk, I still had no clue where to spend the night. Thus, hungry, thirsty and exhausted, I wandered into an inn for carters.

Inside the carters' inn were two rows of connected *kangs* (brick beds) covered with tattered mats, on which several coachmen were sprawled, some wearing socks, some not, but all with stinking feet. The room was a mess of filth, smoke and noise. The April weather in Inner Mongolia was so cold that the clothes I had put on in Beijing could not keep me warm. A shudder swept through my empty belly as a chilly wind swept in from outside. Although the noisy carters' inn reeked with smoke, alcohol and body smells, reminding me of the bandits' lair in the popular revolutionary opera *Taking Tiger Mountain by Strategy*, it was warm enough to draw me in. I chose an inconspicuous corner to sit in.

This inn, located in a small border town, might not have been much influenced by the political winds blowing through China at that time. Since the country was already a 'red ocean', I couldn't become acquainted with the bottom rung of society in Beijing and it was impossible to know the very existence of such an embarrassingly miserable spot. It was eye-opening to see people drinking and playing gambling games. Scenes like that may be commonplace today, but they had all but been eradicated then. I was intrigued to see that several coachmen, speaking in Shanxi accents, were drinking and playing games. After a while, amid the clamour of human voices, they collectively invited someone to tell them a story about a martial contest involving Huyan Zan, a military general in the Song dynasty (960-1279), which was banned during the Cultural Revolution. My curiosity was piqued beyond words, and I listened with relish how the elderly man with a Shanxi accent vividly told the story in Mandarin.

By midnight, the noise had gradually died down, the carters were falling asleep one by one in various postures, and all but one of the oil lanterns in the house were extinguished. The single one that remained lit was turned to its lowest setting. By now, having had no food or drink for the whole day, I could hear my empty belly grumbling. At the least, I needed to get a bowl of water to drink. Seeing that the large room was connected to a smaller one that was lit, I slowly approached the small room in the hope of getting a drink. Inside the room was a man in his thirties and of medium height. He had a slim figure and a face with a rich expression. He spoke fast in soft tones and looked very hospitable. I had no way of knowing whether he was the boss, but he was definitely some kind of manager or person in authority.

He treated me politely on learning that I came from Beijing. It had been quite a while since I had met someone with such kindness and warmth, and I naturally accepted his hospitality. After asking many questions and learning that I had not yet eaten, he immediately produced in front of me a basket that contained several steamed corn pancakes. Next, he shredded a lump of pickle, poured some sesame oil onto it and served it to me in a small bowl. Then, he produced a larger bowl, fetched an old towel from the edge of the *kang* to clean it, and sprinkled a pinch of coarse tea leaves to brew me a steaming bowl of tea.

This simple meal that he took just a minute or so to prepare looked unappetising and in normal circumstances would have repulsed me. But now, having spent the entire day without food, the sight of the corn bread and the pickle made my mouth water. Therefore, I devoured the corn bread one piece after another, stuffing them into my mouth, biting and chewing them without the slightest concern for etiquette. Within minutes, I had wolfed down all of the bread, and then I began to savour the prospect of drinking the bowl of tea. During those two days, I had a total of just three meals. The first was minced meat with vermicelli wrapped up in lettuce. The second, taken on the train and given to me by Zhang Yue, comprised bread, an egg and an apple. The third was corn bread with shredded pickle and a large bowl of tea. These three meals, served with the best sauce of hunger, became so etched in my memory that I could never forget how delicious they were.

While eating, I sensed that the manager was watching me in a strange manner. I wondered if he was shocked by my appetite because I made such short work of six pieces of corn bread. He probably couldn't understand how a city boy like me could eat more than a villager like him. However, what he said next made me think he was entertaining other thoughts.

"You urbanites sure have fair skin. What's your family background? You were born into a rich and noble family, weren't you?"

He spoke Mandarin with a Shanxi accent and asked questions that I hated to hear. My heart raced. I continued eating the corn bread in large and voracious mouthfuls. My sole concern was to eat all the food in the basket and to deflect any questions that came my way. I feared that my limited answers might arouse his suspicion and cause him to take back the food. However, when I was almost done with the corn bread and began drinking the tea, I felt that I could no longer ignore the manager. So I began chatting with him absent-mindedly.

The manager had a lot of questions, and he soon got to know a lot about me. He knew I was an educated youth from Beijing that the Corps had rejected and that I was desperate to find a way to survive. So he began squinting at me, trying to work out how he might best exploit this situation. The way he kept smiling made me feel he was a compassionate man. He might be feeling sorry for me, given that I had been forced to leave my parents and come all the way here only to suffer in this poor, remote village. For better or worse, he was generous enough to treat me to a meal that temporarily quelled my hunger. So I was grateful to him. Such generosity and hospitality reminded me of the virtues of the poor and lower-middle class peasants – simplicity, kindness and helpfulness – that I had so often heard about in the city.

However what he did next puzzled me, and the positive image of the peasants began to fade. He tried to hand me a cigarette he had just made, but I waved it off and told him I didn't smoke. Assuming I was questioning the quality of his cigarette, he grinned and gave me a grimace, as if indicating he was going to treat me to something really special so that I, an uninvited guest from Beijing, would see him in a better light.

He pulled out a small iron box from under his pillow, carefully took out a white pill and put it on the circular cover of the box. Next, he handed me a hollow reed straw, which I held out of curiosity but with no idea what was going on. He inserted an iron bar into the kitchen fire, heated it until its tip turned red before applying it to the pill. The pill soon emitted a blue smoke that he eagerly inhaled with a reed straw. When he beckoned me to join him, I resolutely waved him off. He made no attempt to invite me again, but kept sucking on the straw in greedy mouthfuls. Between each mouthful he would close his eyes and savour the sensation. Having consumed the whole pill in this manner, he looked completely carried away. The pills were most likely drugs that were used to relieve pain or stimulate the nerves, and were probably addictive. For example, long-term use of certain headache tablets can be addictive. After inhaling the smoke, the manager looked excited, his eyes giving off an eerie light. He turned the wick of the lamp to the lowest setting, motioned me to the *kang* and began prattling away in his Shanxi-accented Mandarin. In his 'heart-to-heart' talk with me, he acted as if he could chart out the course of my career, claiming that he was on unusually good terms with the production team leader and citing his lucrative innkeeper job as a personal favour from him.

"Brother," he began. "I really mean to help you out. The production team leader has a very capable eighteen-year-old daughter who is quite a beauty in the village, even though she has a darker skin than urban girls. Indeed, she is quite a capable girl. She's a high-browed and picky shrew, and shows no interest in any of the village guys. Those who dared try to date her were either given a good dressing down or got beaten up real bad."

He bent over towards me with a naughty grin and whispered: "If I could be your go-between, I can guarantee she will fall in love with you at first sight. She likes honest and well-educated city guys, especially those with fair skin like you."

With a short guffaw, he reached over to pinch my arm. I dodged him instinctively. Ignoring my discomfort, however, he kept boasting and selling the course of my life that he had in mind for me.

"Think about it," he said. "Her father is the production team leader, and she is beautiful and capable. With your educational background, what could the villagers do to you if you married her? No one would dare bully you. I bet you will lead a very happy life."

"What do you mean by happy life? Can you possibly be happy living with a bully who scolds and beats you all day? No way!"

I kept fending him off in that manner, but he seemed determined to try to 'enlighten' me that very night.

"That's not right," he continued excitedly. "I bet you haven't touched any girls yet. In the past, men preferred virtuous, obedient and subservient wives. Nowadays, it's the capable, vixen-like and eloquent who are getting the upper hand. In a class struggle environment, anything less than that is a recipe for suffering. I see how honest and simple you are. Imagine how much you would suffer as a couple if you married a submissive wife! Don't you see what's going on in society nowadays? An obedient horse makes for good riding, just as an obedient person is easy prey for bullies. I will see to it that you know the village girls on a personal level, see what Amazons they are and find out how they tame the men in the village. The funny thing is that there are very few promiscuous husbands in the village nowadays, and few of them stay outside the home after work. They obey their women and get rebuked or beaten for doing otherwise. Isn't that fun? By contrast, a virtuous wife could bore you to death! You know what they say? Verbal abuse signifies affection while physical abuse implies intimacy."

As I heard him chatter away with my eyes wide open, I became absorbed by his fancy talk, especially on sexual matters that I had never heard of before. His ideas might well have served as my earliest sexual enlightenment, but I didn't feel comfortable and even found it all a little creepy. He created a kind of chaos in my mind, and I couldn't quite grasp what he was trying to say.

The manager finally became tired, talked less and slowly fell asleep. I too became drowsy, but his words kept ringing in my ears. I dreamed that I got kidnapped by a stout and strong woman, who then locked me in her house, where she teased, bullied and abused me. I lost all freedom and was prevented from returning to Beijing. When I woke up at midnight, I found myself breaking into a cold sweat. I became more scared when it occurred to me that the stout and strong woman was none other than the production team leader's daughter that the manager had mentioned. When I realised that this was not a safe place to stay in, I told myself to take extra care and not get beguiled by sweet words, lest I fall under the influence of that stout and strong woman.

At this moment, I sensed that the manager was also awake and his hands were slowly moving to my body. At first, I thought he was trying to steal something; but he knew I had no money. So I said nothing and simply let his hands fumble about until they gradually reached my belt. Clearly he was making a sexual advance, so I yelled at him: "What are you up to?"

I had never experienced anything like that. Stranded in an unfamiliar place, I was nervous and fearful. I shouted in a trembling voice, like a dog barking out of cowardice rather than bravery. The manager wasn't scared at all. He put his forefinger to his lips, ordered me to be quiet, and then bid me to sit. But I refused to lie in his bed or sleep near him again. Determined to leave this damned place, I fastened my belt, picked up my bag and walked out of the manager's house. I did not leave the inn because it was pitch dark and dangerous outside. To leave this horrible place, I had to wait until daybreak.

I climbed up the big common *kang*, cautiously clambered over the carters sleeping in a disorderly manner and lay down in a corner with my eyes half closed, feigning sleep so I could observe what was going on around me. After a short while, the manager walked out to the vat, ladled out some water and began drinking before he turned around apparently to look for me. When he finally spotted me in a far corner, he put down the ladle and walked quietly back to his room. A few minutes later, the manager came out with an old sheepskin coat draped over his shoulders, ready to leave the house. At the gate, he whispered a few words to the gatekeeper while pointing in my direction. The old gatekeeper tiptoed up and surveyed me for a while. He did not sit down until he was sure he had seen my face clearly. The manager left the inn in a hurry as the gatekeeper continued with his janitorial duties. I started to get scared, wondering if the manager had gone to tip off the production team leader about me. Recalling what had happened, I realised that he might have been coveting me for a long time. All that talk and food were part of a bid to entrap me. I knew a shrewd and sophisticated person like the manager would always be motivated by profit. It might not be long before the production team leader arrived with two militiamen to take me away. And being a non-resident without any ID, they could easily arrest me as a 'class enemy' and then fit me up with the production team leader's daughter as part of a 'honey trap'. In other words, they would deliver the son of a 'black five' to the daughter of poor and lower-middle-class peasants so she would control me and put my entire career at her disposal. The very thought filled me with fear. I made up my mind to flee before they arrived. The day had just dawned. I stretched and rubbed my eyes, pretending that I had just woken up. Next, I made my way towards the entrance when the old janitor stood up abruptly and blocked my way.

"Hey, you!" he said in a strong Shanxi accent. "Where are you going? You can't leave now. The manager told me specifically that our production team leader will be arriving very soon. Good luck is waiting for you. Just don't leave."

He lowered his voice when he uttered the last sentence, revealing a strange shine in his eyes and a demonic smile that was reminiscent of the manager.

I tried my best to hide my sense of panic and nervousness and, pretending to be overwhelmed by the unexpected favour, smiled to him and replied: "If that's the case, I'll go for a pee and come right back."

That said, I walked around him and straight out of the gate. Right after I had finished peeing and tightened my belt, I strode off briskly before breaking into to a run. The clamour of the old man behind me only prompted me to run faster. I ran until I could no longer hear him.

Chapter 7

First Love

After escaping from the carters' inn, I kept running for quite some distance until I was sure no one was coming after me. My nervousness abated, a feeling of unspeakable joy filled my heart, as if I had just emerged from a tiger's den.

I was strolling on a country dirt road. Later on, I learned from a book that pleasure can be derived from several sources: a nice meal, meeting up with long-separated family members, escaping from imminent peril... This last example is similar to what happens when a vulnerable creature manages to escape from a predator. Fleeing is a basic instinct of the weak and vulnerable that applies both to animals and humans. Cowardly since early childhood, I certainly had a keen sense of the joy of being out of harm's way.

April in Inner Mongolia is still a chilly month, though running had kept me warm. The cool and refreshing air on the boundless grasslands was quite a relief for a young refugee from the big city.

But I soon fell into a poor mood again. On this vast, unfamiliar land thousands of kilometres from home, with no money, friends or relatives, I had no idea where I was going to end up. Though out of danger for now, I could easily fall back into the fire at any time. To whom should I go for help? After thinking it through, I knew my only option was the girl I had just met on the train. In my mind, she was more than a saviour. She was Lady Luck herself! And kind and compassionate too. Everyone else had shunned me, viewing me with critical eyes and treating me as if my family was in serious political trouble. Under their scrutiny, what spiritual torment I had to endure. Zhang Yue was a very different person. She not only talked to me and helped me, but she also shared her dinner with me. I knew she would continue to help me if only I could find her. As a matter of fact, she was my only possible source of help.

It was actually quite embarrassing for a young man of twenty to seek help from a girl. But Zhang Yue was no ordinary girl. She was my true saviour. Had it not been for her secret help, I would have been detained on the train. As the saying goes, 'Kindness and help should never be half-hearted'. Did she not say she knew Chief of Staff Wang at the Corps? I might as well swallow my pride and find her, wherever she was. The very thought of Zhang Yue made me flush again, and her beautiful face loomed large before me. My heart pounded as I yelled out her name: "Zhang Yue! My Zhang Yue! My saviour!"

In time, I simply yelled her first name: "Yue! My Yue! I have no one else to turn to."

The sky was still dim when I arrived at the clinic. I sat under a tree about a hundred metres from the bungalows, waiting for the clinic to open. A few minutes later came the sharp, clear notes of a bugle, an ear-splitting reveille that carried far into the horizon. Before long, noise came from the two rows of bungalows. Several women soldiers dressed in army uniform walked out to wash their faces and brush their teeth. I stood up and slowly walked over to see if Yue was among them. On noticing me, one of the women soldiers began gesturing and whispering to her comrade. Knowing that I had been seen, I had to halt because it was quite improper for an insignificant person like me to break into an army camp early in the morning and spy on female soldiers. I could easily get arrested for sexual harassment. A chill passed down my spine as I suddenly recalled my family origin. I turned back and was about to flee like a startled bird.

Just then, I caught sight of a tall, slim and agile woman running out of the bungalow. It was Yue! We recognised each other immediately, and she began walking in my direction. My heart thumped in rhythm with her approaching footsteps. She then sped up, dashed over and grabbed hold of me. I was taken aback by the blazing fury in her eyes. She gripped the front of my shirt to prevent me from sneaking away. I felt like a thief caught red-handed. Fortunately, the large tree in front of us blocked me from being seen.

"Wen Bo, where were you yesterday? I spent all day looking for you. You're driving me crazy," she chided, gasping breathlessly.

I did not reply. I certainly did not want to tell her what had happened to me the day before. I felt it shameful and embarrassing even to mention such things, especially to a girl. So I said nothing. Once sure I would not take to my heels, she loosened her grip but kept on questioning me frantically. I stood still before her, not uttering a sound.

"Where did you eat yesterday? Where did you stay? I got everything ready for you, including food and lodging at the hostel. But I couldn't find you. Tell me, how did you spend your day?"

I kept silent despite her fury, standing meekly in front of her just like a pupil being reproached by a teacher. To my surprise, her scolding only served to warm my heart. I knew her anger and sharp rebuke were nothing but an indication of how much she cared for me. Finally, she could stand it no more. She gave my forehead a sharp poke. Instead of resisting, I willingly accepted her action. Perturbed by my impassiveness, she poked my forehead hard twice more. I was about to collapse and felt like kneeling down before her for mercy, but I held my ground for fear of being seen by others. Yue, however, showed no sign of relenting.

"Speak up!" she continued. "Where did you sleep last night? I even went to the security department to have them help find you. They turned me down because you are not part of the Corps, but they suggested that I check on you at the carters' inn. But how could a girl like me go to that kind of place? Now, tell me, where were you last night?"

I stood stoically before her, still remaining motionless and speechless. Yue's face reddened, her thin, arched eyebrows lifted and her eyes were burning with rage. Her anger, while it carried a special charm, was provoked by my failure to respond. In a fresh outburst of rage, she gave me two loud, burning slaps on the face. The slaps brought me to my senses, and I had no choice but to confess.

"At the carters' inn," I said.

"What? You spent the night there? You bastard! How dare you! The security department staff say it's a dodgy place rife with the scum of the world. Why on earth did you go there? You didn't defile yourself, did you? You left without bothering to let me know, Wen Bo. You fucking arsehole!"

Yue kept on swearing at me. She looked a very different person to that gentle girl on the train, but I fully understood her. She was only acting in this manner because she was infuriated. I could imagine the kind of desperate anxiety she had to go through while looking for me the previous day. Right now, she was just giving full vent to all those suppressed concerns. The degree of harshness in which she scolded me was a reflection of the depth of her love and care for me. But Yue seemed to be determined to teach me a lesson in order to get the whole story from me. She grabbed me by my ears, lifted my head and snapped: "Wen Bo, raise your head and look me in the eyes. Tell me, how did you spend your night at the carters' inn? Where did you eat? Did you pick up any bad habits?"

She then released my ears, but only to give me another punch on the nose, causing tears to seep from my eyes. As if that was not enough, she kicked me hard on the bottom three times. I was dumbfounded. But all the while, I felt she had truly fallen in love with me, for the innkeeper's words of sexual enlightenment were now ringing in my ears: "Verbal abuse is a sign of affection, while physical abuse is a sign of intimacy."

All this happened in a matter of minutes. I was convinced she had fallen deeply in love with me, while at the same time realising that I was now her captive. So, stammering, I confessed: "I slept in my clothes in a corner on the communal *kang*. Since I knew nobody there, I left straight after daybreak."

Yue's anger died down a little bit, but her chiding did not.

"Damn it! Didn't you know it would be filthy in there? Were you aware you could get lice?"

I chuckled at the way she talked and cursed. Swear words from the mouth of a beauty have a particular sweetness. She responded with another heavy punch, and continued with the interrogation.

"How dare you laugh? Be serious. Where did you eat?"

"I was starving to death, so I asked someone for baked corn bread."

"You got that?"

"I kept begging him. I told him I was a runaway from Beijing. He took pity on me and gave me one."

I spoke with a tearful tone in my voice, hoping that she would forgive me. The trick worked. Her anger subsided as her heart was softened by kindness and compassion. I saw two teardrops roll down from the corners of her eyes. She failed to contain her lust just as she had failed to contain her fiery temper. In the end, she threw herself on me and put her arms around my neck. Her prominent breasts pressed hard against my chest, and I felt the passionate heaving of her body and the turbulence within my own body.

Her face, wet with tears, was pressed to mine. She was no longer crying out of compassion for me, but out of excitement that two devoted hearts were now joined together. For me, this spontaneous love was a godsend that I willingly and naturally accepted. As a man who had never touched a girl before, I now put an arm around her slender waist. I knew I was in love, for the first time in my life. She slowly released her grip and gently stroked my cheeks.

"I'm sorry. Did I hurt you? I was heavy-handed. I lost control. I didn't mean it. I am just hot-tempered. Everyone is scared of me. Are you?"

"Of course. I'm a born chicken. I was scared to death just now and felt like kneeling down before you. I held my ground just because I didn't want to get noticed. Even so, I adore girls like you who dare to love and hate in such an honest and real way."

Yue burst out laughing. She must have been touched by my frankness, especially my last remark, for she began a frantic round of kissing my cheeks. I was worried about being seen by other female soldiers, but Yue did not seem to care at all. Fortunately, the thick tree blocked us from view.

"I have been very mean to you," she continued after she had finished kissing me. "Please don't take it to heart. I don't normally swear."

I had no idea what I could say to help release her from her sense of guilt. On remembering what the innkeeper had said, I replied: "Never mind. I actually enjoy being scolded, beaten and controlled by you."

She gave me a surprised look, giggled and said: "Really? You're so cute. What if we live together in future, so I can control you, scold you and beat you up every day? How about that?"

I nodded my head, sending her convulsing with laughter again. She threw her arms around me, and showered my cheeks and neck with even more fervent kisses. I leant hard against the tree, propping up straight to avoid being seen, but she didn't seem to be at all concerned. Intoxicated in her tender caresses, I indulged myself in her almost unbridled love and fantasised about her kissing my mouth. But she did not. It looked like she still had reservations about her love for me.

Our passion was cut short by a voice calling for Zhang Yue. In five minutes, she would have to head to the fields to work, and she wouldn't be back until late at night. Suddenly, it occurred to her she had a lot of important things to tell me, so she gave me some quick instructions.

"Don't go anywhere, just stay put at the hostel. I've asked the manager to provide you with meals and accommodation. But remember, you must visit Chief of Staff Wang tonight."

I balked at the idea of seeing a high officer, although I knew I had to do so alone because Yue wouldn't be able to accompany me. She didn't yell at me for being timid this time, but patiently encouraged me instead.

"Don't worry," she said. "I've told Chief of Staff Wang that your mum used to be my dad's physician, and he has promised to help. I have just been assigned to work at the health clinic. Try to plead with him, and you may be able to stay with me at the same clinic. Your mum was an army surgeon after all."

I did not hold any great expectations. I would be happy just to stay in the Corps, even if it meant taking on the most gruelling job. Yue read my mind but kept inspiring me: "Just plead with him. His words carry quite some weight."

"OK," I replied, lacking all conviction.

It was time for her to leave. She took off but ran back to repeat what she had said earlier: "We won't return until midnight, so I won't be able to see you today. Listen to me – you're not to go anywhere tonight. Just stay in your room at the hostel. I have asked someone to keep an eye on you. Watch out how I deal with you tomorrow if you decide to stray! See Chief of Staff Wang at seven tonight. Don't you dare forget. And don't pull a long face. Cheer up! This is going to be vital for you. See to it that you do a good job. You'll be in hot water tomorrow if you mess things up."

Yue talked with the speed of a machine gun. I truly loved her personality. She ran back to me again after walking some distance. My heart pounded with excitement because I knew she was coming to say goodbye and perhaps wanted to kiss me again, maybe even on my mouth. So I closed my eyes, offered my face and pursed my lips. But she merely smiled and said: "No way!"

Instead of kissing me, she playfully punched me on the nose again before drifting away like a breath of wind. I rubbed my sore nose and watched entranced as she disappeared into the distance. After running a few steps, she looked back and made a face that soon blossomed into a sweet smile.

Yue darted off to meet up with her comrades. These newcomers were beaming with a vital energy. Singing songs of Chairman Mao's quotations, they strode in the morning sun across the loess land until finally disappearing into the woods. How I envied them. And how I wished to join them.

I stood still by the big tree. All was quiet now except for the sound of rustling trees and the occasional tweets of birds. My nose and face were still sore, but my heart was swelling with joy. It was a feeling that I had never had before. It came so suddenly and powerfully that I felt as if I had been thrown into a dreamland. I started singing in a low voice as I walked into the hostel next to the clinic.

I was treated cordially when I mentioned the name Zhang Yue. Everyone looked at me with curiosity instead of discrimination, as if trying to find something extraordinary in my ordinary face. My unkempt appearance was no longer synonymous with a lack of hygiene or country living. Instead, it carried with it a sense of mystery that caused people to look at me with fresh eyes. From my awkward appearance they were expecting to discover some hidden potential, some magical element or distinctive intelligence that would cause an outstanding girl like Zhang Yue to become attracted to me and even somewhat obsessed with me.

As a favour to someone special, I was provided with a single room at the hostel plus a large and delicious lunch, after which I lay on the bed alone. I obeyed Yue without question because I thought I belonged to her, now and forever. So I had to act according to her instructions and be at her beck and call. Still stressed from having been on the run for several days, I slept deeply, and my body could finally unwind.

By the time I woke up, my fatigue had largely gone. Yue's face floated before me again as I lay in bed. The more I thought about her, the more she reminded me of a certain movie star who had short hair but was a little older and a little fatter than Yue. Yue was also wearing short hair. There was something special and captivating about the way she threw back her hair. Her voice, crisp and sonorous like a bell, was so sweet and appealing, even when she was swearing. To close my eyes was to hear the echo of those curses again. Strangely, I seemed to enjoy reflecting on them again and again.

I knew I was truly in love. How did I see love then? For me, to love a woman was to love everything about her and to obey her unconditionally. I would not complain even if she abused me or bullied me. For better or worse, I would love her and obey her forever. That was my understanding about love then. Even today, I cannot tell whether my concept of love was the result of the innkeeper's sexual advances or something natural that issued from the deep recesses of my soul. Anyway, I loved her deeply. Whether she said good words or bad, was smiling or burning with anger, the way she threw back her hair or the way she bounded, I found her gorgeous and fascinating in every way. I guess that's typical of all first loves.

Chapter 8

Loss and Gain

After eating a rich and delicious dinner at the regimental headquarters hostel, I was faced with the daunting task of seeing Chief of Staff Wang. I walked out of the hostel into the office compound of the Corps headquarters but found Wang's office locked, so I paced back and forth waiting. If Yue were there, she would have no doubt taken me direct to Wang's house. Now that I was alone, I couldn't imagine doing that all by myself. Just to go and see him in his office took a lot of courage.

By 7pm, the lights in Wang's office were finally turned on. He had arrived for the appointment. As I approached the door to knock, my legs went soft and I began to backtrack and paced in circles along that row of houses, until a vision of an angry scowl on Yue's face came to me. If she had seen my wretched state, she would have started kicking me again. Stirred by this thought, I returned to the office door and called out: "Excuse me?"

"Do come in."

On entering, I saw a tall and burly army officer seated behind two connected wooden tables. He had thick eyebrows and a moon face with a stubbly beard. His voice was sonorous and penetrating, and sounded like a bronze bell when tolled. He had the look of an important person to me. So I stood to attention and asked him respectfully: "Are you Chief of Staff Wang?"

He was busy going through some papers. On hearing my voice, he raised his head to look at me. Maybe because I was dressed in plain clothes, he instantly knew who I was.

"Hello. Are you Wen Bo? Little Yue told me your mum was her dad's physician, is that right?"

I nodded hurriedly after a short pause. Yue must have told him that so he would take my case seriously, but she made no mention of my mum's current status, probably out of concern that it would impact my job application. Wang, however, was inquisitive.

"Since your mum is a military surgeon, are you interested in medicine as well?"

Sensing that something positive could soon come my way, I felt a new strength in my body, and I was bold enough to speak louder.

"I know something about medicine, and I know how to do acupuncture."

"Then why were you not approved to come here?"

"My family background did not pass political review. I have a couple of uncles in the US and Canada."

Chief of Staff Wang put down his pen and gave me a sombre look. He frowned before saying in a slightly grave and deep voice: "These are serious issues in a border area like ours, so I can't put you in an important position. But since your mum treated her father, and he was actually my former boss, I will have to honour Little Yue's request. I can keep you in the Corps, but you won't work in the health clinic. You'll have to go to a grassroots company and get reformed in a tough environment."

My heart raced before finally settling down, and I heaved a deep sigh of relief. Wang tore off a piece of paper from a notebook and scribbled on it before handing it to me.

"Take this with you to see Chief of Staff Li, and let him make the arrangements. Don't try to compare your problems with those of Little Yue. Her father is a venerable army officer. He has entrusted his daughter to me, so I have to take care of her, provide her with a good job and be responsible for her."

Wang's sharp eyes stung me, as if he had discovered something about my intentions towards Yue. Could my close physical contact with her early that morning have been revealed to him? I lowered my head as my face blushed under Wang's stare, and my heart beat so violently he could probably hear it. My limited life experience made it impossible for me to hide anything from him.

The chief of staff must have seen my guilty look because he seemed to be changing his mind, and he took back the note he had written for me.

My heart sank, and I thought he might be revoking his promise or at least rethinking the whole thing. I felt it was going to be a bad night, and with Yue away I was left to fend for myself.

I slowly raised my head to sneak a glance at the chief of staff, who had just lit a cigarette and put it in the corner of his mouth. A wisp of smoke drifted upwards as he began questioning me.

"If your mum is an army doctor, what did she do before liberation?"

"She was a college student."

"Is your dad an army man? What did he do before liberation?"

"No, he is an intellectual. He was a senior clerk at a pharmaceutical plant in Shanghai before liberation."

"What is your family background then?"

"Corporate employee."

"That can't be right! A senior officer in a factory is an agent of the principal. What was your father's position? Who owned the pharmaceutical plant?"

"My father was the general manager, and the factory was owned by my grandpa."

"So your family origin is capitalist, and you are part of the 'black five'!"

It felt as if I had been punched, and my mind went blank. The chief of staff was clearly a professional politician, good at persecuting people. Through aggressive questioning, he managed to expose my family background in just a few minutes. I was immediately turned into a criminal who was trying to conceal his family background. I began to fear that the Corps would escort me back to Beijing on charges of concealing family background, cheating on a female soldier or even hooliganism.

Seeing my wretched state, the chief of staff seemed to deem me a poor match for Zhang Yue, so he continued to press me in order to have me give up. He took another deep puff on his cigarette and blew out several rings of smoke.

"Little Yue comes from an impeccable revolutionary army family. She is one of the 'red five' categories, while you belong to one of the 'black five' categories. Any union with her is out of the question. However hard you try, the authorities will not approve it, and nor will her father."

Each of his words pierced my heart like a dagger, bruising my soul and demolishing the tender buds of my love. I was losing all hope, but the chief of staff took no heed of my feelings. He was getting carried away, and stood up while he continued with his non-stop preaching. The room, containing just two tables and two chairs, was by no means large, but there was ample space for him to pace up and down with his hands clasped behind his back.

"Little Yue, who grew up under my guidance, is a pretty, kind-hearted and pure-minded girl, but she does have a will of her own and quite a little temper. She is committed to whatever she sets her heart on. Her waywardness has a lot to do with her dad's indulgence. She very much has her own mind. She insisted on joining the Corps even though she had the chance to become a real soldier. So her father entrusted her to me and asked me to keep an eye on her lest she made boyfriends too early. I must tell you seriously that the Corps does not permit new recruits to date during the first three years. Little Yue is young and has never dated anyone. She is easily fooled. If you want to stay in the Corps, I suggest you break up with her straight away."

The chief of staff gave me another stern glare. He obviously took me for something of a Lothario. Otherwise, how could a 'black five' pariah win over a slim, pretty, kind and innocent 'red five' girl in just a matter of days? By now, I found myself in no better a position than those who had been openly criticised in public. I simply bowed my head and said nothing. A person without hope can become indifferent to his fate. I thought I would just leave everything to him.

As a seasoned army man, the chief of staff felt he couldn't go too far, since he knew Zhang Yue had fallen for me; otherwise, she would not have bothered to ask him to help me. So he had to come up with some clever way of dealing with this issue.

On seeing my honesty, weakness and vulnerability, he decided to give me a glimmer of hope so that, in the end, I would be grateful to him. He now began to speak in a gentle voice.

"Despite the fact that your father is a bourgeois capitalist, your mother, after all, is a revolutionary soldier who will give you proletarian influence. In you we see a kind of tug-of-war competition for the next generation between the proletariat and the bourgeoisie, and in you we see the important issue of whether socialism will overcome capitalism or vice versa. I will accept you as an educable young man, but I will assign you to the most difficult company in the entire regiment so that you may be turned into a new man."

After hearing all that, I felt like a bird tossed by a storm into the wet mud but somehow managing to regain consciousness after the storm had relented. Or like a withered seedling on a parched land that was about to receive its first rainfall in months. I slowly straightened my limp body and adjusted my posture, trying to sit straight in front of the chief of staff and listen attentively to his instructions. At that point I was happy to accept all conditions and do whatever was asked of me so long as I was employed. The chief of staff lit another cigarette, gave a deep puff and blew out an even longer trail of smoke. He paced up and down beside me and began to make specific demands of me.

"If you want to stay in the Corps, you have to promise me one more thing: don't tell Zhang Yue what I told you today. Stop all communication with her, especially letter-writing. If you fail to do so, and I find out about it, I will ask you to leave at once."

I slumped my head down, wondering if this was the end of my first love. Would the blossom of my love be snapped and gone forever? I found it hard to reconcile, so I whispered: "I can do it, but I think Zhang Yue will definitely come looking for me. Even if I keep quiet, she will still ask around and eventually find out where I am."

On hearing this, the chief of staff laughed so loud that the whole room shook. He paced about, circled around me and said emphatically: "Rest assured on that score. Tomorrow morning I'll get you a car ride to the company. In the meantime, I will tell Zhang Yue you have been assigned to the Yunnan Corps and that you will head back to Beijing early in the morning. I trust she will give up on you after hearing this. Should you ever get together again in future, it must be because of you. I will then show you no mercy. If I have the authority to keep you in the Corps, I also have the authority to kick you out."

The words of the chief of staff were premeditated and his strategy watertight. He was certainly a wily man and I was no match for him. He kept staring at me after I had finished talking, and then he asked me slowly and deliberately: "So, are you close to making a decision? Do you agree to my conditions?"

Exhausted and stressed, I nodded in acquiescence. The chief of staff walked over to me and grabbed my slender and cream-colored hands in his firm and sturdy ones.

"Tomorrow at 6am, I will have a jeep pick you up and send you directly to the company. Work hard, reform yourself and become a new man. In three years, you will surely be able to mould yourself into a member of the revolutionary ranks."

He patted me on the shoulder as he sent me to the door. I thanked him again and again before backing out of his office. Only now was I aware of the fact that Yue and I belonged to two utterly different classes. However much indebted I was to her, and even though I had a crush on her from the very beginning, the chief of staff made my true status very clear. I knew any union with Yue would be impossible. She was the adorable swan while I was the ugly duckling. From now on, I dared not harbour any dreams about Yue. Being able to stay in the Corps was a blessing in itself. I owed it to the chief of staff. I could no longer cry for the moon or expect anything more than that. I made up my mind to follow his instructions and head to the toughest place to reform myself, and follow my father's advice of keeping a low profile, bringing my youthful impudence under control and casting out all fancy ideas.

After leaving the office of the chief of staff, I did not return to the hostel, but kept circling around the clinic. The two rows of windows of the clinic were still dark and the female soldiers who had gone to work in the company had not returned home. Yue had told me they would not be back until midnight.

Feelings of exhilaration and depression were intertwined. Being accepted by the Corps was a key moment in my life. I did not have to return to Beijing. I no longer had to run around aimlessly, nor would I be dispatched to a place I did not want to go. My basic needs of life were being met to pave the way for a good future. I would soon get two sets of clothes, a quilt, a mattress and a monthly subsidy of six yuan. This would be the first time that I would live on my own. I felt indebted to the bearded chief of staff, even though his belligerence and craftiness had enabled him to unearth my family background. He was kind enough to use his authority to find me a position in the Corps. He was like a boxer who had knocked me out before coming over to pick me up. On reflection, however, I knew he would not have done any of this had it not been for Yue. So my true benefactor was Yue.

Thinking of Yue brought back memories of Beethoven's ninth symphony. I had heard my father play this piece many times when I was young. He had a passion for classical music. Before the founding of the PRC, a British friend of his had given him a French gramophone that could play six albums at a time. The gramophone accompanied my father for most of his life. His favourite record was Beethoven's ninth, and I grew up to the sound of its stormy melodies. It was once again thrilling me now, but I was fully aware the chief of staff forbade me to have any further contact with Yue. It was a command that I had to obey. Was I doomed to swallow the bitter fruits of love when I had just smelt the sweetness of its flowers? The very thought that I would not be able to see her anymore sent my heart into agonising spasms of pain. How disappointed and distressed would she be if I simply left without word? A feeling of melancholy and hopelessness eclipsed my earlier joy and excitement.

Without thinking, I walked to the large tree where I had met with Yue. I leant against its thick trunk as I recalled everything that had happened in the morning. In that short span of just twenty minutes, the passionate Yue had boldly proclaimed her love for me. Her beautiful face reappeared before me. Once again, I seemed to be smelling her sweet breath and hugging her supple waist. The bitter expression on my face at the time of our parting would probably remain with me forever. A tremor went through me, and a torrent of emotions swept over me. I knew my life would be nothing but suffering for a long while to come, and my memories and longing for Yue would probably provide my only spiritual sustenance. And the tree that witnessed our embrace would be a symbol of our eternal love. I would come to see it whenever I came to the town of Xin'an, and a holy tree of love would also grow out of my heart – a tree that I would worship constantly.

I had no sense of the time when I trudged back to the hostel and threw myself down on the bed. The next day at dawn, having washed my face and brushed my teeth, a driver woke me up and led me to his jeep, which would take me to my future company. As the jeep passed the clinic, I strained to look at Yue's house through the window. How I wished she would come out now so I could see her for the last time! But the reveille had not yet sounded, and everything was quiet and still. I could barely hold back my tears. The chief of staff wanted me to forget Yue, but how could I? All I could do was bury her in my heart, like the moon cast out in the water, or like the coral in the depths of the ocean. In a secluded company dozens of miles from Yue, I would miss her quietly and keep loving her without her being aware of it. Meanwhile, I knew a new page of my life was about to begin in an unfamiliar, lonely and loveless place far away from Beijing.

Chapter 9

New in the Company

The company I was assigned to was the First Company, Twelfth Regiment of the Second Division. On my way there, I asked the driver many questions. The reason it was the first company, he said, was probably because it was the most remote – about thirty miles from Xin'an, where the regiment was based. Its location, Shatou, has a chilling association because the word sounds like 'chopping off the head' when spoken in Chinese. Shatou was originally said to be a gulag for felons or major criminals who were sentenced to prison or death. With a precipitous terrain, Shatou had for years contained nothing but a single building resembling a pillbox and dozens of tomb-shaped sand dunes, with no signs of human habitation. Prisoners had no chance of escape because, even if they had managed to get out, they would be easily caught in this bleak environment.

Probably for this reason, the First Company became a special gathering place for the Second Division. Any 'delinquent' or individual with a politically incorrect family background would be sent here first. Especially in its early years, all manner of *guanxi* (social connections) were needed in order to join the Corps. The earliest arrivals were mostly children of the privileged class who had grown up in official compounds. Their family origins were either revolutionary officials or soldiers supposed to be part of the 'red five', but their family status had taken a turn for the worse during political campaigns. Some of them became children of the 'black five' after their parents were labelled 'capitalist roaders'. There were children of 'red' family origins who had become juvenile delinquents due to their involvement in criminal activities such as vandalism, looting and robbery. So, on careful consideration, many of the pioneers in the First

Company had extraordinary backgrounds, and a number of them enjoyed quite some fame in Beijing. For people who had lived through that era, it easy to imagine what those youths looked like in the capital. Wearing classy army overcoats and armbands, they rode their bikes alongside one another, passing quickly through the noisy evening streets. They could have easily joined the army but were prevented from doing so because of their problematic family backgrounds or personal records. In the end, the Inner Mongolia Corps became their best possible option.

The Corps was made up of six divisions. The Second Division with a total of ten regiments was located in the Urat Front banner of Bayannur union. Those with solid *guanxi* joined the Nineteenth Regiment located near Ulansuhai since it enjoyed the best terrain. I was allocated to the headquarters of the Twelfth Regiment because of Yue's special relationship with Chief of Staff Wang. Those who were assigned to the First Company were mostly either children of the 'black five' or simply hooligans given to brawling or street fighting. Hence, the First Company included the most problematic and troublesome elements. Although Chief of Staff Wang kept saying I was educable, he still sent me to the company because he saw me in the back of his mind as a type that deserved nothing better. Sensing that I had special connections, the driver kept telling me stories about the First Company.

"The guys in your company are all good at fighting! They deploy strategy, tactics and careful planning. They must have been influenced by their parents, and now they are notorious throughout the regiment."

He told me how soldiers from the First Company had raided neighbouring companies in Victua and Qiaowan. He said those soldiers were good at fighting because most of them had military backgrounds. They were especially good at surprise raids with knives, cleavers, bricks or shoulder poles, he said. In small groups, they would steal into the camps of other companies and act on predetermined signals. They were given specific tasks: some were there to fight, others to 'make peace'. When their target was set, several young men would break into the room to fight. Creating such a clamour at the dead of night would draw people out of their rooms. The 'peace-makers' would then step forward to block them, failing which they would drive them back into their rooms with bricks and axes until the fight in the main battlefield was won. They would then retreat in unison. By now, heads would be sticking out of every window to see what was going on, but no one would dare breathe a word. About ten minutes later, cries of bloody murder would be heard...

The jeep arrived at the headquarters of the First Company in Shatou before the talkative driver was done with his stories. All the soldiers of the Corps were heading out to work in the fields. Almost everyone was looking at me with curious eyes because of the vehicle. Maybe they thought I had powerful *guanxi* or family background. Knowing that I came from Chief of Staff Wang, the company commander would naturally treat me seriously. He told me to get some training in the farming platoon before offering me a better position. No one knew I had been an outcast just several days ago, an unwelcome intruder who, without any official paperwork, had managed to sneak onto a train and make it to the Corps. Had it not been for Yue, I would never have been treated with such courtesy. With these thoughts, I felt the onset of tears and a vision of Yue emerged. I forced myself to stop thinking about her.

I was assigned to the Second Platoon whose leader was a veteran called Zhou. Tall, with a large face and a dark skin, he spoke like a man of real authority. He put me in Squad No.1 whose leader was called Zeng. I was led to a room in a mudbrick house in which lay a *kang* big enough for four people to sleep on. The vacant spot on the edge was for me. A mat supposedly made of reed leaves from Ulansuhai was set on the berth and on the mat were a cotton-padded mattress, a quilt and pillow. This would be my sleeping place. I received two new army uniforms. I gained some confidence after putting one of them on. Just a couple of days before, I had been crouching in a filthy corner in the carters' inn like a beggar suffering from hunger and cold. And now I was a true soldier of the Corps wearing a green uniform. My heart was filled with joy.

A short while later, there came the loud dinner bugle, which gave me a special feeling of warmth. It was company dinner time. I followed my roommates into a large auditorium whose mudbrick exterior wall was painted with four large Chinese characters: '*Tun ken shu bian*', which means 'Farming and safeguarding the border regions'. In the middle of the auditorium were two large baskets filled with cream-coloured steamed bread. Next to the baskets lay two huge vats of vegetable soup. Diners could take as much bread and soup as they liked. In addition, each person was served with a dish from the kitchen window by two female soldiers. Diners typically lined up to wait for their turn. Normally, everyone would get a large ladle of food. However, the amount contained in that ladle could vary. So, when the male soldiers reached out their hands for the food, they would open their eyes wide to stare at the ladle. Some would smile or even put on flattering expressions to please the female servers so they could get a full measure. However, such tricks would often backfire because the servers did not appreciate them. Their hands would shake and the food in the ladle would spill, the sight of which would bring despair to the male soldier at the head of the queue and the sound of guffaws from those waiting behind. When it was my turn, I simply walked quietly to the window and gave my bowl to the server, who took a curious look at me as I lowered my head sheepishly. To my surprise, she gave me a full ladle, which made me feel I had finally arrived at the right place.

As a newcomer who knew no one, I chose to squat in a corner to eat by myself until Li Yi and Liu Wei approached and engaged me in conversation. The medium-sized Li appeared spirited and energetic, and had bushy eyebrows and a pair of large, shining eyes. The slightly taller Liu had a clean-shaven head, a strong and muscular build, and a unique personality. As children of families in the Beijing military region community, they assumed that I lived in a military compound just like them. However, the only military connection I had was Mum's former employment at the General Hospital of Beijing military region, where she was never allocated any housing. So my family and I actually lived in an alley near Beijing railway station, in a courtyard house all by itself, though we had to share it with another family during the political movement. By Chief of Staff Wang's analysis, I did not count as part of the military community because I had never lived in a military camp. The isolated bourgeois style of life I experienced with my dad made it impossible for me to receive a proletarian education, Wang reasoned. The fact that I had been brought up by two nurses and trained as a young master was ample proof that I carried the stamp of the bourgeoisie.

Since no one knew I had arrived here by irregular means and I didn't have any personal papers with me, no one could possibly know my capitalist family origins. All they knew was that I came here in a jeep, which meant I had special background or *guanxi*. I thought it would be profitable to pretend to be something I was not, so I told them I came from the compound of the General Hospital of Beijing military region.

However, the conversation became embarrassing when Liu Wei mentioned several names that I didn't recognise. It turned out that they were all well-known street fighters in the compound. Anyone with only a fleeting social contact would have known them.

"You must be a very meek and humble person," my two new friends commented.

They began to think of me as a bookworm who spent his time reading and studying at home all day, and who never played with the wild kids on the street, let alone mix with those from the army community. They left after failing to find any common ground with me. They must have been very disappointed, I thought.

That evening, I sat blankly on the kang recalling all that had happened during the day. I thought it would be hard to make any close friends here, let alone date anyone of the opposite sex. My only option would be to keep a low profile and face the trials and difficulties head on so as to change myself in profound ways.

At this point I recalled what Mencius had said: "Thus, when Heaven decides to give a great responsibility to someone, it first makes his mind suffer. It makes his sinews and bones experience toil, and his body endure hunger. It inflicts him with poverty and knocks down everything he tries to build. In this way Heaven stimulates his mind, stabilises his temper and develops new abilities."

Although Mencius' ideas had long been criticised for being feudal, I felt they made good sense when I related them to my personal circumstances. So I took out a notebook and scribbled down several so-called 'poems'. In the process of writing this book, I came across these poems in a dog-eared notebook. Though my handwriting is squiggly and the sentiments naïve and laughable, readers may get a glimpse of my honesty, purity and mental state at the time. Here are some segments:

I choose to live a life of heated struggle.
I enjoy doing the hardest, dirtiest and most gruelling jobs.
Let the onerous physical labour crush my laziness.
Let the blizzard break my brittleness.

For me there are no comfy houses, fancy food or mellow wine,
Nothing but barren grassland, roaring winds and endless snow.
Ahead of me trials and tribulations abound,
And twists and turns multiply,
But I am marching on the broad way of glory,
Wielding a banner that bears these shining words:
'Farming and defending the border'.

I will leave the city and my home for Inner Mongolia,
To defend my country's northern border.
I will go and farm the wasteland,
I will rush to the frontiers to guard our border.
Let the cold winds temper my will.
Let the sunshine reform my thinking.

Mount Daqing is a mountain of mountains.
Ulansuhai lake is a sea of waves.
They seem to be beckoning me warmly.
The barren land of the Gobi desert,
Which has slept for a thousand years,
Seems to have opened its drowsy eyes,
To call me over for a mission,
To turn this wasteland to farmland.

Let me use the big brush of revolution,
To write the most fabulous poem,
To paint the most brilliant landscape.
Let me be a brave trailblazer,
Under the fiery red banner.

After finishing the poem, I closed the notebook and fell asleep. My new life started the next morning, when the loud and clear bugle sounded.

I knew where I had come from. I was a social outcast without any means of survival. I knew the value of the rice bowl I had just found. So I went out of my way to work hard and devoted my whole being to whatever assignments or tasks I was given. I took the lead rushing into the fields – to remove the weeds; to the tunnel digging sites – to keep shovelling the earth; to the wheat fields of summer – to harvest with a sickle, sparing no strength under the scorching sun.

I gave the impression of being a quiet dynamo who would at times just sit there grimly and stoically daydreaming. My withdrawn and solitary ways also somehow cast a veil of mystery over me. Few people were aware of my background, but everyone knew I was sent to the company in a jeep, so the people around me would never look down upon me. In the eyes of my fellow soldiers, I was a hardworking labourer who would never harm anyone and I would consistently avoid potential conflicts. Therefore, leaders at all levels of the company were happy with my performance. Meanwhile, I managed to earn goodwill and respect from my peers.

Chapter 10

Transferred to the Horse-keeping Squad

Before I knew it, I had already spent two months in the Corps. One day after wheat harvest, Platoon Chief Zhou called me to his house for a private talk, which made me feel somewhat flattered.

"You've been doing well since you came to the company," he said, smiling. "Everyone can see that. The leaders have a good impression of you and plan to give you a new position. The horse-keeping squad, which has just received some new horses, needs a responsible and hardworking helper. After discussion, we decided to give the job to you. Are you willing to take it?"

That was exactly the job I wanted. Though usually an introvert, I jumped into the air and yelled: "I am! I am!"

There was an unspeakable sense of blessing in being able to find my dream job in a new environment full of hardships and far away from friends and loved ones. I was easily satisfied back then. Many weird things had happened since I came to Inner Mongolia. I was the only person who sneaked onto the train and got away with it. I ran into Zhang Yue and got to stay in the Corps with her help. Though I could not remain with her and continue our love affair once I had been assigned to this remote and tough place, I still felt lucky because I was asked to raise horses. Despite the difficulties in my life's journey, Lady Luck has been consistently nice to me.

The stable courtyard where the horse squad was based looked huge – about the size of a football field. Although the walls, stables, cowsheds and houses were built with adobe bricks, they gave a sense of spaciousness, openness and solidity. At least they looked outstanding in this setting. The entrance to the stable was huge. Two massive mud mounds were connected with two thick wooden balustrades. Close to the entrance was a deep well with a high platform equipped with an iron-handled compression bar that looked simple but solid. Buckets of water were drawn from the well to fill three tanks large enough to provide water for a herd of horses or cattle.

As I carried my luggage to the horse squad, a smiling oval face was there to greet me. It was Little Li, the squad chief, a kind, handsome man of average height. He took my luggage and put it in the house that was prepared for me. No longer able to contain my curiosity about the horses, I raced to the fence and saw an adorable herd playing in the enclosure. All of them held their heads proudly in the air. Full of vim and vigour, they shook their necks and manes and playfully bit and chased one another. Sometimes two horses would lift up their front legs and touch each other with their hooves. On other occasions they would kneel down before each other like newlyweds at a Chinese wedding ceremony. Quickly immersed in the horses' world, I was enthralled in what they were doing. An admirer of animals as a child, I fell in love with those horses at first sight. Attracted by their vitality, an unprecedented pleasure enveloped me and swept away all my grievances and troubles.

The company had recently bought a herd of horses from Xilingol league, most of which were local Mongolian racers that were characterised by their small size and well-developed muscles. At the time, Mongolian horses typically went for about five hundred yuan each. The company also kept Kabardin crossbreeds from the former Soviet Union, costing fifteen hundred yuan, which was quite a sum back then. We soldiers at the Corps commonly made six yuan a month in allowance in return for all our hard work. This tall, long-eared 'foreign horse', with slender legs, a relatively slim waist and a short and scant mane and tail hairs, ran fast and nimble like a gust of wind. All of the horses were named, some after their colour, such as Little Green, Little Yellow, Little Black, Old Mixed Hair and Big Old White. Others were named after their own characteristics, such as Snow-white Hooves, Bandit and One Eye. Still others were called by the numbers branded on their croups.

When I first arrived at the squad, I was not allowed to ride the horses. My job was to graze them on a strip of grassland in between some crop fields. Walking around the horses with a small branch in hand, I would watch over them, yell at them or wield the branch whenever any of them got bored with the grass and were tempted to try the crops nearby. I would be filled with envy whenever a horse-riding villager darted past like a valiant warrior. I would seriously wonder if I qualified as a horseman when I couldn't even ride a horse. I decided to learn the skill at whatever cost.

One day at noon, I secretly led a horse to the backyard of the stable for my first trial ride. Called Mixed Hair because of its brown, black and white coat, this horse was the tamest in the entire herd. Being over ten years old and looking like a typical Mongolian horse, Mixed Hair was bought by the company from a neighbouring village through *guanxi* for 180 yuan, the price of just an average horse. It was obedient in every way. It could pull a wagon or millstone, and would walk, jog and gallop with real patience and ease no matter who was riding it.

I stroked the hairs on its back before slowly climbing on. It was meek and quiet at first but started moving and jolting as soon as I had steadied myself. And that was when I lost my balance, flipped over and fell heavily on a wheat stack. Feeling no pain, I climbed up again. I was so keen on riding and wanted to master the skill so badly that I would continue even when my body was battered black and blue.

Persistence finally paid off. After practising for a couple of weeks, I finally grasped the key elements of riding. When mounting a horse, you need to be quick, quiet and gentle. Keep your legs clamped around the horse's back, relax your upper body, maintain your balance, hold the reins tight and grab the mane if necessary. When the horse is running, position yourself comfortably and keep your balance. Tilt your body slightly when the horse turns. Sit back when it stops abruptly. When it comes to saddling the horse, you need to first adjust the stirrup based on your height. It should be neither too long nor too short, so that your feet and legs can work effectively. There are also some basics for quick mounting. Take the reins in your left hand and hold the pommel towards you with your right hand. Put your left foot into the stirrup, bounce gently and throw yourself in the saddle with a swing of the waist. As you sit on your horse, keep your heels pointing down so you can stretch and kick. Do not clinch the horse with your legs the same way you would ride an unsaddled horse. Release the bit when the horse starts to run, bend your waist or even move slightly away from the saddle, as if you were half squatting, and the horse will start to gallop. Once you learn how to control the horse with ease, you will become a great rider roaming on the steppe.

I lived in an area where riding a trotting horse was the fashion. Riding a trotting horse is much different from riding a galloping one. A trotting horse wiggles like a race walker while a galloping horse surges forward like the billows. An excellent trotting horse is no slower than an average galloping horse. The former can provide a stable and comfy ride over long distances.

With a trotting horse, you need to tilt your body slightly, with one foot exerting force sideways. The bit needs to be neither too loose nor too tight, and your body should rock gently in tempo with the horse's movement. Otherwise, the horse will not be able to move in a smooth and steady manner. Such equestrian skills are never acquired quickly. Probably only one in a thousand horses would know how to trot smoothly with the rider by itself. The vast majority need training and guidance from a skilled rider. An extraordinary trotting horse would be known throughout villages and towns, while those cared for by an expert vet would be worth huge sums.

A novice rider can easily get addicted to horse riding. I would feel quite uneasy physically and mentally if I stopped for a couple of days. The horse-keeping squad had a rule that forbid the riding of horses while they were being pastured. So the herder had to walk. During regular meetings, I frequently motioned to change that rule, giving various reasons. For example, I would emphasise the need to graze the horses in more remote places because the grass nearby was about to run out. I would also cite individual cases where some solitary horses tended to run into the fields and cause damage to the crops.

My efforts eventually caused the horse-keeping squad to modify that rule. The new rule allowed herders to travel back and forth on horseback, but disallowed riding during grazing time. In order to gain more riding time, I sometimes went as far as two miles away to graze the horses.

One day while herding, Squad Chief Li pulled out a mule for me to look after. The mule and the horses were incompatible. So I had to keep an eye on the mule all the time we were walking. During grazing time, I planted a stake in the ground and tethered the mule to it by its ankle with a long rope, so that it would graze all by itself. On our way back, Li looked a hero, directing the horses on horseback while I trudged in step with the mule. It gave me no joy. As I walked and walked, an idea struck me. I stopped to examine the mule and found it could be ridden. So I coiled the reins, grabbed its bridle in one hand while touching its neck with the other, and jumped on its back before it knew it. Startled, the mule ran off at high speed.

Mules are actually more powerful than horses and have greater endurance when it comes to pulling a cart. No wonder my mule started racing as soon as I got on its back. Struggling to keep it under control, I felt I could be thrown off at any time. It was just like a riding a hungry tiger because I had no way of getting off. Filled with regret, I simply gripped the mule tightly with my legs and pulled the reins hard so that I may jump off as soon as it slowed down. Unfortunately, it was impossible to keep it in check because it had no bit in its mouth. The more I tried to stop the mule, the faster it ran, and it took only a split second for us to fly past Li.

Li was stunned. By the time he realised what was happening, I was nearing the barn. Seeing me riding a mule in the distance, soldiers of the First Platoon of the Corps who had just finished their day's work raised their hoes to cheer me on. Their cheers in turn alerted others in the horse-keeping squad, who all came out to witness my unusual act of bravery.

By now, however, I felt I could no longer hold on. How I wished the frightened mule would stop right there when I saw a four-foot-high railing at the opening in front of the stable. But it didn't. It simply leapt over it and carried me across. The next thing I knew was that it came to a halt in front of a manger inside the stable. The ordeal was over.

Later on, Li said that this mule had never previously been ridden by anyone. I was the first person to do so, and that gave me confidence in my horsemanship. Through interacting with the horses in the process of raising and riding them, I emerged from my cowardice and became more and more daring. Had she witnessed this, Yue would certainly have admired my progress. I never rode that mule again, having being told that mules were poor riding animals because they could play dirty tricks on riders. Before long, I had finished riding all of the horses that the company owned. My only regret was that I had not acquired a really top horse.

Chapter 11

Death of a Wild Horse

One day, Platoon Chief Zhang of the horse-keeping squad brought an untamed wild Ferghana horse. The Ferghana is a very rare species, worth up to ten million yuan today, so I wondered if it was just an ordinary chestnut-coloured Mongolian horse. Now, however, I am quite certain that it was a Ferghana.

Ferghana horses existed in ancient China. In *Records of the Grand Historian*, Zhang Qian wrote: "The western region abounds in fine horses that sweat blood." Ferghana horses have been thought to exist in China for two thousand years, although purebreds are hard to find because they have been integrated into some Mongolian breeds.

I am certain that this horse had at least some Ferghana blood because it was taller than the average Mongolian horse. Irritable and unyielding and nicknamed 'Bandit', he was the wildest of all of the horses in the company. Bandit would not normally allow anyone to get close to him; if you did, he would prick up his ears, open his nostrils, breathe heavily and dig at the ground with his hooves, as if confronting an enemy. Bandit seemed to have boundless energy and power. It would take more than a dozen people just to rein him in.

"What a mighty wild horse," I exclaimed. "If tamed, he would be the finest horse ever."

Platoon Chief Zhang was a cavalryman of medium height. He had a baby face even though he was in his late twenties. His bright eyes under bushy eyebrows bespoke his sharpness and capability. He led out Bandit on Sunday in the hope of taming him. Because of a lack of alternative entertainment at the Corps, horse training was the most popular pastime.

Zhang was the one who took the lead in training Bandit. The stable was so packed with spectators there was hardly any space to move. At the beginning of the training, two soldiers held the reins tight as another brandished a whip to keep the horse going in circles until he was exhausted and drenched in sweat. Next, Zhang walked over to grab Bandit by the ears and saddle him. A cheer erupted among the crowd, followed by complete silence when everyone held their breath to wait for the most exhilarating moment when Zhang would leap onto Bandit's back.

However, the former cavalryman lost his nerve. After several attempts, he could no longer mount the horse, and one of his feet was visibly shaking. Determined to save face and not be shown up as a coward, he turned his eyes to the crowd and asked: "Who dares go first?"

As he said this, he swept his look at every soldier in the stable before his eyes settled on me. Either because my craving for horse riding had not been satisfied or because I was young and wanted to prove myself, or perhaps out of a need to vent my long-suppressed feelings and energy, I suddenly found the courage to stand up and walk over.

Platoon Chief Zhang grabbed Bandit by the ears. The horse's defiance seemed to be temporarily held in check. I jumped onto the saddle and pulled up the snaffle bit. He did not budge. As soon as his ears were let go, however, Bandit sprang to his feet like a Spanish fighting bull and kept bucking until I was thrown to the ground. Just then something unexpected happened. One of my feet got caught tight in the saddle iron, which is the most perilous thing to happen to a rider. Although someone was holding the reins, I still got dragged along on the floor for several metres and got trampled several times by Bandit. Fortunately, a few brave soldiers grabbed Bandit by the ears and pulled me from under his hooves. My groin was hurt and was oozing blood. I was left with a permanent scar after it healed.

I was scared as I lay in bed that night because the injury I sustained was just five centimetres from my testicles. I could have been disabled for life, if not killed. The worst part would be that I would never be able to marry. My impulsive act did not mean I was brave, but reckless. I had no idea how I had been transformed from a genteel scholar into a macho and foolhardy young man. I do not attribute it to my Corps training, nor to any courage acquired through frequent interaction with horses. To be honest, it could only be an abnormal outbreak of the ego after prolonged psychological repression.

There was someone who was in love with me, but I could not approach her, not even by mail, even though she was just several dozen miles away. Sustained inhibition had twisted my mind and created a mental imbalance, and the need for relief turned me into an impetuous risk-taker. Such a change, I later reflected, was not something that Yue would have wanted to see. Had she known of my actions, she would have deterred me – she would never let me risk my life in that way. For Yue's sake, in future I should deal with situations in a calm and poised manner, keep walking humbly and stick to the virtues of kindness, honesty and integrity.

After the accident, as a gesture of apology to me, the platoon chief ordered Bandit to be given a good whipping. But I felt it wasn't fair to punish a horse just because he had kicked me. My thinking was that horses could never be tamed by violence alone. A better approach would be to treat them humanely, with patience and love, because they are similar to human beings in many ways.

Since my fall, no one else dared to ride Bandit again. Instead, it was used to pull a wagon. According to Coachman Song, Bandit was always the most hard-working wagon-puller. He needed no whipping at all. I felt sorry for this exceptional wild horse being used to pull a wagon. What a terrible waste. If trained by the right person in the right way, it should become an excellent riding horse, one of the best on the grasslands.

After a few months, I got the sad news of Bandit's death. It happened when the company sent all the soldiers to Ulansuhai to cut grass. To prevent the horses from running away, an inexperienced coachman fastened the reins connecting the bridle to the ankles of the horses' forelegs. While grazing, the horses got closer and closer to the deep canal. When they saw the water, they went ahead to drink and then jumped in out of excitement. They forgot their heads were actually tied to their ankles by the reins. Unable to raise their heads, they started sinking as soon as they entered the water, and the more they struggled, the faster and deeper they sank. Though several soldiers dived in to rescue them, four of them drowned, and Bandit was one of them. The coachman said Bandit put up such a violent struggle that nobody could get close to him. All they could do was watch him die.

Bandit's death broke my heart. I deplored the manner of his fate despite my own near-death experience. Bad-tempered horses are said to be good horses. Though irascible by nature, Bandit was powerful, speedy and steadfast. All he had needed was a good trainer. I could only regret that Bandit was born in bad times, times when even countless talented people were neglected or persecuted. The death of Bandit was soon forgotten as an accident. But the subsequent death of another horse in the company stirred up the compassion of many.

Xiaojunma (Little Army Horse), so-called because he was a veteran from the cavalry, was in his teenage years when it was assigned to our company. He had done a great service during the quelling of the Tibetan rebellion. Xiaojunma was a Sichuan breed, smaller than a Mongolian, which explained its muscular, sturdy and dynamic appearance and the fact that he ran like an arrow. Having received formal training and shown an ability to lie down and stand up as instructed, he won the acclaim of many. However, his special talent and brilliant achievements in combat did not save him from a fate of drudgery. He still needed to pull heavy loads. Fortunately, he was led by a kind-hearted coachman called Zhou Ying, and he could share the work with three other horses, each with the same dark blue hair.

The four horses were well cared for. They had plenty to eat and drink, and were often tied to a tree where they could bask in the sun. Thin and oval-faced Zhou Ying had a pair of small, smiling eyes. He had a deep love for the horses he herded. He enjoyed doing a thorough job of combing them with a bristle brush from top to bottom, so the four dark horses always had smooth hair. If the combing failed relieve their itching, the horses would play happily together and lick and nibble at one another. When put to work, they would do it quickly and share the load evenly. Seated in the driver's seat, Zhou Ying could encourage the horses without using his whip, as if saying: "I let you out to exercise rather than toil."

During long journeys, Zhou Ying would lie on the wagon and hum a tune as the horses ran happily to the same beat. When they stopped by a hostel to rest, as soon as the excitement dissipated, the horses would roll over on the ground to dry their skin and then shake the clay off themselves. Zhou would then throw the reins on their backs instead of tying them up to the wagon. He would simply fill up the wooden grooves in the back of the carriage with hay and then go to attend other things. The horses would never step away from the carriage. When it was time for the horses to drink, all Zhou needed to do was to lead any one of them and the rest would follow. And when he moved away, none of the horses that were drinking would return to the carriage until all of them were done. In this way, they acted like real brothers.

One day during a labour contest, under the orders of a political instructor, two soldiers from a losing platoon stole into the stable and dragged Xiaojunma to the contest site to pull the roller. Xiaojunma was tied to a large tree and was basking in the sun. The soldiers thought he would be easy to manoeuver, but he refused to leave his partners, and nor did he want to obey strange new voices. When the whips and sticks came out, he felt insulted and turned around abruptly, struggling out of the hands of the intended rider and running back frantically.

Startled by the rapid sound of hooves, I rushed out of the house. Horses would charge like this only when they were frightened or out of control. I sensed something terrible was about to happen. On the boundless salt marshes, Xiaojunma ran desperately, creating huge clouds of dust. All of a sudden, it turned around and ran in the direction of the stable, and to the tree to which it was usually tied. That was the place it was most familiar with, the place where it spent the happiest times of its life and, most of all, where its brothers were. Xiaojunma ran frantically towards the tree. Rather than slowing down, it sped up until it crashed into that huge tree. I dashed over to find him lying on the ground, with no blood apparent on his head. As I lifted his eyelids, I saw his dilated pupils. There was no breath or heartbeat. He was dead.

A few hours later, I saw something that I would never forget. The other three horses were licking Xiaojunma all over his body until his hair was wet with their saliva. Zhou Ying stood there stupefied, with tears streaming down his face. The tragic scene awakened me to the existence of a soul-stirring love. In an era devoid of human love, I saw the purest love in nature, the great love in the natural world. Our quiet comrades-in-arms, horses had bravely demonstrated their pure and natural love, which had an irresistible appeal to me. If no human love could be found in that strife-ridden age, wouldn't it be better for me to seek love in the natural world?

Chapter 12

Horse-keeping

People who live in unfamiliar, depressing or distressful circumstances often feel the sluggishness of time. Once they have adapted to those circumstances, when things go more smoothly, time passes more rapidly. That's what happened to me in the Corps. Since I was transferred to the horse-keeping squad, I became obsessed with horses. I loved my job so much that I became indifferent to everything else around me. Even memories of my beloved Yue began to fade. One reason was that I had never left Shatou and had no opportunity to revisit the town of Xin'an, where the Corps headquarters was located. Hence, I had no chance to meet with her, or even catch sight of her. Immersed in the paradise of horse-keeping, I hardly noticed the passage of time. My first year at the Corps had passed like a flash. I was now twenty-one years old.

My main job was raising and herding horses. I worked mostly at night and occasionally during the day when the horses were not working. This was because, as the saying goes, 'horses need to eat green grass at night in order to stay healthy and strong'. They were let loose to graze in spring, summer and autumn, when the land was covered in green grass. Usually before dinner, cart-pulling horses, farm horses and riding horses would return to the stable. Released from their saddles and other restraining devices, they would roll on the floor to dry their sweat-soaked bodies before being locked in a stable with a wood frame door. Our company had dozens of horses in those days. Between 9pm and 10pm a colleague and I would start working. I would fetch buckets of water from a well to fill the three troughs before letting out the horses, and the horses would eagerly gather around the troughs to drink.

I would then equip myself with a raincoat, long whip and flashlight before heading off to the pasture. At the start, when the horses were most hungry, they would typically finish off an area of grass before moving on to a new spot under the guidance of one or two leaders. So the horses would keep moving during the first half of the night.

There was no need to ride the horses at night. All I had to do was follow the horses and prevent them from eating the crops. If some of them were tempted, I would shine the flashlight on their leader and yell at it, and if that failed I would brandish my whip and make a loud cracking sound to scare them away.

After five or six hours' continuous grazing, the horses would be full. Some of them would begin to doze off, some would nibble or bite each other, and others would roll on the ground to ease the itching caused by mosquito bites. In the end, all the horses would gather together and begin a collective nap with their lowered heads facing in the same direction. They would rarely move at this point, and I would feel sleepy too. I would find a spot by the horses, cover the ground with my raincoat and lie there for a short while and practise *qigong*. I would exercise breathing through the abdomen, absorbing the fresh morning air, drawing in the inner strength of the earth and learning to become at one with nature. It was a heavenly feeling. Lying flat on the ground, I would look up and sometimes see shooting stars flash across the sky.

Such pleasure is not easily found in modern life. As I lay on my raincoat, I would revel in the gentle sounds of nature: the croaks of frogs and toads from afar or the snores of the horses close by. Every now and then, a horse would relieve itself and set off the others; each pee would last longer than the previous one. When they were all done, the horses would lower their heads once more and continue to nap. And the pasture would be peaceful and quiet again.

As the sky brightened, heralding the dawning of another day, some of the horses would raise their heads as they began to sense the mist of early morning. They were now ready for breakfast – 'dew-soaked grass', otherwise known as 'night grass', which is crucial for the healthy development of a horse. I would lead the horses to the alfalfa fields and let them eat the most nutritious dew-soaked grass. Sitting close by, I would watch them devour the alfalfa and hear their constant munching that reverberated like a symphony in the silence of dawn. At that moment, I forgot all about my relatively privileged city life, the sadness of being away from my parents, the humiliation and trauma my family had gone through, and even the sweet memories of my beloved Yue. My heart would rejoice and my soul would be content with all the pleasures that nature had to offer.

Grazing in winter was impossible because the grassland turned dry and desolate. In preparation, the company had prepared carts full of reed leaves in Wuliangsuhai during the autumn. In the daytime, we would scythe the grass and stack the processed grass in a thatched shed. By night, the horses would feed on the grass as usual. The horses' barn, consisting of more than twenty stables, was made of adobe bricks. Each stable had a stone or wooden trough that stood more than one metre high. Above the troughs lay crossbeams, on which the bridled horses were tied. One of my duties was to fill the troughs with chopped grass.

Each stable could accommodate two to three horses. Stallions, valuable horses and bad-tempered horses would be allocated to different stables. In front of the mangers was a long corridor. I enjoyed feeding the horses alone in the dead of the night, something that called for plenty of courage. I liked the task mainly because it allowed me to read in perfect peace. I usually wore a sheepskin overcoat, not in order to appear like a country fellow, but because the cotton overcoat provided by the company was insufficient to keep me warm in the chilly northern winds. I would read by the light of a lantern, which was much brighter than the kerosene lamp typically used in the army camp.

At that time there were very few books to read. Besides some philosophical works by Chairman Mao, Karl Marx and Friedrich Engels, I had a book entitled *A Handbook for Country Doctors*, widely used as a training textbook for 'barefoot doctors' (farmers who received minimal basic medical and paramedical training and worked in China's rural villages) after Chairman Mao had called on officials and institution staff to receive re-education in May 7 cadre schools and on educated urban youths to settle down in the countryside. I paid four yuan for this thick book from a Xinhua bookstore in Beijing's Wangfujing Street after queueing up for a long time. I arranged for it be sent to me from Beijing after I had settled down in the Corps. Because I loved medicine even as a child, the book soon became my favourite. Other books that I loved included a bilingual collection of foreign fables in English and Chinese and a small English-Chinese dictionary. Thanks to these books, I was able to improve my English proficiency during my six years with the horses. As a matter of fact, I managed to commit to memory a dozen or so fables in English.

Holding the lantern, I would walk along the dark corridor, past one stable after another, and when the horses saw me, they would raise their heads, and some would even snort for food. I would stroke their heads as I walked on until I reached the thatched hut at the end of the corridor. After putting the lantern on the floor, I would then pick up a large basket, fill it with chopped grass and spread it evenly in the troughs. After I had eventually filled all the troughs, the whole barn would echo with the sweet sound of the horses chewing on the grass. After that, I would walk back along the corridor and stop in a larger room in the middle section. Inside was a square adobe table and a square adobe stool. I would put the lantern on the table, take out the books from under my arm and begin reading. This was my favourite pastime during my years in the Corps.

I did my reading to the background sound of the horses' chewing, which seemed particularly loud at dead of night. When the sound died down and eventually stopped altogether, I knew that all the grass had been eaten. I would then get up and add more grass. After feeding the horses five or six times, I would walk to the well in order to fill up the water troughs. Next, I would be faced with the daunting task of providing water for all of the horses in more than twenty stables. I needed to unfasten all of their bridles, lead them to the water one by one, and then take them back and leash them up again. By then, a new day would be about to break and it would be time to prepare for the horses' last meal before I went to bed. This last big meal, which included corn, black beans or soybean cakes, was so enticing to the horses that they could be heard munching from a long distance off. Exhausted and sleepy, I then carried the lantern and walked back to my dorm. My work was now done.

Since the barn was some distance from the company and I did night shifts, my life was quite removed from the workings of the company. Frequent absences from company meetings made it possible for me to become detached from various political activities or rectification and criticising sessions. The Corps did have rules that precluded all soldiers from dating during their first three years of service. I strictly abided by those rules, particularly because of my previous history in this regard. Since I seldom showed up at the company headquarters, many of the girls would only see me during occasional meal times. I walked at a slow and steady pace, dressed in an untidy manner and was often late in arriving at the dining hall. So it was hardly surprising that many girls would fail to notice me and did not know who I was despite the fact that I had been with the Corps for some time. During the first two years, I would rarely talk to any girl. Even inside the dining hall, when I had to interact with girls at the service window, I would simply hand over my lunchbox without a word or a smile. Nor would I care how much food they gave me. However, my indifference bordering on arrogance did not arouse any antipathy from the servers. Instead, I would invariably receive a full scoop of food.

Compared with those who worked in the fields, I had a job that was much more comfortable and rewarding. The horses in my keep were all healthy and strong, and they were all distributed to different carters. So I never had a horse of my own. The death of Bandit and Xiaojunma, both excellent horses in my eyes, made my heart ache for a long time. I firmly believed that, if treated with love, a wild horse like Bandit could have been trained into a hero galloping on the prairie. But in an age dominated by hate, I could only blame its treatment on its bad fortune.

A year had passed, and my interest in horse-keeping kept growing. I had always been on the lookout for a real top horse, preferably an untamed, wild one. Through true love and good training, I wanted to shape it into a real champion on the grassland. Above all, I wanted to be its sole rider. My thinking was that, if I could not find true love in the human world, I might as well seek it from the natural world. Could I possibly form an attachment with a wild horse, treat it with real love and be loved in return? Such thinking was soon to develop into a fascinating dream. By then, Yue was beginning to fade from my memory. Each time I recalled her image, the bearded Chief of Staff Wang would appear simultaneously. My contractual arrangement with him served to dissolve the love I had for Yue.

Chapter 13

Silver Needles

B efore joining the Corps, there was a period of time when we were all relatively idle. Because we had been out of school for quite a while, I began missing the classroom. However, because schools were all closed and no classes were offered except in arts and sports, I could only choose to learn subjects such as music or table tennis. I spent eight yuan on a *yueqin* (moon guitar) from a junk shop in Dongdan. When two weeks' practice failed to yield a single tune, however, I realised I was not cut out for music and decided to quit. As for table tennis, although I couldn't call myself an expert, I had mastered the basic shots and the advanced techniques of both attack and defence. This expertise was later put to good use at the Corps, and it benefited me for the rest of my life.

However, at that time, what I really wanted to learn was some more useful skills that could provide me with work and an income. One of my senior high school classmates had learned some basic skills of acupuncture from an older sister who was a professional acupuncturist. I was able to observe him when he gave a demonstration in class. He wiped a stainless steel needle with an alcohol swab, cleaned the *hegu* acupoint on the back of one of his hands, held the needle in the other hand, pointed the needle tip to the *hegu*, gave it a twist and stabbed it in. Could acupuncture be that easy? I decided to try it myself. I bought a few silver needles from a pharmacy, prepared a bottle of alcohol and some cotton swabs, and began to try acupuncture on myself by imitating what my classmate had done. I applied the needle to my *hegu* and pushed it in. Next, I tried it on my family members and classmates, and it worked too. Thereafter, I bought *Handbook of Simple Acupuncture* from a local Xinhua bookstore and began giving acupuncture treatment to patients around me according to what was written in the book. The healing effects of acupuncture were a great encouragement to me.

I always carried a glass tube and glass bottle in my pocket. The tube held several needles and the bottle contained alcohol cotton swabs. I made a habit of volunteering acupuncture treatment to those who were ill and the habit almost evolved into a hobby. From then on, I began to think I had mastered the discipline, and I wished for the opportunity to make a living out of it. On the day I decided to leave for Inner Mongolia, I packed the tube and bottle in my baggage and took them to the Corps. After joining the company, especially after being assigned to the horse-keeping squad, I made it a routine to treat the sick with my needles, and it worked pretty well. Given that my mum was an army surgeon, patients confided in me even more, thinking that she might have passed on some medical knowledge to me. Soldiers who suffered from backache, headache and other common ailments would come to me for treatment instead of going to regular doctors. But this was limited to the horse-keeping squad only.

I had a friend named Shunzi who worked in the carters' squad. A man of below average height and with a pair of eyes that shined with ingenuity, he had a flexible body that made it easy for him to do somersaults, stand on his head and perform other acrobatic feats. Though just a junior high school graduate, he was pretty good at writing, and he frequently wrote stories that proved very popular within the company. Probably due to his active mind, he had a hard time falling asleep at night and enjoyed wandering about. Sometimes he would accompany me as I herded the horses, which I quite enjoyed since I often felt lonely. Before we left to herd the horses, I would ask him to bring a raincoat with him, not just to provide shelter from the morning mist, but more importantly to prevent mosquito bites. But he declined, claiming that his thick skin made him immune to mosquito bites and that, even if he did get bitten, he would not be infected. However, because he was such an outgoing sort, he inevitably picked up injuries such as a sprained ankle. Knowing that I was good at acupuncture, Shunzi would turn to me for help every time he got injured, whereupon I would take out a needle, insert it into the right spot, and he would find immediate relief. So he truly admired me for my skills.

Another younger soldier in the horse-keeping squad was thin and had small cross eyes that earned him the nickname 'Little Rooster'. One day, he got afflicted with hives and asked me for treatment. I inserted the needle in the *quchi* acupoint on one of his arms, and quickly twisted it until feelings of soreness, numbness and swelling spread throughout his body and tears came his eyes. Ten minutes later, however, all the symptoms of hives had disappeared completely.

However, as a nonprofessional I had few opportunities to show off my acupuncture skills. As time went by, I developed an urge to seek a platform to demonstrate my proficiency. One day, I saw a teenage villager with a crippled leg pass by the horse-keeping squad with great difficulty. He seemed to have suffered from polio as a child. I saw opportunity knocking at my door. It happened to be midday when everyone else was napping. I followed him into a farmhouse in Shatou village. When I told his family I wanted to treat the child with acupuncture, they immediately saw me as a saviour. I stabbed a long needle into the boy's *yanglingquan* acupoint and began twisting like crazy. After the treatment, I noted a slight improvement in the way he was walking and felt secretly pleased. Sensing a possible miracle, I scheduled an appointment with him for a second course of acupunctural treatment.

Three days later, I went to the appointment, only to find the patient's acupoint infected and oozing pus. In a state of nervousness, I repeatedly rubbed the wound with alcohol and then fled on the pretext of returning for medicine. Worried about his condition, I stole back into the village a week later to check on his condition. I saw the child walk out to fetch a bucket of water and then head back, his crippled leg looking nimbler than before. I didn't pursue the matter now that I believed the infection was gone. I never took the initiative to treat him again. The case convinced me of the wisdom of the old saying that a doctor shouldn't go to the home of a patient if he hasn't been invited.

When I was about to leave Shatou, a woman in her thirties grabbed me. She had witnessed me giving acupuncture treatment to the boy when she was visiting his home. I thought she was going to take me to the village committee and then maybe escort me to my company to hold me accountable for medical malpractice. I started shaking, my legs went wobbly and I found myself unable to run, no matter much I wanted to. So I had to do her bidding. But the woman just wanted me to treat her mother-in-law in a neighbouring village. Knowing that I had no room for manoeuvre, I was willing to do whatever was necessary. So I followed her to Liangdi village, which was about three kilometres away. Liangdi, which was larger than Shatou, had a long-distance bus station where we would normally take a bus in order to get to Urat Front banner.

She led me to some impressive, tall brick houses. Since there were no brick houses in my entire company – all we had were adobe houses – I started to look at this woman with new eyes. I soon found out this was the home of the production team leader, and she was the leader's spouse. Her mother-in-law was suffering from a severe headache that could not be controlled by tablets. I entered the room to find her in terrible pain. So I inserted a needle in her *baihui* and twisted it with intensity. By the time I pulled out the needle, her mother-in-law's pain was gone. The leader's wife immediately changed her attitude towards me. She insisted on having me stay for dinner and kept trying to persuade me to become a frequent visitor to her house.

I had been transformed from a frightened chicken to an honoured guest. I sat on the *kang* to scrutinise the woman before me. She had a strong build, a square face and a twinkling pair of large, scalding eyes. She had a glib tongue, a quick temper and deft hands. She made homemade noodles for me by kneading the dough on a cutting board, flattening it with a roller and rolling it again before chopping it into a stack of wide noodles. All done in a matter of minutes.

Just then, the production team leader returned home. He was about my size, tall and stocky with broad shoulders, a ruddy face, bushy eyebrows and large eyes. Clearly an outstanding rural youth befitting his title, this mighty man became subservient on stepping into his own home. Frequently yelled at, he was at the beck and call of his wife. He busied himself lighting the stove, adding firewood to it every now and then and constantly fanning the fire with the bellows. Fearing an instant and loud rebuke from his wife if he slowed down a beat, he almost ran to get the potatoes, carrots, cabbage and a chunk of pork from the cellar. Maybe because he was accustomed to his wife's quick temper, he always had a cheerful disposition in her company.

From what was my first visit to a rural family, I got a glimpse of the true nature of married life. So perhaps what the innkeeper at the carters' inn had said about marital relationships was actually true.

The production team leader's wife was probably a spiteful woman who wouldn't bother to show her husband the slightest respect even before guests, and in her presence he acted like a mouse. If the production team leader was like that, could other men in the village be any different? Imperious as she was, the team leader's wife was not spoiled and was diligent in doing the housework. In a short while, several steaming hot plates of food were laid out on the small table placed on the *kang*. The production team leader and I started eating and drinking, something that we men could particularly enjoy. The food was good and the local sorghum drink was strong. We ended the meal with a bowl of hot noodle soup, and we didn't stop until we could eat or drink no more. It was wintertime, and the chilly winds outside were howling, but this wonderful meal warmed my body and heart in a special way.

After dinner, I hurried back to the company before it got dark. I considered it a day of blessing because, instead of getting into serious trouble in Shatou village, I got to enjoy a good meal and experience real life in a typical rural home.

From then on, I never volunteered acupuncture treatment again. I later heard that several villagers came to look for me at the company clinic, and one of them even left me with a thank-you note. Company officials wondered what was going on and even investigated the case. Because I was an obscure character and the horse-keeping squad was never in the spotlight, I remained that undiscovered, mysterious acupuncturist who had served the local villagers.

Nevertheless, my peers in the horse-keeping squad knew I had this wonderful expertise, and some of them even felt sorry for me, thinking that I deserved something better than horse-keeping. When the regimental headquarters was ready to train a group of vets for the companies, Platoon Chief Zhang who had lived with me in the same dorm and had heard of my expertise, recommended me to my company without bothering to consult me. In his opinion, I was particularly suited to this job. I thought it was a golden opportunity for me to develop my talent in medicine in the future.

Chapter 14

Veterinarian Training Class

The veterinary station was located in a courtyard house near a bridge in the town of Xin'an. In the middle of the courtyard was a wood-framed, six-column stable built exclusively for vets to treat large animals such as horses, mules, cattle and donkeys. All large animals that got sick had first to be tied and bound to the columns before being treated. Hence the six-column stable became a symbol of the veterinary station. The courtyard contained a total of six rooms: a pharmacy, clinic, kitchen and several bedrooms furnished with *kangs*. At the entrance of the courtyard hung a banner that read: 'First company-level veterinarian training class for the Twelfth Regiment'.

Carrying a schoolbag on my shoulder, I showed up in the courtyard and joined more than thirty fellow trainees, who were divided into two classes – one for men, the other for women. The station hired two vets. One of them was Li, who had been transferred from a cavalry unit. He was a humble man of few words and he always wore a firm and serious expression on his weather-beaten face. In addition to being a classroom teacher, he was a clinical expert with more than ten years' practical experience that was put to ready and calm use in crucial moments of the treatment process. Moreover, he excelled at equine physiognomy, and he rode an illustrious dark-grey trotting horse that was bought from Xilingol league. On arrival by train, the horse looked so emaciated that nobody wanted to take it, but Li loved it at first glance. Li thought that it was a horse of great potential based on its physical features: ears resembling chipped bamboo, a nose that looked like a square rafter and hooves in the shape of bells. As a result of his training, the horse soon became one of the few trotting horses in the whole of Bayannur league that had the capacity to go hundreds of kilometres a day.

The other vet, surnamed Xue, was a man of modest height and a ruddy face with high cheekbones that resembled shiny and juicy red apples. He was entirely Han Chinese and spoke perfect Mandarin even though he looked a little Mongolian or Uyghur. A recent graduate from the famous Zhalantun veterinary school in Inner Mongolia, he talked like a typical student and was dressed in plain clothes. Since we were about the same age, we had a lot to talk about and soon became close friends. Probably because of that, I was appointed monitor of the men's class, which took me by great surprise. This was the first time in my life that I had ever been made a leader.

Like tens of millions of barefoot doctors then in rural China, the vet assistants from the Corps received nothing more than short-term professional training, usually of three to six months, before being rushed to clinical practice and on-the-job learning. Training time could be as short as one month, even though our services were not limited to horses, but also covered other animals such as cattle, sheep, pigs, chicken, ducks and rabbits, which all contracted different types of disease. Restricted by the fact that animals can never talk about their ailments, vets have to diagnose through observation before rendering treatment. Within the space of just a month, it was impossible for us to know everything about the pathogenesis, pathology, diagnosis, symptoms and therapies concerning all common animal diseases, and it was extremely difficult just to get a rough idea. Xue was in charge of all classroom training. He could only focus on the main points of several diseases per session. Since there were no textbooks, we had to depend entirely on class notes.

In fact, we did not receive a textbook until the training was about to end. We referred to *A Simplified Version of Veterinary Science* as the 'Red Brick' because it had a red plastic cover. Though a science book, each chapter began with a quotation from Chairman Mao and continued with a brief introduction about a certain disease and the corresponding therapy. Shallow as it was, the book was as valuable to me as a slice of bread is to the hungry. As a high school student who had been deprived of attending college, I loved this book so much that I devoured its every word. For the time being, it quenched my thirst for knowledge.

In those days, learning and practice were intertwined. When the month-long training was over, all of the trained vets were provided with supplies for independent practice in their companies. No matter what type of animal was sick, be it cattle, horse, pig, sheep or chicken, they would have to act independently and treat it by themselves. During the training sessions, any horse that got sick would be hospitalised in the regimental veterinary station so that we could observe and practice. For example, the first step for treating a large animal was to take it to the six-columned stable and have it bound and tied before giving it an injection or administering medicine.

Horse drenching is a basic veterinary skill that involves the following process: immerse a rubber tube in water, insert it into one of the horse's nostrils, slowly push it into its larynx, tentatively provoke its throat and cause it to perform a swallowing act so that the tube can be pushed past the oesophagus and into or close to its stomach. Next, connect the other end of the tube to a funnel, have an assistant pour cups of medicinal liquid into it, and flush it with a cup of clean water so that all of the medicine finds its way into the horse's stomach. I happened to carry out my first procedure when Commissar Ma of the regiment was inspecting my company. The regimental chief was interested in seeing it because I had just graduated from the regiment's first company-level veterinarian training class, which later turned out to be the only one of its kind.

We first watched Li carry out the procedure before doing it ourselves. I took the lead because I was the squad chief. With Commissar Ma standing by my side, I was a little nervous and my hands became stiff, leading to a mistake that caused the horse's snout to bleed. I grew more nervous and seemed to lose control. At that moment, Commissar Ma encouraged me by saying: "Don't panic. Don't panic just because there is blood."

These words of encouragement, said in a casual way 43 years ago, have stayed with me and continued to benefit me for the rest of my working life. They not only spurred me on to be a good vet, but also inspired me to become an accomplished medical doctor. Commissar Ma was certainly a much better leader than Chief of Staff Wang.

Unlike a medical doctor, the vet has to bring his patients under control before they can be treated. This is relatively easy for smaller animals such as chickens and rabbits, which were usually raised by women and could be easily treated by them. Larger animals such as pigs and sheep were raised by women as well, but they were not easily subdued by a single woman. So female vets usually worked in teams of two or three who were strong in terms of build and personality, and they were usually quite daring in their ways.

However, larger animals could only be handled by men. To treat them, strength and courage alone are not sufficient. Special devices and fixtures were needed as well. For example, six-column stables were established to bind the bigger animals and make them stand so that the vet could carry out procedures. The western way of drenching a horse involves using of a thick nasogastric tube, while the traditional Chinese way is to lift the horse's head, hold the medicinal liquid in an ox horn and spoon feed it through a corner of the horse's mouth. However, some of the medicine could easily leak out. For this reason, vets at the Corps would also use the tube for horse drenching so that all the medicine was consumed.

Medicine for horses usually took the form of powdered Chinese medicine ground by machines in veterinary medicine factories. Each packet weighed as much as 500 grams, which was about the amount of medicine used for each drench. A commonly used method was to pour a packet of powdered medicine into a basin, add boiled water and blend it into a thin paste. Next, a funnel and catheter were used to drench the medicine completely into the horse's stomach. Chinese medicinal herbs that had not been processed had to be crushed into powders fine enough to be poured into boiled water and blended into thin paste that could be tube-fed into the horse's stomach. This is different from Chinese medicinal herbs for humans that can be brewed into a decoction for drinking. As trainees, we often took turns walking on a big steel roller in a large iron groove to grind the medicine into powder.

Nasogastric intubation cannot be used for drenching cattle, but I'm still not sure why. Maybe because cattle are stubborn and uncooperative. Though cattle have large nostrils easy for intubation, they are highly sensitive. Besides, cattle heads are not easily tied still to wooden pillars as are horse heads. The best implement to subdue cattle is the nose clamp.

Once the nose is clamped, however, it is very hard to insert the tube. The only way to do so is to tie the clamp into the steel ring on top of the six-column pen so that the cattle's head can be lifted for spoon feeding through a corner of its mouth.

Pig castration is another basic skill in veterinary medicine. Chinese vet skills in this respect are far superior to western skills. While lecturing on this subject, Xue invited Xiao, the best-known local vet, to demonstrate the procedure. The optimal time for castrating a pig is one or two months after its birth, when it weighs about ten kilograms. Because the vet has to independently complete the procedure, he or she will have to frequently practise squatting, usually for more than half an hour at a time, without shaking or going numb.

Vet Xiao grabbed a piglet and stepped on its ears so that it lay face up for the operation. After having a trainee fetch a barrel of well water, he took out a scalpel, grabbed the piglet by its testicles, slashed the scarfskin, squeezed the testicles and then plucked them out with a twist. Then, he asked a trainee to flush the wound with a cup or two of cold well water in order to clean the blood and stop the bleeding. Finally, he had a trainee spray some disinfectant on the wound and let the piglet go. Relieved from this ordeal, the piglet scampered about the yard.

Next, Xiao showed us how to sterilise a sow. He grabbed a little sow and had it pinned to the floor in the same way. He took out a scalpel with a half-inch blade on one end and a solid ball on the other. He slashed an opening in the sow's lower left abdomen, inserted the ball end of the scalpel into the wall of the abdomen through the slashed opening, felt around inside, and brought out a mass of white tissue resembling intestines, which were actually the oviduct and the ovary, which Xiao quickly removed. He then let the sow go without using any disinfectant, and she began running about in the yard just like the castrated boar.

As a new trainee, I was greatly impressed with Xiao's superb veterinary skill and nimbleness. I now knew that veterinary medicine was by no means easy to learn and that it would take a long time to master pig castration and sterilisation techniques. But I made up my mind to study hard and do my best to cross these hurdles.

Chapter 15

Reunion

A t that time, all soldiers in the Corps had a scheduled nap time. From noon to 2pm, almost all of us would take a good nap on a *kang*. On my first day at the veterinary station, I was kept awake on the *kang* by thoughts and memories of Yue. I wondered if she was still working at the Corps headquarters health centre. How I wished to go and see her! But the very thought of that domineering, bearded chief of staff, especially the memory of our face-to-face talk, sent a chill down my spine. With Yue under his direct watch, breaking a covenant I had made with him was almost unthinkable, so I had to contain my initial impulse. The following day, I tossed and turned on the *kang* once again, unable to fall asleep. Being so close to her, I thought I would forever regret failing to seek her out when I had the opportunity. At least I could ask whether she was still working at the health centre. If she had left, my hesitation and fear would have been quite unjustified. I would be just wasting time and energy imagining things.

This perspective led to a resolve to find out her whereabouts at nap time on the third day. At noon, I crept out of the regimental veterinary station and headed towards the regimental headquarters clinic. It was a hot summer day. The loud and repetitive sound of cicadas in the trees was occasionally interrupted by the barking of a dog. A walk of approximately twenty minutes took me to the clinic. The two rows of bungalows had remained the same. The sight of that familiar big tree made my heart pound. I walked to it without thinking and relived that morning of a year ago. Memories cascaded through my mind as the blood in my veins leapt like streams of fire.

How I wished that Yue would somehow walk out of that clinic then and there. But no miracle happened. All I saw were two girl soldiers, maybe nurses, each holding a quilt that they would soon drape over a long rope to dry. I was about to go and ask them if they knew Zhang Yue, but kept hesitating until they went back in, leaving me in bitter regret. Fortunately, after a while, they came out again with another quilt in their arms. I plucked up courage to approach them, although I felt I was no longer my former self of one year ago. I was a coward no more, but only before horses. In front of girls I wasn't any different – I was still shy.

I walked over noiselessly, as if stepping on cotton. They did not sense my presence and turn back to the room. This time, I made up my mind not to hesitate anymore, because for me this could be the last chance. Believing they would be back, I stood under the rope to wait. Sure enough, they came out with a third quilt. On seeing me, they began sizing me up in a way that made me flush and stammer with embarrassment. They smiled at each other and asked: "What are you up to?"

"I, I… I want you to do me a favour."

I must have sounded like a coward to them, because the shorter of the two girls became impatient and asked: "What is it? Speak up!"

"I am looking for somebody."

"Who?"

"Zhang Yue."

The name had a startling effect on the pair. They began gazing at me, making my face turn red again. They took turns questioning me: "Why are you looking for her? How do you know her? What's your relationship to her?"

"I, I …"

I was stuttering again, because Yue was not supposed to know I was working at the Corps and had been here to look for her. This meant I could not even mention my name. On top of that, I was worried that the girls may inform Chief of Staff Wang of my suspicious behaviour. So I was at a loss what to say and ended up lying: "We used to live in the same compound. I just wanted to know if Zhang Yue still works at your clinic."

On hearing these words, they relaxed their guard, and I got to see them more clearly. The taller girl was pretty, gentle and kind. I later knew her name was Shan Ying and she told me what had happened to Yue.

"She's still at the clinic, doing a good job as our boss. She's now away at the divisional headquarters hospital for some training, and she won't be back for a few days."

I heaved a deep sigh of relief. Now that my goal was attained, I thought I had better leave. But the shorter nurse blocked me path. She had two small dimples on her round face and a glint in her shining, big eyes. Her name was Lin Na, as I found out later. She asked me mischievously: "Who are you? Where are you from? What's your name?"

Unable to withstand this cross-examination, I quickly told them the truth: "I come from a grassroots company. I am on my way to attend a vet training class at the regimental headquarters."

They started giggling. Shan Ying smiled without showing her teeth, while Lin Na laughed out loud, bending her back and touching her belly with her hands.

"What? You are learning to be a vet? You mean your patients are animals? That sounds like a hoot!"

She simply couldn't stop laughing. I felt so embarrassed that I wanted to dive into a hole. Fortunately, Shan Ying spoke up on my behalf: "Whether human doctor or animal doctor, you are still a doctor and our future co-worker."

Her words comforted me somewhat, but I felt I should leave them as soon as possible, before they got to know me any better. So I pretended I had to leave at once.

"Gosh, I'm going to be late for class. Got to run," I said and fled without looking back, leaving their hearty laughter behind.

Because the veterinary station was still under construction, we trainees had to work while studying. Inside the compound, several temporary workers were hired to work day and night. They did odd jobs early in the morning and late in the evening. As the class monitor, I had to take the lead every time. I sweated a lot. One day, I felt particularly thirsty. I went into the kitchen to get a bowl of boiled water, but found the thermos bottle empty. So I pushed away the cover on the water tank, scooped out a ladle of well water and drank it down.

By night, as I slept on the *kang*, I found my belly making a lot of noise, followed by fits of abdominal pain. I had to get up several times and go to the toilet. By midnight, I could stand it no more. I couldn't help moaning as I felt my temperature rise. When Ma Ming sleeping next to me was awakened, he touched my scalding forehead before sitting up and calling out: "He's running a high fever. Quick! Go get a doctor from the regimental headquarters clinic."

"Quick! Give him water. He has been to the toilet several times already. He'll dehydrate if he keeps on like this."

Ma Ming's yelling woke everyone in the house. A soldier named Guo Peng put on his clothes and went to the clinic to call for a doctor. Others served me boiled water, to which Ma Ming added a little salt and poured it into my mouth. Although we were only studying veterinary medicine, we had some general medical knowledge too. That very morning, Mr Xue the teacher had just finished lecturing on how to deal with acute gastroenteritis in larger animals. In addition to antibiotics, the timely addition of liquid, preferably saline solution, to prevent dehydration was an important part of the treatment.

Dr Wang, who was on duty, came with two nurses. One of them placed a thermometer in my armpit. As I opened my eyes slightly, I saw with surprise that the nurses were none other than the ones I had met at the clinic the other day. Being barely conscious, however, I could only hear them whisper.

"Forty point three degrees. How come it's so high?" Lin Na said as she checked the thermometer.

Dr Wang walked over and felt my pulse before listening to my chest and belly with a stethoscope. Next, he opened my eyelids, looked at my conjunctiva and said decisively: "Acute intestinal gastritis. He could pass out at any moment. Quick! Send him to the divisional headquarters hospital. He is in a critical condition."

Shan Ying gave me several pills with water. After taking those, I collapsed on the *kang*. The doctors and nurses took off running and were ready to send me to the divisional headquarters hospital located in Urat Front banner as quickly as possible. About half an hour later, a jeep was driven to the veterinary station. I was still running a high fever and was feeble and delirious. I soon found myself carried onto the jeep. I thought I was dying, especially when I heard the doctor say I was in a critical condition. But the moment I was lifted into the vehicle, I immediately knew I was in good hands and would survive.

Shan Ying was sitting next to the driver, as I lay flat on the back seat. As the old military jeep bumped down the rugged country road, I slowly gained consciousness and sensed myself lying on the other nurse's thighs.

"Check his temperature, boss." I heard the indistinct voice of Shan Ying. Only now did I realise I was lying on the head nurse's legs. Could the head nurse possibly be my Yue? People can entertain foolish thoughts when they run a high fever. I was doing exactly that. I knew my feet were resting on the inside of the jeep door while my head and upper body lay on the head nurse's soft and supple legs. In truth, her feminine body had already turned me on in the most intimate way. I could feel her leaning close to me and her chest pressing towards my face. In fact, I was right there in her bosom. Although I was only half conscious, I still felt her heaving chest and smelt the intoxicating perfume of her body. What a sweet and fascinating scent.

The head nurse put a thermometer in my armpit. A wave of happiness spread through me as I felt her cool hand touch my scalding body. Feeling somewhat energised, I opened my eyes slowly and saw the head nurse's beautiful, goddess-like face. Thinking that she resembled Yue, I opened my eyes wide and took a better look: she had a fine countenance, rosy cheeks and large, attractive eyes that reminded me of a well-known film actress. I strongly sensed it was Yue but I wasn't quite sure, so I refrained from making any rash moves.

The head nurse took the thermometer out of my armpit, looked at it again and again in the moonlight, until she said happily. "Thirty-nine point eight degrees, down a little bit now."

On recognising her sweet but high-pitched voice, I knew immediately that it was Yue. I shuddered instinctively, as a force of life erupted once more in my sapless body. I cried out with all my strength: "Zhang Yue!"

My voice, though weak, was sufficient to touch Yue. She exclaimed fervently: "Wen Bo! Wen Bo! So you've finally woken up. You really scared me."

She gave me a tight hug, something that was very rare in those days, and it endowed me with the courage and strength to overcome the illness.

"Wen Bo," Yue said affectionately, oblivious to the driver and the other nurse as her tears kept falling on my face. "Your fever is down a little bit now. You will be OK. You must hold on. We will shortly get to the divisional headquarters hospital. They will hook you up to an IV and give some you good medicine, and you will be fine. So please hold on."

She took out a handkerchief to wipe my face and left it with me.

Xin'an town was only about twenty kilometres from Urat Front banner, but it took more than an hour to drive there because of the bumpy dirt road. The driver tried hard to speed up so I could get to the hospital as quickly as possible. But I was wishing the opposite because I wanted to lie longer in Yue's arms. The car jolted along the pothole-strewn road. Yue's hair frequently brushed my face, and when the jolting became worse, her prominent breasts would push up against my chest, which gave me pleasure even in sickness. I was immersed in happiness.

As the journey became smoother, I could feel Yue gently kissing me on my cheeks. Seeing how excited I had become, she abruptly turned her mouth to my ears and whispered: "I thought you had returned to Beijing. I was so mad at you leaving me without you telling me that I went sleepless for three days running and I lost clumps of hair."

She gave me a furtive pinch as she said this. She was playing the bully even when I was sick, making me wonder if such aggressiveness was something in her blood. But she seemed to have a reason for it.

"I was trying to stimulate you lest you passed out. I'm going to press your philtrum too," she said, smiling.

She did exactly that and it wakened me even more. I couldn't help crying when I realised she had spent sleepless nights and had lost hair for my sake. She again embraced me and slowly sucked the tears from my face before poking me on my forehead.

"Why didn't you tell me where you were? Why not even write to me?" she asked.

"Chief of Staff Wang wouldn't let me. We had an agreement that I couldn't breach. Or he would send me back to Beijing."

"Why are you so scared of Wang? You could have come and looked for me without his knowing it. You fool!"

She poked me again and put the thermometer back in my armpit. My temperature was now down to 39.5 degrees. Obviously, Yue knew my illness had not worsened. I would be out of danger as long as we reached the divisional headquarters hospital in time. We would arrive at Urat Front banner in about half an hour. We suddenly felt our time together becoming increasingly precious. We had a chance two-hour meeting after a year's separation. Who knew if we would reunite in future? Who could predict our destiny?

The car kept moving as I felt Yue hold me tighter. We stopped talking altogether because words could no longer express our feelings. Our faces were now pressed together, her hair touching my skin. I smelt her perfume and heard her rhythmic breathing in tempo with the swell of her heaving breasts, which were pressed hard against mine. I was thrilled.

As we got closer to Urat Front banner, the road conditions improved. Sensing that she was about to lose me, Yue started kissing my cheeks once more, which culminated in her resting her wet lips on my hot and dry lips. I felt my heart melting and my soul revelling in her love. The driver and Shan Ying were either oblivious to all that was going on behind them or they were simply turning a blind eye. As kind-hearted people, they probably did not want to interfere but wished that the rose of our love would be allowed to blossom.

Chapter 16

Lovesick

In the makeshift ward of about twenty square metres at the single-storey divisional headquarters hospital were eight large plank beds occupied by Corps soldiers. They lay in a variety of positions and those in a serious condition were constantly moaning. I had been confined to a bed next to a wall for a week with no one to look after me. I started to get better thanks to the IV, my temperature fell and the frequency of my bowel movements decreased to once or twice a day. While still looking sallow and worn out, my face began to get back some of its natural colour.

Tian Yu, the nurse, came in and gave me a thermometer. At the divisional headquarters hospital, every patient took his own temperature by putting the thermometer in his armpit. She left to fetch cotton swabs on finding the IV bottle almost empty. When she came back, she removed the needle and reached out her hand for the thermometer.

I took it from my armpit and passed it to her.

"Your fever is gone," she said, "and you're looking better after a whole week's IV."

"Really?" I responded as I tried to crack a faint smile.

Tian Yu was a talkative and energetic girl of below-average height. She wore two small pigtails and had a childlike smile. On seeing me open up, she began to prattle away.

"No kidding! You looked terrible when you first arrived. Luckily, you were brought here quickly in a jeep. A patient from a company of the 16th Regiment was suffering from stomach flu and shock just like you. We failed to save him because he was brought here in a pony cart," she said before hurrying away, leaving the ward in silence.

The patients gazed at one another while I fell into deep and troubled contemplation. It was scary to imagine what might have happened had I fallen ill in a place more remote from the hospital. If not for the regiment jeep, would I not have died like the man from the 16th Regiment? At that time, the life of a Corps soldier was cheap. Upon death all the relatives got was a pile of dust. In luckier cases, their bodies were cremated after the parents were given the chance to take a final look. With these thoughts, my heart sank into an abyss of sorrow, and I began to mourn my unknown deceased colleague. I could have so easily followed him into the grave.

I had been in bed for a week now. Possibly due to the high fever, I had passed in and out of consciousness, and felt as if I had been in a dream. I did not sober up until my temperature returned to normal. Once awake, a myriad of thoughts about what had happened that night crowded into my mind. Did I actually meet Yue? Was I really lying in her arms? How her juicy lips had caressed my cheeks and mouth! How soul-stirring and inebriating! But now I began to think it was all just a dream.

What made me believe it had really happened was the handkerchief Yue had given me, the one with the sewn head of a black horse that I so loved. I gazed at it from different angles over and over again until I fantasised it as a galloping black horse. It ran fast, in a gallant and graceful way until I imagined it turning into the glamorous Yue, the elegant figure I first encountered on the train and who shared my journey on the jeep that brought me to the hospital. And I remembered clearly how she had used that handkerchief to wipe the tears off my cheeks.

She had saved me once again. She had been there every time I was in danger and had helped me pull through before quietly departing. I couldn't help seeing her as a goddess sent by Providence to rescue an unfortunate princeling, although I might sound presumptuous in describing myself in that way. But my father had mentioned that we, as a family, might be descendants of Xie An, commander of the historic Battle of Feishui during the Northern and Southern dynasties (420-589). Besides, two generations of my ancestors had lived in the Humble Administrator's Garden in Suzhou. So I later truly saw myself as an unfortunate prince and Yue as the goddess who came to the world to save me.

Lying still in bed while holding the handkerchief, I missed Yue all night long. I knew I had been living under restraint and fear. I was effectively under the control of Chief of Staff Wang. Unlike Yue, I did not have the courage to express my feelings directly, but surely I could have done so in private. What was holding me back? For my sake, Yue did not sleep well for several nights running, and she had lost a lot of hair. I began to blame myself and felt so guilty that I made up my mind to look for Yue as soon as I recovered and returned to Xin'an. I wanted to throw off my cowardly image, apologise to her and express my true love in a brave and sincere manner.

I thought about inviting her out to that sacred tree in the moonlight where I would bow before her and apologise. I imagined reciting words of repentance over and over again, but ended up stammering when I said them in her presence. I would envisage my embarrassment and picture the way she would react – either a smile with pursed lips or chuckle with her head and waist bent. Anyway, I made up my mind to please her and boldly express my love for her. She had already explicitly professed her love for me, and now it was my turn to reciprocate and speak out loud. Having managed to overcome a wild horse like Bandit, I would surely dare to tell Yue clearly how much I was in love with her.

I would also practise the love words I was going to say again and again. It was a touching declaration of love. I would read out loud those poetic words in a rich baritone, in a way that would touch any girl in the world, even the most hard-hearted. Throughout the night, when everyone else in the ward was asleep, I would lie awake missing Yue. I would then recite my declaration of love again and again and be moved to tears. She was a warm and passionate girl, not cold and icy. She would certainly have been moved by my confession of love. Even so, I would take the initiative and hold her in my arms and press my less-than-muscular chest hard against hers and kiss her fondly on the cheeks, her beautiful neck and lips. I kept daydreaming about Yue in that way until dawn, when I fell fast asleep.

I fully recovered after two weeks in hospital. Before being discharged, Tian handed me a quilt that she wanted me to give to the regimental headquarters clinic. So I actually had a quilt over me when I lay in the backseat of the jeep, or to be more accurate, when I was in Yue's arms. She gave the quilt to me when she saw the ones in the hospital ward were too thin. The instant I held the quilt in my arms and smelt Yue's special scent, I felt happy that I finally had a solid excuse to go and see her at the clinic. I would have no fear, even if I ran into Chief of Staff Wang. Just the prospect of being able to see her made my heart swell with joy and excitement.

By the time I returned to the veterinary station, the training class for the vets had ended. Each of the trainees returned to their respective companies with some medicine. Now that I was all by myself, I decided to stay for a couple of days. My spirits rose when it occurred to me that I was obligated to return the quilt. But I wavered when it came to leaving for the regimental headquarters clinic. So I asked a vet called Xue to accompany me.

With the quilt in my arms, I followed Xue to the clinic. I lacked the courage to move forward. Luckily, Xue knew the nurses well and asked Shan Ying and Lin Na to come out. Their scrutinising eyes made me flush. I immediately offered the quilt to them in the hope of covering my embarrassment.

"You're looking well," said Lin Na. "Are you feeling better now? We thought you were at death's door when you arrived here."

Both girls burst out laughing.

"Is everything fine now?" asked Shan Ying. "We were all scared that day, and Zhang Yue even began to cry. It was she who came to knock at Chief of Staff Wang's door at midnight to get permission for the jeep to be sent."

Whether it was because I had not fully recovered or that the idea of seeing Zhang Yue had made me overly excited and nervous, I found my legs locked up, as if frozen. It took me a long time to get my mind together to say thank you. "Had it not been for you," I said, "I can't imagine where I would be now."

Both nurses were very eloquent and were not content for a tongue-tied man like me to walk away having uttered such simple words. Assuming a haughty manner, Lin Na said with folded arms: "How will you thank us properly? We saved your life!"

Sensing my embarrassment, Shan Ying came to my rescue, saying meekly: "Well, don't thank us! Thank Zhang Yue instead. She was the one who played a crucial role in saving your life, but she…"

At this point, the two girls stopped talking, and the smiles on their faces disappeared abruptly. I immediately sensed something wrong and asked anxiously: "She what? What's happened?"

After a long pause, Lin Na finally answered: "She has left the Corps. You won't see her here anymore."

Shan Ying felt an urge to tell me the whole story. "Don't you know what's going on? All those with parents serving in the military have left the regiment to join the PLA. They all went without a word right after they had received a letter from home. Zhang Yue told no one except the two of us, and she gave us all of her stuff before leaving stealthily the other night."

I felt like a chicken drenched by a bucket of icy water. I couldn't remember how I left eventually, nor did I fully absorb what they had said. All I wanted to do was to find a quiet place to clear my thoughts. I left behind Shan Ying, Lin Na and Xue, hurried off to the open spaces and started running until I was exhausted. I then wandered aimlessly and somehow found myself at the sacred tree. I leant against it and sank into painful contemplation.

Was life playing tricks on me? I felt as if I had been riding on a roller coaster. After experiencing so much turbulence, so many twists and turns, now that the journey had taken a smoother and more fortuitous path, when love and happiness were within reach, things were suddenly taking a reverse turn. Those things that I was so ready to embrace with a passion were suddenly disintegrating. I used to think love in the human world was within reach, but I came to realise that it could never be easy in those days. I could dream about love and long for it, but I could never obtain it in real life. If I really wanted love or could not do without it, I would only end up bringing endless pain and trouble upon myself. But I had a benevolent heart that was filled with love and which, if crushed, would cause me to slide into distress and despondency, and lead to a miserable death. So I had to let the love within my heart blossom in liberty. I had to release it naturally. If I could not find it in the mortal world, I would have to seek it elsewhere.

Chapter 17

Serving as a Vet

Only after returning to the company did I realise that Zhang Yue was not the only one who had left unannounced. It was actually a class act relating to every Corps soldier who had parents in the military. They all did what they believed to be right after receiving letters from home. None of them bothered to inform their superiors or comrades before departing. They got to join different field armies with the help of their *guanxi* or through a back-door route. In my company alone, about twenty such people vanished from the Corps.

In those days, universities were all closed, making the military an attractive career option for young people. Once they joined the army in that era, they would be lauded. Therefore, it was obvious to me that Yue would never return to the Corps just to seek a coward like me. So I had literally lost her forever.

However much I had wanted to serve in the army, there was no way I could ever join. My mum's incarceration (she was even prevented from wearing a regular army uniform), my overseas relatives and my dad's identity as a capitalist would have barred me from the army even if I had hardcore *guanxi*. Perhaps my only option was to remain in the Corps, which meant Yue and I belonged to two different classes and our union was out of the question. I was totally disillusioned.

For months after Yue's departure, I felt extremely lonely, as if I had lost my soul or had been left hopelessly stranded in the wilderness. However, I had at least undergone more than a year's hardships and had learned how to adapt in times of adversity. I strove to readjust my thinking and decided that the most effective way was to distract myself by focusing on the study of veterinary medicine.

When I returned from the veterinary station to the company, I had with me some veterinary medicine and a copy of the 'Red Brick'. Platoon Commander Zhang set aside an unfurnished room for me to stock the medicine. Since wood was hard to come by, I made a shelf with cement and bricks to hold the medicines according to type. I went on to build some concrete grids for stocking medicine and I asked my comrades-in-arms to gather medicinal herbs with me while pasturing. I took out *A Concise Handbook of Chinese Medicinal Herbs*, a thick pocket book that my mother had posted to me. I showed my friends pictures of the herbs so that they could verify what they had collected against the pictures. We had dandelions, Pulsatilla, gentian, Rhizoma Anemarrhenae, Semen Cuscutae, medlar, Schisandra chinensis, Semen Platycladi seed, Cistanche, globeflower, plantain seed and Vaccaria segetalis seed. Gradually, I established a veterinary pharmacy that had an inventory of both Chinese and western medicine, which was unique in the entire regiment.

Following that, I built a stable that had six solid wooden pillars for the First Company in Shatou to which I belonged. The project was carried out under the leadership of the newly appointed squad chief Jieshi and with the help of comrades Baozi, Little Rooster and Little Zhao (I can only remember their nicknames). Similar in size to the one at the regiment, the stable later came to be known as a symbol of my company, thus giving me a strong sense of pride. Though I was just an assistant vet by title, I was a true vet in practice. From then on, I would take under my care all beasts of burden – horses, mules, cattle and any other large animals – and I would soon feel comfortable injecting and drenching them and dressing their wounds.

My career as a vet began. As long as those 'silent comrades' were sick, I would consult the Red Brick, identify the symptoms and look for cures. It's quite unthinkable to practise veterinary medicine after going through just one month of training. Fifteen years later, when I told a group of American students about my experience both as a vet and doctor, they were all shocked because medical students in the US had to undergo eight years of training before they could qualify in either profession.

I enjoyed treating horses with traditional Chinese medicine. Patent Chinese medicine for animals was usually milled by machine. Veterinary drugs, such as phlegm-clearing powder and spleen-warming powder, were packed in bags of half a kilo. I would usually use egg white or cold water to dilute a whole pack of powder into a mushy paste before using it to drench a horse. Drenching was a job that required skill. I was able to perfect the procedure because I had been through a lot of practice, especially when it came to drenching using a stomach catheter. Sometimes my job involved drenching dozens of horses in half a day, but I never hurt any of them like I did on my first occasion. In those days, the horses in my company all enjoyed what is now called 'special treatment'. Each horse was given four different kinds of medicine a year, one for each season. They were liver heat-clearing powder in spring, anti-inflammatory powder in summer, lung-moistening powder in autumn and kidney-tonifying powder in winter.

One spring, when the company had run out of medicine, the regiment veterinary station decided to try a new preventive care strategy on the horses – bloodletting. This new measure, which was developed by a local vet, was actually quite effective, even though letting out between half and one litre of blood per horse at a time looked quite scary to me. The animals that shed blood stayed healthy all year round, while those that did not either grew boils or coughed because of heat in the lungs. Many years later, when the company I worked for called for a donation of blood, I signed up happily because I wanted to try the same measure myself. The health benefit I had in mind was to reduce the heat in my liver.

In the company, I also took charge of disease prevention for smaller livestock. As a result, I had the opportunity to interact with female soldiers who were raising sheep, pigs and chickens. They would come to the stud farm and ask me for help whenever their animals got sick. I would naturally be excited when I heard them call me by my name, but I had enough self-control to hide my feelings and keep my poise. I would walk at a steady pace, casually ask about the sick animals' conditions, carry my medical kit with me and happily follow the women to their workplace.

I visited the sheepfold most often because it was closest to the stud farm where I worked. Whenever I walked away with a shepherdess, my co-workers would look at me with envious eyes. Since sheep needed to be drenched every spring, I would sometimes go to the sheepfold together with some male friends so they could help me catch the sheep. The male co-workers would vie for such an opportunity.

The most impressive sheep that I have ever treated was one born without an anus. The shepherdesses told me the lamb was dying of constipation because it could not empty its bowels. When I arrived at the sheepfold, I saw the lamb groaning on the floor with a bloated belly. This difficult case embarrassed me because I had no idea what I was supposed to do. As I stood there scratching my head, I found myself facing three charming and graceful young women. Guo Sheng, the sheep squad chief, was about my age, tall and slim, with a jadeite complexion, an oval face and eyebrows that resembled willow leaves. Below her long eyelashes glittered a pair of large eyes, indicative of a refined personality. She carried a certain pride as she rested a hand on her waist, her glossy black hair blowing in the air. I could hardly bring myself to look into her eyes and felt unable to turn down anything she asked me to do for her. Pan Jing was an unfathomable woman with the light of wisdom gleaming in her eyes. Slim, noble and elegant, and a lover of philosophy, she usually wore a pair of sunglasses while shepherding, which set her apart from the others. The third girl, Zhang Juan, was equally slim and no less beautiful. She had a milky skin, thick, black eyebrows, a high-bridged nose, cherry lips and sparkling eyes.

In order not to disappoint these three beauties, I racked my brains trying to figure out a solution, all the while feeling and acting like an ant in a hot pan. Finally, I came up with an odd idea – cutting an opening in the animal's anus. As expected, the lamb immediately discharged the faeces and stood up slowly. A life was saved temporarily. However, just a few days later, the slit closed and I was called to deal with the same problem again. I repeated the previous procedure by cutting another opening. When the third incision healed, however, I had no choice but to try something more radical. I used a pair of burning chopsticks to scald the opening so as to create a fake anus. The lamb managed to survive a couple of months before dying of intractable constipation. The artificial anus was not much help because it had no contractile function.

The two girls at the chicken farm, Xiaoli (her full name was Huang Xiaoli) and Niuzi, were both of modest height, but I was strangely drawn to them. Xiaoli was the more attractive because of her well-balanced facial features and her crystalline, shining eyes that looked as limpid as a well of pure water – eyes that spoke of righteousness and fearlessness. Even boys had a healthy fear of her, and many of them regarded her as a legend. But I was attracted by her chivalrous nature. I was both curious and fearful of her at the same time. Niuzi was a cute, humble and meticulous girl who was highly coordinated. Her compatibility with Xiaoli made their work at the chicken farm smooth and orderly.

At that time, chicks were vaccinated once a year to prevent fowl plague. The day of vaccination was always busy. After breakfast, Xiaoli and Niuzi would drive all the chicks into a big room and then pull them out one by one. They would grab the chick's body in one hand and its two feet in the other. I would aim a special injector at the fleshiest part of the chick and give it a shot right there. The whole task usually took several hours. In the end, a few mischievous chicks would be left scuttling around the room, refusing to get treated. Xiaoli and Niuzi would chase them while I just stood there laughing and having fun watching them instead of offering any help.

I had a certain tacit agreement with Xiaoli and Niuzi. Sometimes I would even see the chicken farm as my 'refuge'. On one occasion, probably because some horse-keepers had got involved in a brawl, Deputy Company Commander Zhou of the company was sent over to us to chair a disciplinary action meeting. This kind of meeting would usually go on for ages. Attendants would experience a sort of spiritual torment even if they were not being targeted. As a countermeasure, I deliberately scheduled the chicken inoculation day on the day of the meeting. So, prior to the start of the meeting, I arrived at the chicken farm with my medicine kit on my shoulder. I deliberately worked slowly that day. However, Xiaoli and Niuzi had no clue what I was thinking. Instead of slowing down, they were actually speeding up, thus adding to my anxiety.

At this point, Little Rooster came to look for me and told me Deputy Company Commander Zhou wanted me to attend the meeting. I replied that I couldn't leave my job and had to stay there at the chicken farm. After a while, however, he came to call me again because nobody could leave the meeting until all the participants had made a statement.

Before leaving, I told the girls to take a break, but when I came back, I saw them still working. Xiaoli was giving shots to the chicks as Niuzi was catching them. They had seen how I inserted the metal syringe by an inch every time I gave a shot. Xiaoli had mastered this trick a long time ago, so she had temporarily assumed my veterinary role. I took back the syringe from her and began to act in a professional manner while Xiaoli showed a certain degree of reluctance in her eyes, as if indicating that being a vet wasn't such a difficult job.

Though I finished my work early that day, I did not immediately leave as I usually would, but sat still on the bench in their house trying to strike up conversation in order to kill time. I did not leave until I reckoned that the meeting at the stud farm would be over. Forty years later, after I had posted this story on my blog, Xiaoli and Niuzi replied to say how confused they were by my unusual behaviour at the time.

I also had a lot of contact with the girls in the pig-raising squad. The most memorable event about that experience was related to pig castration. Gilts over forty days old had to be sterilised by having their ovaries and fallopian tubes removed. The procedure, which I had seen Xiao of the regiment veterinary station perform, was probably the hardest part of being a vet. Anyone who failed to master the procedure would not qualify as a vet. The company blacksmith had prepared a sharp castrating knife a long time ago, but I never had the opportunity to use it. In fact, I had learned the basics of pig castration a long time ago, but had never had any chance to practice. So I really wanted to practise on one of the pigs, though I could hardly mention that to the pig-raising girls. After much thought, I came up with a very dishonourable idea.

Early one morning, I woke up Little Rooster, gave him a flax sack and asked him to steal into the pigsty to get me a gilt. To my great excitement, he managed to get one and I immediately found an empty room where I could carry out the procedure. Based on what was described in the book, I put one foot on the pig's left ear, and the other on its right lower leg before pulling out my scalpel to cut a slit in the gilt's abdomen, between the third and fourth nipple. The next step was to insert the scalpel and gently scratch out the white fallopian tube. However, as a novice, I had a hard time trying to get it out. Half an hour later, after much sweating, I threw up my hands in frustration.

I had to have Little Rooster send the gilt back. After a few days, Little Rooster told me that Wang Feng, chief of the pig-raising squad, had learned of our clandestine act. Thereafter, my heart was filled with shame and fear, especially when I caught sight of Wang Feng and her co-workers. Wang was attractive and robust, but she also had a strong personality and a hot temper. For quite some time, I felt she was staring at me in a scary way. I would bow my head before her lest she informed the authorities of my scandalous behaviour. Actually, Wang and her squad showed mercy and magnanimity by keeping it secret for decades.

However, the pig-stealing and gelding incident did have a positive effect. I kept looking for the cause of my failure in gelding. By carefully comparing the anatomy chart of pigs with what was described in the textbook, I discovered that the textbook was wrong about opening a small cut between the third and fourth nipple on the pig's belly. I found out that the opening should have been in the iliac crest joint at the root of the pig's back thigh. Later on, I practised this skill so diligently that I eventually reached the point of perfection. One year later, when I went to the May Seventh cadre school in Hunan to see my father, I carried a scalpel with me ready for use. I did use it and was something of a success over there.

Chapter 18

Little Black

Setbacks and misfortune are unavoidable in life, and different people react in different ways. The feeble-minded get discouraged; the cowardly, who are in the majority, try to hide from them; while the disillusioned, who are in the minority, occasionally take the drastic step of committing suicide. The truth of the matter is that, sometimes, just a little more persistence is sufficient to turn around our fortunes.

The bumpy journey of my life provides enough material to write several novels. A proven measure I have taken in pain management is to divert the focus of my attention and try to delve into things that interest me. For example, in times of despair, I commit my feelings to paper in order to pacify my heart. I was traumatised when Yue suddenly left. It was my commitment to the study of veterinary medicine, the joy of work and the bonding with female comrades that slowly healed me and enabled me to slowly forget Yue.

However, the emergence of a hybrid mare called Little Black made me think of Yue once again. The small black horse was sent to my company from the Corps headquarters because of her petulant and unyielding nature and because she had already kicked quite a few people. According to Vet Xue at the regiment headquarters, Little Black's mother was a mixed Sanhe and Mongolian horse. Her father was a thoroughbred Kabarda horse. The combination of these three noble breeds in one made it possible for Little Black to bring out the greatest strengths of each individual breed. Xue also said that Little Black's hair was pitch-dark and glossy as silk because her parents both had dark hair. She was tall, had a protruding upper chest, slender legs that were straight as lute strings and hooves as stable as bells.

She had a straight neck, alert ears that resembled sharpened bamboo stalks and square nostrils shaped like the end of a rafter. In common with many famous horses, her forehead featured a white spot which, matched with a pair of glowing, bronze-coloured eyes and a head held high, endowed her with an inviting charm.

Whoever saw Little Black would be attracted to her, just like a man is attracted to a beautiful woman. One day in the 1980s, when I was waiting for a bus in Beijing, I suddenly found myself standing next to several female fashion models. Models were then just beginning to emerge in China, and it was the first time I had ever seen one. My eyes were immediately fixed on them. The same thing happened to me when I first saw Little Black. It was an eye-opening moment followed by ecstatic joy. As a horse expert and vet, I had a deep sense of dream fulfilment – the pure breed that I had for years been dreaming of at the Corps was now suddenly right there in front of me.

One day I happened to be herding the horses with Jieshi, the squad chief. He had thick eyebrows, huge eyes and a large, square face reminiscent of General Guan Yu, a hero of the classic novel *Three Kingdoms*. The only difference was that he did not wear a long beard like Guan Yu. The stocky Jieshi, standing 1.85 metres tall, had managed to build a physique that matched his nickname, 'Jieshi', which means 'strong' in Chinese. Our shared interest in horses gave us much to talk about as we worked the horses together. The day Little Black was sent to the company was the day she grazed with the company's herd of horses for the first time. Our pasture was an expanse of green grass dotted with ponds and footpaths. Though eye-catching, Little Black was not gregarious. She was constantly running, full of inexhaustible energy and drive.

Unlike Bandit, Little Black was a beautiful and long-bodied mare with an irascible temperament. She would give a high-pitched scream to whoever approached her before raising her hooves to kick. She instantly reminded me of Yue. I took out the small handkerchief from Yue that I always kept with me. On it was the embroidered head of a black horse that resembled Little Black in an amazing way. There was something mystic about Little Black's arrival six months after Yue had left, and I was surprised to see so many similarities between them. They both had an aggressive temper and shapely figure, which made me wonder if one was the incarnation of the other. Maybe she had turned herself into a horse to accompany me when she saw how lonely I was in the Corps. Early one morning, on their way back to the stud farm after being let loose for a whole night, maybe due to the fact that they had just fed on dewy grass, the horses found themselves in very high spirits. They chased one another, jumped and started frolicking. I had just got up and was standing with my colleagues on a wall of the stud farm to enjoy the scene of the galloping horses. I saw clearly how Little Black could easily overtake all the others. When she ran, her legs and body seemed to have merged into a single line, her belly brushing against the tall grass tips. She was such a beauty.

"What a rare horse," I couldn't help whispering to myself.

I felt like Bo Le, a legendary horse tamer from the Spring and Autumn period, who had just discovered a wonderful but unruly horse. I set my mind on training it in my own way, which was to conquer her power with love. So I was eager to develop a strong bond with her. My initial method was rather simple, maybe even vulgar. When dining in the cafeteria, I would take a couple of extra steamed buns and take them to Little Black in an attempt to curry favour with her. However, as an honourable lady of noble descent, Little Black was indifferent to my actions, and maybe she even saw me as a man of poor taste. She pushed me to a corner as soon as I entered the stable. Pinning me with her rear end, she gave out a shrill neigh as she kicked me on the legs several times.

As I rubbed my bruised legs, I felt frustrated and depressed, but not angry. Little Black's beauty and demeanour made it impossible for me to bear any grudge against her. Instead, I respected her strong personality and had a desire to show her love. This was because she reminded me of Yue and the time we had spent together. I remembered how she had slapped my face for good reason – the affection and love hidden behind it all and how my tolerance had won her heart. Little Black's kicking may not reflect the 'principle' that 'beating is a sign of care, scolding a sign of affection and kicking a sign of deep love'. However, from the perspective of animal psychology, she was mean to me simply because she did not understand why a stranger would force steamed bread on her. She probably kicked me because she thought I meant her harm. I realised that, before making friends with her, I first had to disarm her of her vigilance against me and let her feel my true love. So I patiently waited for such an opportunity.

A few weeks later, there suddenly came news of Little Black's stabbing injury. That day, a labour competition led by the company's political instructor was taking place right next to the stable. The soldiers were working at full tilt. At the behest of the political instructor, several field platoon soldiers took two big horses from the stable and forced them to work at the mill. Little Black was one of them. But they had little idea that untamed horses were unwilling to work. As a result, Little Black reared up in the crowd of people and neighed out loud. As she kicked wildly, one of her hooves caught the political instructor's face. The instructor flew into a rage and yelled with a finger pointed at her: "Beat her! Give her a good whacking!"

So the soldiers rounded her up and used the farm tools they were holding to beat her. Amid the commotion, someone stabbed a pitchfork into her hindquarters, causing a lot of bleeding. A soldier then went forward and led the limping horse back into the stable. Little Black's hindquarters kept bleeding. On seeing the injury, the soldiers in the horse-keeping squad felt sorry for her. I was saddened to the point of tears.

Jieshi, the squad chief, went ahead and took hold of the rope that was tied to Little Black. "Who stabbed him? That was incredibly heavily handed," he said.

"I've no idea who stabbed him, but she kicked the political instructor first," said a soldier from the field platoon.

On hearing this, all soldiers in the horse-keeping squad fell silent, because at that time a company's political instructor was like an overlord who nobody dared challenge. Wasn't it a big deal when an overlord got injured? This was something only a young horse like Little Black could have done. Jieshi could only respond with a sigh and left the reins of the horse with me.

I led the limping horse into the six-column stable and secured her with a rope. They all pitched in to help. Little Zhao brought in a basin of disinfectant and put it on the floor. Little Rooster brought a stool, and Jieshi came with a white plate and put it on the stool. On it was some gauze, a pair of flat-headed scissors, tweezers and the like. I picked up a pair of elbow scissors to cut the hair around Little Black's wound, and then I used some tubing to draw up some disinfectant and rinse the wound repeatedly. Next, I used the tweezers to pick up the gauze, dip it in the disinfectant before inserting it deep into the wound to clear away the congealed blood. As I dressed her wounds, Little Black felt the pain and struggled hard, but because she was firmly tied, all she could do was let out a high-pitched whinny.

Several days later, Little Black's hindquarters got swollen and began oozing blood and pus. She didn't take food for two days, probably because of the high fever caused by infection. With sunken eyes and a drooping head, she lost all her previous pomp and power. I once again led her into the six-column stable and had her tied up with a rope. This time, she was so weakened by fever that she couldn't move at all. Nor did she try to struggle, because she gradually came to understand that I was utterly different from the man who had stabbed her with a fork. She knew I was curing her so she kept her body still as I treated her. Once again, I picked up the elbow scissors to shear the hair that was matted with pus and blood, disinfected an exposed pustule with alcohol and iodine, and then stabbed a sterilised scalpel into it, which caused the pus and fluid to spurt out. Next, I rinsed the wound repeatedly with sterile water and filled it with an ointment-soaked gauze to absorb the residual fluid. Although Little Black was experiencing a lot of pain, she seemed to know I was treating her. So she remained quiet and still, except for a slight shake of her tail.

After changing the ointment and dressing, I gave her an injection of penicillin in oil suspension. Then I untied her and led her out of the six-column stable to an open field behind. She followed me in slow and heavy steps. Sometimes I would stop, pluck some handfuls of green grass and let her sniffle before she rolled it with her tongue into her mouth for a slow chew. I enjoyed walking with Little Black on the salty land because it made me feel as if I were promenading with Yue.

In those days, I would walk the horse several hours a day, sometimes going more than five kilometres. On our way back, the horse seemed to have regained some strength, and she followed me quietly without being led. I continued to pluck green grass from the roadside and I called her Little Black. Sometimes, I would deliberately walk faster than usual and call her by her name, and she would make an effort to catch up. That way, we got familiar with each other and managed to gradually build up a special friendship.

I also cleansed her wound and changed the ointment daily. I often had to lead her into the six-column stable but she would sometimes go there on her own. Before applying new ointment on the wound, I would first use tweezers to pick up the gauze soaked with blood and pus and discard it. Next, I would pick up a cotton swab with forceps, soak it in sterile water and then insert it in the wound. Finally, I would wiggle the cotton swab gently to remove the residual blood and pus. The procedure had to be repeated numerous times without using anaesthetics. The kind of pain felt by Little Black was not hard to imagine, but she did pretty well. She made no noise or sudden movement except for an instinctive tremor of her tail and wounded rear. One day after dressing her wound, I took a routine walk with Little Black. I carried fodder beans in my pocket. This time I fed her with these beans instead of roadside grass, And, of course, I called her by her name. Under my dedicated care, she healed very quickly as the pus and stale blood drained out and the wound began to close. She did not limp as before but began chasing me with her outstretched neck. Later, when the fodder beans were gone, she would still follow me like a faithful dog behind its master. A special friendship had been established between us.

After recovery, Little Black was allowed to rejoin her peers. She resumed her usual wild ways and kicked and neighed in the brilliant sunshine. One day, when Jieshi and I were feeding the horses, I was surprised to notice that a tacit understanding had been reached between me and Little Black even though she was still her former self in terms of temperament. During grazing time, whenever I shouted 'Blackie' to the herd of horses, Little Black would turn around abruptly, look in my direction and then walk over until her body touched mine. She would then slowly raise her beautiful head, rest her long neck on my shoulders and softly stroke my face. In return I would hug her neck, comb her mane with my fingers and feed her fodder beans. Such endearing acts made her feel comfortable by my side, and when she lowered her head to graze, she would press her hindquarters to me as a sign of happiness and contentment. She would never kick me or yell at me again.

As a mare, Little Black's mission was to give birth to ponies; so drudgery was not her call. And because mares were normally supposed to give birth at the age of four, the two-year-old Little Black was actually carefree and enjoying the best time of her life. She was at liberty to do whatever she pleased. Her natural glamour and purity were very appealing. I loved her deeply. I loved her for her silken, charcoal black hair, her slender and comely figure, her wild and unbending character and her astounding speed. She was the best horse I could have encountered since I came to the stud farm. I treated her like a real treasure, and cared for her in all possible ways.

One Sunday, I led Little Black out of the stable, tied her to a pillar and combed her fur from head to tail with a stiff brush until her entire body glistened. Basking in the sun, she stood motionless before me, with her head lowered and her eyes half closed, looking a picture of ease and comfort. Next, I fetched a bucket of water from a well, poured it over her and cleaned and combed her fur meticulously. She was so happy that she not only licked her own fur, but also licked off the water that had spilled on me.

During my moments of leisure, I would sometimes have some fun with Little Black. I would take the bridle off her head, stuff my trouser pockets with fodder beans and begin to tease feeding her. She would chase me to be fed, thus attracting many of my colleagues to the scene. In front of a big crowd, I played hide and seek with her, dodging into the house and hiding behind the door when she wasn't looking. I wanted to see what she would do. When done with all the soybeans, Little Black raised her head to look around before moving back and forth, neighing out loud and charging straight out of the stud farm. She ran towards the vast wilderness at a breathtaking pace. Everyone inside the stable came out to watch. Little Black moved with great style. She ran at a leaping gait, at more than a dozen metres per leap. That meant she could cover a hundred metres in just seven or eight leaps. Though she was slender, her explosive power made it possible for her to fully extend her legs at every leap in a way that allowed her belly to rub against the grass tips. All those who watched her run were overcome with admiration. I was completely carried away. I was astonished at her speed – she was so much faster than I had expected.

How could she run so fast? Of course, horses could become startled sometimes, and I had no way of knowing whether that was the case with Little Black then, but she certainly was anxious to find me. That was why she was running like crazy in the wilderness. Stunned by her reaction, I didn't know what to do at first. When I realised what was going on, however, I rushed out of the stable and yelled in the direction in which Little Black was running: "Blackie, Black-ie! Black-ie…"

On finally recognising my voice, she came to a sudden halt, reached out her neck and pricked up her ears as I continued screaming: "Blackie, Black-ie! Black-ie…"

She immediately turned around and ran back towards the stud farm. Her speed scared me, for she reminded me of Xiaojunma who had died after crashing into a tree on his way back to the stud farm. Now that Little Black was travelling even faster than Xiaojunma, if she were to run into me at such speed, I would perish for sure. I got scared and ran quickly back to the stud farm. When Little Black followed me there, I changed course by going in circles around the house. Little Black kept coming after me, but obviously slowing down. When she finally reached me, she bit into my clothes and belt, tossed her head and threw me onto the floor before pulling back her hooves. Obviously, it was a good-willed gesture. She just wanted to tell me that my joke went too far.

Initially, I raised Little Black like a dog. Whenever I called her name, she would run to me promptly. If called upon during grazing, she would step to my side and not let other horses approach me. If any of them did, she would close up ears, charge forward and take a big bite on the other horse's rump. At that time, the stud farm also kept a few dogs. When a stranger drew near, we would say "Whoosh, whoosh" to the dogs, and they would rush out barking to scare that stranger away. I taught Little Black the same trick. For example, I would point a finger at a horse and say "Whoosh, whoosh," whereupon she would close her sharp ears, charge forward and bite into that horse's rump. I would then reward her with fodder beans so that she would get into the habit of obeying me. I enjoyed playing this game so much that the other horses became wary of me and kept their distance. Only Little Black would stay by me while grazing. Later on, she effectively became my herding assistant. When a horse was about to intrude into a crop field, I would 'whoosh' Little Black into action and drive that horse back.

Liang Yi from the propaganda team was a versatile man with a talent for dancing, playing the accordion and table tennis. Having a good eye for horses, he often came to the stud farm to watch them. He knew a long while ago that Little Black was a rare individual. When I saw how much he liked her, I boasted to him that she was so obedient to me that she would bite any horse I indicated. Liang didn't believe me, and he wanted to bet with me with two photo studio coupons. So I called 'Blackie' over. After feeding her a handful of fodder beans, I pointed to a horse and 'whooshed' Little Black forward. Sure enough, Little Black closed her ears and bit the horse right on his rump. She then quickly returned to me for her reward of soybeans as I subsequently pointed her to a second and a third horse. Each time, she carried out my command. So Liang had to surrender the two photo studio coupons, and I got to take two pictures with Little Black, which I managed to keep to this day.

Chapter 19

Conquering Little Black

Through that game of hide and seek I got to appreciate Little Black's amazing racing ability. What a pity it would be if such a fine horse lay idle without being ridden. Since she wouldn't be pregnant for at least another two years, why should I not train her to become my own exclusive riding horse? All the local vets travelled back and forth on horseback, carrying medicine kits on their shoulders. And they looked great! If I were able to train Little Black into a riding horse, I would be riding on a big, foreign horse carrying a medicine kit, and I would look even better than the local vets. In addition, I would be able to fetch medicine from the regiment headquarters on horseback instead of taking a vehicle. The thought gave me every reason to be excited, and I dreamed of riding Little Black someday.

It took me an entire week to figure out the best approach to conquer Little Black. Judging by my previous horse-riding experience, untamed horses typically make desperate attempts to throw their riders off when being ridden for the first time. They would not willingly submit to a rider unless the rider learned how to hold his ground and conquer them. My previous attempt to ride Bandit was extremely rash because we never got the chance to know each other. It was only natural that he should make every effort to dismount me. Ever since he threw me off, no one dared ride him again. So Bandit never got tamed. Little Black was somewhat different because I had already spent months trying to befriend her. Because she was grateful to me for treating her injury, I knew she would not intentionally throw me off when I rode her for the first time, but she could become startled when she suddenly felt the sudden weight of a person on her back, and this might cause her to run even faster. If I failed to maintain my balance, I could get thrown off and fall hard on the ground. Therefore, I decided not to saddle her so that I wouldn't get injured by the saddle, which meant I would at least stay alive.

Another Sunday arrived. I pulled out Little Black, brushed her all over, bridled her and led her out into an open space just behind the stud farm. I fed her some fodder beans from my pocket and kept a few in reserve. The open field was deserted and far from the stud farm. I was ready for my first ride on Little Black. In retrospect, my decision to ride her in such a remote area was unwise, even dangerous, because no one would know where I was if I fell off. I wanted to remain unseen because I felt falling off Little Black's back would be so humiliating. I might have been overconfident to think that I would conquer her, but I did have a secret weapon that I did not want to reveal to others.

After serious consideration, I decided to ride without a saddle. I replaced her halter with a bit. Since it was the first time she had worn a bit, she shook her head up and down. I tried to calm her by touching and feeling her, hugging her neck and kissing her head so that her mind would be at peace. Then, taking her by surprise, I grabbed her by the mane, clenched the reins that were connected to the bit, leaned on one side of her body and quickly jumped onto her back. Clearly shaken, Little Black instinctively put up a resistance against what would be her first ride. But the rider happened to be me, the one who truly loved her, whom she could not just throw off. So, with a shrill neigh, she charged forward like a shot arrow across the vast stretch of grassland.

My legs gripped tightly and I clutched the reins with one hand and the horse's mane with the other. I hunched over as much as possible to balance myself, and in the process almost merged into one with Little Black. I saw ditches, trees, weeds and mounds fly by on both sides; I heard the sound of the whistling wind; and I felt as if the earth was constantly moving. Little Black ran like an antelope, with cadence and rhythm, striding across in spans of dozens of feet. The staccato sounds of the hooves still echo in my ears today. Recalling the basic skills of horse riding, I made sure that my centre of gravity was as low as possible and that my body movement was consistent with that of the horse. That way, I would blend into one with Little Black so that we could safely move across the vast salty land.

I can say without exaggeration that this was the fastest horse ride I had ever experienced. Although I would later completely tame Little Black so that she would become my regular riding horse, she would never attain the same speed again. The reason why she could reach such a phenomenal speed was because she was startled after I jumped on her back. Stress response is a reaction to fright that is common to both humans and animals. Their bodies secrete excessive hormones that cause the cardiovascular system of the organism to function at high levels of efficiency, which also explains why a person in crisis can produce energy level many times higher than usual. So there was nothing unusual about Little Black's startling top speed. Ten years later, when my wife and I were watching a horse race in Cleveland, Ohio, we did not think much of those staggeringly expensive horses. I told my wife proudly that Little Black was much faster than them.

After I had conquered her, Little Black became my exclusive carrier; no one else could approach her. Once saddled and bridled, she would quickly turn around if anyone else wanted to take her for a trial ride. One day, as I took Little Black out of the stable, I came across Platoon Commander Zhang, who used to be a cavalryman.

"I hear Little Black is now ready for rides. Is she fast?" he asked.

"Absolutely! The fastest I've ever ridden."

"Can I try her?"

"I don't know. She is choosy. You'd better be careful."

While I hated to see other people ride my Little Black, I had no option but to cede to his request. Not surprisingly, as soon as Zhang took the reins, Little Black turned around and lifted her hooves in the air and neighed in that shrill tone. Zhang stepped back in embarrassment.

I patted Little Black on the back and said proudly to Zhang: "I told you. She won't let anyone else ride her."

Zhang looked at me and Little Black with puzzled eyes. He must have wondered what magic I had used to tame such a wayward horse. But he didn't want to interfere, for he knew I needed a horse as an exclusive ride in order to be an effective vet.

A new rider must have a good horse, a good saddle and a good pair of boots. My fondest dream then was to own a good pair of boots, and I told my mum about it in a letter I wrote her. She then had a pair custom-made by a well-known tanner in Beijing using top-grade hide.

When the boots were delivered by post, my peers mistook the package for food, and they all gathered round me in the hope of getting a morsel. But when the package was opened, we saw a new pair of shiny boots. Everyone was surprised and I jumped with excitement. From then on, I would love to put on the boots and race across the open fields on the leather-saddled Little Black. It was my greatest passion at the Corps.

At that time, I frequently visited the pharmacy at the regiment headquarters. The company base of Shatou was between thirty-five and forty kilometres from the regiment headquarters in Xin'an town. Travelling by a horse-drawn coach would usually take more than half a day, but on horseback it would take only a couple of hours. Little Black ran like the wind. Once we came to the open expanses, I would loosen the horse's reins and let her run as fast as she could. A good horse needs no whipping because running is second nature. Little Black never missed such an opportunity. She raced to her heart's content with her hooves high off the ground as I raised a tree branch the way those mighty knights of ancient times wielded their sabres in battle.

Chapter 20

Trips on Horseback

U nder clean, bright skies and refreshed with crisp air, autumn is a fascinating season in Inner Mongolia. On sunny days, when white clouds float in the blue sky and the earth emits an intoxicating scent, I would travel to the regiment headquarters to fetch medicine. I enjoyed these excursions because they gave me the opportunity to relax and the liberty to be on my own. I cherished those trips because I was fully aware I was the envy of many of my peers in the Corps.

One day, I led Little Black out of the stable and tied her to a pillar, and then went to fetch a beautiful saddle from my house. After saddling up and putting on my new boots, Platoon Commander Zhang came over and said: "With that saddle on, I'm sure I can ride Little Black."

But I was quite sure Little Black would only accept me as her rider. She would not let anyone else get close to her. But even so I gave the reins to Zhang without objection.

"Try then," I said.

"But do help me control her," Zhang replied.

As soon as I had helped Zhang onto the saddle, Little Black quickly evaded him, kicked its hind legs twice and threw the former cavalryman onto the floor before giving out a loud whinny.

I chuckled to myself as I continued preparations for my trip. I put the empty medicine box on the saddle and led Little Black on the way after saying goodbye to Zhang. I told him I was going to fetch medicine from the regiment and wouldn't be back until the next day. I lifted myself onto Little Black's back, and she immediately gave a loud whinny before galloping away. When I looked back, I saw Zhang wiping off the mud from a corner of his mouth. He had just got back to his feet, and he seemed to be mumbling with a puzzled look on his face: "That's crazy. Why would Little Black be so obedient to him? How did he train her?"

Little Black was not a pure breed, but a mixture of the Kabarda, Sanhe and Mongolian breeds and was a head taller than a regular Mongolian horse. I wore an informal army uniform that was enough to distinguish me from the average herdsman and vet. The old leather saddle that I was riding on came from Xiaojunma, who got it when he was serving in the cavalry. Once equipped with this saddle, Little Black looked no less valiant and spirited than the youngsters in the army compound who wore flannel army overcoats that their high-ranking parents had given them. Moreover, my boots were made of the finest leather. With a large medical kit on my shoulder, I was filled with vigour, and my face shone with pride and excitement.

Vectu, where the Third Company was located, is about four kilometres from Shatou. If I had meant to seek attention, I could have whipped Little Black and galloped through town. However, as a reserved kind of person, I merely tightened Little Black's reins and strolled past the Third Company. Even so, I could not prevent many eyes from gazing at me because on horseback I looked a lot taller than the other riders. Besides, Little Black was such a graceful-looking horse. I acted nonchalant, but I clearly saw many female Corps soldiers giving me the glad eye.

Being scrutinised by female soldiers made me embarrassed and uncomfortable, so I loosened the reins to allow Little Black to go faster. However Little Black took it as a signal to sprint. So, like a brave knight, I flew out of the Third Company without looking back. All soldiers of the company must have seen my gallant ways.

The propaganda team of the Third Company was well known in the regiment. They had come to my company to perform a modern revolutionary ballet called *The Red Detachment of Women*, which fascinated me at the time. A pretty hostess in the show turned out to be the daughter of my high school Chinese teacher. The star of the ballet who played the role of Wu Qionghua was a terrific dancer and she had a charming figure and graceful gait. I was so enamoured with her that for several nights I had trouble falling asleep. Later I learned that her parents both worked at the General

Hospital of Beijing military region as departmental chiefs, and her father was in custody in the same 'cowshed' as my mum. How I wished both girls had seen me riding Little Black!

After passing through Vectu where the Third Company was based, I covered several miles more and arrived at Qiaowan, where the Sixth and Tenth Companies were based. Qiaowan had much more vegetation than Shatou. There was also a river that flowed through the base, which helped cool the area during summer. By contrast, Shatou was much more exposed to the sun. The houses at Qiaowan were also more spacious and orderly, and many of them were brick and tile structures.

So I took a liking for Qiaowan as soon as I arrived.

To avoid the same mistake I had made at the Third Company, I dismounted before entering Qiaowan. Little Black held his head high and walked with irresistible charm, like a fashion model. Under her influence, I too began walking with my chest out and chin up, swaggering in tempo with Little Black. Because I was born premature, I grew up with weak bones, which caused me to develop a sort of pigeon breast. Back in high school, I would do fifty push-ups a day to improve my physique, and this helped considerably except that my chest remained underdeveloped. I was tall, thin and slightly hunchbacked.

I was hoping that more female soldiers of the Sixth and Tenth companies would see Little Black and me pass by. But unfortunately, none of them showed up. Only a few horse-keepers came up to chat with me on seeing the beauty of Little Black.

"Which company are you from? She's a tall girl! How does she run?"

"Extremely fast. At least twice as quick Mongolian horses."

On saying that, I was motivated to demonstrate my riding skills in the presence of my co-workers, and I wanted to show them the glamour of a really swift horse on the grassland. I mounted the horse in the normal manner, holding the snaffle bit in my left hand and throwing the surplus reins off to the opposite side of the horse's neck. In the meantime, my booted left foot was already in the stirrup, and as I grabbed the pommel with my right hand, I lifted myself into the saddle. By now, Little Black was accustomed to my unique way of mounting and knew it as an order to start running. She immediately set off like a shell discharged from a cannon. I did not look back, but I was pretty sure the spectators were all stunned.

The twenty kilometres from Qiaowan to Xin'an town comprised mostly white and yellow salty land overgrown with wild grass. The flat and spacious terrain made it smooth riding country. In a happy mood, I hummed a song from *Taking Tiger Mountain by Strategy* (one of the model revolutionary Peking operas filmed for the purpose of promoting the Cultural Revolution) as I sped through the desolate fields. No one was there to upbraid me even though I frequently sang out of tune. The horse was running so fast that we overtook every moving vehicle on the road – chariots, tractors and trucks. We did not stop until we reached our final destination – the regiment veterinary station at Xin'an. I had a great time riding Little Black.

Chapter 21

Feast of Fish

A one-way trip to the regiment headquarters to fetch medicine would usually take only an hour. I could easily get back to the company on the same day after having a meal up there. But I didn't want to rush in that way because I regarded riding Little Black on business as an opportunity to relax, and I enjoyed a slower pace. It so happened that Vet Xue was going to the Ninth Company to deworm the horses and vaccinate the cattle against foot-and-mouth disease. The medicine I was fetching from the regiment dispensary was going to be used to vaccinate such animals. Since the Ninth Company had no male vets and Xue had to do everything himself, he was more than happy to have me on board as a skilled horse-drenching assistant. I was thrilled to take on this additional job because I saw it as a precious opportunity to learn two veterinary procedures under the tutorship of a seasoned vet, not to mention the additional benefit of working in a different company.

The Ninth Company of the Twelfth Regiment was the only company based on the shore of Wuliangsuhai lake. Unlike my company that was solely concerned with farming, the Ninth Company engaged in reed harvesting, reed weaving and even fishing, thanks to its proximity to the lake. So they had plenty of fish to eat, which made me envious because, during my two years in the Corps, I never tasted any fish.

By the time Xue and I arrived at the Ninth Company, the stud farm had already tied all the horses and donkeys to stakes. These animals, which had not been fed for the whole night through, were now ready to be drenched with vermicides, the most commonly used being Dipterex. The horses were given vermicides twice a year, in spring and autumn, so that they would stay strong and healthy. When they were purchased and brought over from Xilingol league over a long distance, each of the horses resembled a bag of bones, and they looked no better after more than a month's feeding. Later on, when vets saw their wizened skin and hair, they concluded that they had worms. Although many herders had raised horses throughout their lives, they never knew how to deworm them. They sold their horses cheap when they saw them become emaciated. However, once those horses settled down in the companies and went through a single deworming procedure, almost all of them grew fat and their hair turned shiny, as if they had regenerated, and many of them were actually good horses. Since then, the Corps had been implementing strict deworming procedures.

After estimating each horse's weight, I would put an appropriate amount of Dipterex solution in a measuring cup. Because there was no six-columned stable in the Ninth Company, we had to tie the horses' heads to stakes. During drenching, one person would hold the horse's head as I slowly inserted a rubber catheter that was the thickness of a thumb into one of the horse's nostrils after dipping it in a basin of water. Next, I would push it slowly forward until it reached the larynx, where I would gently push and pull back and forth to induce deglutition. As soon as I saw signs of swallowing, I would push the catheter into the horse's oesophagus and send it slowly down into the stomach. Then, I would put the other end of the catheter to my ear to listen.

If I heard the sound of breathing, it would mean the catheter was inserted into the trachea, and I would have to pull it out and repeat the procedure until it was properly inserted into the stomach, whereupon I would connect a funnel to the catheter and pour in the Dipterex solution. Following that, I would pour in a glass of clean water to make sure that all of solution was into the stomach.

It was soon springtime. Xue told me to carry out bloodletting on some of the hot-tempered horses. I looked for veins in the horses' necks. On locating a vein, I would use a pair of flat-headed scissors to cut off a patch of hair, disinfect that area with iodine and alcohol, and then insert a thick needle into the vein, following which blood would quickly ooze out. Seeing bloodletting for the first time in his life, one of horse-keepers at the stud farm grew scared and felt compassion for the horse, and kept asking if I was close to being done. But I simply followed the normal procedure and did not stop until half a litre of blood was let.

The next task was to vaccinate against foot-and-mouth disease among the cattle. I would begin with the placid ones in a large pen. First, I would insert a needle into the cattle's rump, and then I would inject the liquid vaccine. The hardest part was dealing with a certain bad-tempered bull. It was panting heavily, with its eyes wide open, its waist bent and its horns pointed at us, as if it was going to attack. Just then, a brave man from the Ninth Company jumped into the pen and clamped its nostrils with a pair of tongs. I immediately stabbed the needle into its rump. Just as I was connecting the syringe to the needle, the bull began struggling valiantly. Right after I had finished injecting, the bull managed to get free from the tongs and came straight at me with its head down and its horns up. I ran as fast as I could. Fortunately, I was young and agile at the time and managed to get over an adobe wall about half my height. As it turned out, the bull's horns pierced the wall and got stuck there.

Since Xue and I were exhausted by the end of the day, the stud farm of the Ninth Company decided to treat us to a good meal. So they invited us to go fishing with them in the evening and then they would cook fish for us. This was a new experience for me, and I was looking forward to it. At about 9pm, we found our way to Wuliangsuhai lake where a boat was waiting for us. After we got on board, a soldier from the Ninth Company rowed the boat through an area thick with reeds. On reaching the centre of the lake, they cast two fishing nets borrowed from a villager. The meshes of the nets differed in size – one was the width of three fingers, the other five. Metal weights were attached to the bottom of the nets to cause them to sink, while the tops were attached to floats. That way, the nets would open out fully when they were cast into the water. The idea was that small fish and fries would swim through the meshes while the larger fish would get stuck as they opened their gills to breathe. Nets with bigger meshes were used to catch bigger fish.

After casting the nets into the lake, we marked their locations, rowed the boat to a wetland near the reeds and went ashore. Then we all sat down in a circle to smoke and chat. It was a starry night, and there was a crescent moon in the sky. The lake was all peace and quiet, with only the slightest ripple on the surface. It looked like a mirror reflecting the stars and moon. Occasionally, a fish would leap from the water, cracking and shining in the moonlight. In the reed area, a few water fowls would occasionally take flight, flapping their wings and splashing across the surface of the lake, the sound of which would then die out as the birds flew off into the distance.

By 5am, we returned to our boat and headed towards the centre of the lake. By now day had dawned, and we began collecting what we had caught during the night. When we pulled up the nets, I was elated to see so many fish jumping into the boat. My heart was filled with joy. As designed, the net with the smaller mesh trapped fish that were about three finger-breadths wide. The net with a larger mesh caught bigger fish, including carp and catfish. In total, our catch exceeded a hundred kilos. We cheered and sang as we moored the boat on shore.

My peers from Ninth Company brought out a full set of cooking utensils, the most important of which was a large iron wok, which was set on top of a mound of mud. They cleaned up the fish pretty quickly, and they knew how to cook it too. Into the pot they poured the right volume of lake water – supposedly better than well water for cooking fish – and let the water steam dry, by which time the fish was done. Next, they put spring onions, ginger and salt into the wok, covered it and lit up the firewood under the pot. We then sat together in a circle chatting and smoking as we waited for the food.

About half an hour later, the appetising smell of the fish spilled out of the wok. It made my mouth water because it had been a good two years since I last ate fish. When the wok lid was removed, I could barely wait any longer. As a guest, I was served a large bowl of fish. The first bite was heavenly, and I continued to eat ravenously, mouthful by greedy mouthful, right by the lake. Some horse-keepers brought along plum wine which we called 'coloured wine'. The hardened drinkers drank a spirit called '139', so named because it cost 1.39 yuan a bottle. We kept eating until noon and almost all of us got drunk. Because I had not eaten fish for a long time but now had the chance to eat all I could, I soon found my belly bloated. In my drunken state, I lay in the wilderness, and then got sent back to the stud farm in a donkey-cart where I slept for hours. When I got back to the regiment veterinary clinic with Xue, it was already evening.

Chapter 22

Saving the Master

A t the veterinarian station I ate only a bowl of congee and some pickles because the fish in my belly was not yet fully digested. It then suddenly occurred to me that the platoon leader had mentioned I had to head back to the company that day. So I led out Little Black, saddled him and packed the medicine I had taken from the regiment headquarters on either side of the saddle.

Just as I was about to get going, Xue came out, took a look at the sky and said to me: "It's too late. Why don't you stay here tonight and set out tomorrow?"

"Sorry I can't. I promised the platoon leader that I would return today. And there are so many horses and cattle waiting to be drenched and injected that I have to get back tonight."

"Then be careful about riding alone at night. Stay safe."

"Don't worry. With Little Black, I have nothing to fear because no one can go faster!"

I said goodbye to Xue and led Little Black on the way to the regiment health clinic. It wasn't dark yet and on the streets of Xin'an I saw a number of Corps soldiers ambling in twos or threes having finished their dinner. I knew I still had something important to do, something of special significance especially when I was alone with Little Black. After walking some distance, I dismounted Little Black, and she followed me close behind. I unconsciously stopped in front of the divine tree that reminded me of Yue and our love for each other. It was now more than a year since she had left. I had no clue where she was now, as if she had evaporated from earth. In the first two months after she left, I was so lovesick that I

137

thought I was going to die. However, knowing that I had made her suffer before and had caused her to lose some hair, I felt I deserved all the pain I was going through.

In the past, Yue had time and again rescued me from big trouble. She hid me in the train toilet when I was close to being arrested by the military guards. She then made it possible for me to stay in the Corps to make a living. Still later, when I fell ill with acute gastroenteritis, Yue phoned for a jeep and personally escorted me to the divisional headquarters hospital until I recovered. So I owed my life to her, and I was happy for her when she could move to develop her career in a better environment. I could only wish her all the best.

There is a saying: "As water flows downwards, so man struggles upwards." It's all part of human nature. I wanted her to have a happy future. Maybe she was now a head nurse in some field hospital; maybe she had decided to continue her studies and had become an army surgeon. Or perhaps she had found a position that matched her 'super girl' personality, and become a soldier in the special forces. Whatever she was doing, she was like a goddess to me. Whether in the past, present or future, she will always be the queen of my heart. Probably out of concern that I would feel lonely, she might have shapeshifted into a horse to keep me company. Or she may have prayed to heaven that Little Black be sent to me for companionship. With these thoughts, I grabbed on to Little Black's neck, pressed my cheeks into her face and rubbed her continuously. She seemed to know what I was doing and began moving her long neck up and down before giving out a high-pitched whinny.

The sweet whinny caught the attention of two female soldiers, or more accurately, two nurses from the regiment health clinic who were walking towards us. There were several good horses at the regiment headquarters, but none of them had the tall, slender stature and glossy black hair of Little Black. The seductive beauty and the gentle whinny of such a horse would attract anyone.

The nurses stepped closer, hoping to get a better look at the beauty, but unconsciously, their gaze eventually landed on me. As they approached, I saw that the nurses were none other than Shan Ying and Lin Na, who used to work under Yue. They recognised me at the same time and were surprised to see this once sick man now wearing riding boots and standing with a horse in front of them in such high spirits. They looked at me in amazement as we began to chat.

"What are you doing here, Wen Bo? You look great," Lin Na began.

"Yeah! You're looking full of life. You've become a different person," Shan Ying echoed with admiration in her voice.

I smiled and said nothing.

"He's quite a proper vet now! You know how capable he is just by looking at his horse!"

Lin Na walked over as she spoke, trying to touch Little Black, but the horse closed her ears and turned her rump around, ready to jolt. Her sudden whinny so scared Lin Na that she immediately drew back her hand and withdrew nimbly.

"Be careful. She kicks those she doesn't recognise," I said quickly.

"Does she recognise only you?"

"Of course, because I trained her."

I decided to show off a little bit in front of them so that they might one day pass on a favourable impression of me to Yue. So I jumped on the horse and yelled: "I have to get back to the company today. Let's talk next time I come to the headquarters. So long!"

"Wen Bo, do see us next time you come. Don't forget us! We saved your life once, after all. Come and see us if you need any help."

"OK! I'll let you take some pictures with Little Black next time. I have to go now. See you!"

I spurred on Little Black and sped into the darkness.

Night had fallen when I left the regiment headquarters, and it was completely dark in under half an hour. The night sky was full of clouds and there was no sign of the moon or stars. With not a single road lamp over the next forty kilometres of dirt road, it all looked dark and ghastly until we came close to a village dotted with dim lamplights. It was my first solitary horse ride in the dead of night. There were no vehicles, no pedestrians, nothing but the rustling of leaves in the wind. It would have been scary walking alone on that dark road, but I was young and had Little Black with me. At least I did not feel that scared in the beginning.

I dared not let Little Black run for fear of having an accident.

So I reined her in in order to slow down. At a slow pace, it would probably take five to six hours to get back to the company. But I preferred going slow and steady, for if the horse started running and tripped up, we could end up falling in a place where no one would find us. This prospect gave me reason to fear, and I began to regret my decision to head back to Shatou during the night. I thought I should have followed Xue's advice and left the following morning instead. I had probably made another rash decision.

I thought about singing a song, like one of the arias in *Taking the Tiger Mountain by Strategy*, just to lift my spirits. On reflection, however, I felt it was simply an attempt to conceal my fear, just like when a timid dog barks. If indeed there was a 'class enemy' hiding in the woods and I shouted out loud, wouldn't that be the silliest thing to do? So I simply kept quiet and kept going. But deep in my heart I was losing my poise, and I became increasingly scared.

There were few recreational activities for soldiers in the Corps, so we often went to bed early and told ghost stories just to entertain ourselves. I was never frightened by those stories, but now things seemed a little different. I really did think there might be monsters hiding in the groves, ready to jump out and scare me. I began to shiver on horseback, and my whole body seemed to be shaking.

After travelling for another three kilometres or so, I felt a pain in my back and decided to dismount and walk a while in order to relax. As I was walking, I thought that previously I would never have been brave enough to walk alone at night on such a road. It was the presence of Little Black that emboldened me.

But I still felt insecure. What if a 'class enemy' ran out of the tall grass with a knife in hand and stabbed me? I would have no escape. Eventually, I decided that staying on horseback was the safer option, because in case of emergency, I could quickly escape. So I jumped back on Little Black. But Little Black was quick, and she did not appreciate the way I was dawdling. My decision to remount lifted her spirits because she thought I was ordering her to run. She sped up, and I felt I could no longer hold her back. So I simply let her pick up the pace.

However, after walking briskly for less than two kilometres, for some unknown reason Little Black suddenly pricked up her ears, began looking around suspiciously and quickened her pace. It's still a mystery to me what she had seen. It could have been a wolf or a raiding 'class enemy'. Whatever it was, she got startled and began to gallop. No longer able to restrain her, I had to let her run free, not on the dirt road, but on the barren, salty land.

Just then, something unexpected happened. While Little Black was crossing a ditch, she stooped down before suddenly stopping, which caused me to be thrown hard into the ditch. I must have passed out. When I regained consciousness, I was glad to be alive but I could not move, my backside being pinned by a thick, forked tree stump. I felt a sharp, piercing pain, and my backside was bleeding.

I knew I was in serious trouble. I was injured, and my horse was gone. Maybe I had to stay in the wilderness bleeding for the whole night until I passed out again or died. Stranded in the middle of nowhere in the dead of night, I stood little chance of being discovered. Even if Little Black ran back to the stud farm and my friends knew I had been hurt, where could they possibly find me? No doubt people would look for me, but it could take days to locate me. By then I would have been long dead, and my friends would only be in time to collect my body.

But then I heard a familiar high-pitched whinny in the distance. Little Black was looking for me! It was the sound of one form of life calling another. It was the kind of worldly love I had been seeking and waiting for. It thrilled me in a special way, and I felt strengthened and energised. "Blackie! Blackie!" I shouted at the top of my voice.

My words from that ditch were by no means loud, but because it was so quiet, they still managed to carry. Little Black stopped neighing. She seemed to have heard my voice and was trying hard to discern where it had come from. So I shouted again from the bottom of my lungs: "Blackie! Blackie!"

Little Black must have heard my voice reverberate in this remote wilderness. I soon heard approaching hooves. It was the sound of Little Black trotting up, a sound only too familiar to me. I tried to climb out of the ditch, but a new spasm of sharp pain forced me to lie down again. The ditch was deep, almost deeper than a man's height. Lying there, I could do nothing but look at the dim stars in the sky. I had no idea if Little Black would ever find me. Even if she did, how could she possibly rescue me from this deep trench?

But something miraculous happened, something that I would never forget. I saw Little Black's head peering down. She was obviously looking for me! To my great relief, the reins were drooping down naturally into my hands. I grabbed them immediately. Little Black seemed to be aware of what I was trying to do and began to pull me up. She was very good at it. She bent her lower legs, sat low on her hooves and kept pulling backwards. Meanwhile, her neck was pulling back and up too. Little by little, Little Black dragged me out of the ditch.

Later examination showed that I did not have a fracture, but my backside was so badly bruised that I could not even stand up, let alone ride a horse. Little Black strutted around me anxiously and kept licking at the bloodstains on my trousers. I motioned her to lie down, but because she never been trained in sign language, she couldn't make out what I was trying to convey. So I kept dragging down her reins until she finally understood and lay down by my side. I struggled onto her back, or rather climbed onto the saddle, but I did not insert my feet into the stirrups. I feared that she would start running and throw me off, so I lay prostrate on the saddle, my arms hugging her neck tight.

Little Black was so considerate. Knowing that I was hurt, she got up slowly and walked steadily rather than ran. We naturally got lost. The pain made it impossible for me to sit or direct her. Besides, my poor sense of direction could not be trusted. As the saying goes, 'An old horse knows the way'. Although Little Black was just two years old, I knew she was clever enough to find her way home. So I simply let her saunter freely and steadily in the wilderness, believing she would eventually carry me to safety and maybe even take me directly back to the stud farm.

Probably due to the bleeding, I was hungry, thirsty and exhausted. I could pass out at any time. Head swimming, I lay on Little Black's back and held on to her long neck, and after an unknown period of time, I would awake for a while and then fall back to sleep. While the saddle was uncomfortable, the steady and rhythmic pace of Little Black made me feel as secure as a baby in a crib. So I believe I did not pass out, but was just in deep slumber.

Carrying me on her back, Little Black walked the whole night through until dawn and the first rays of morning shone on us. I knew my life was no longer in danger since in daylight I would be found very easily. Anyone seeing a horse carrying a wounded person would surely come to the rescue, but I would much prefer to be able to return to my own company in Shatou and to the stud farm.

These thoughts gave me hope and strength, and raised my spirits. I began caressing Little Black's neck, and I recalled every detail of her efforts to save me. I was amazed at the horse's love and wisdom. She was perhaps repaying me for what I had done for her in the past. Her love for me was true. I became more certain of my training methodology. Termagant horses should not be trained with a whip, but with tender love. They need to be won over with human love because horses are spiritual beings that know about human feelings. They will repay kindness with loyalty and compassion.

Knowing that I was touching her, Little Black turned her head towards me. She looked relieved when she saw me still alive. Determined to get me home as soon as possible, she walked at a firmer and more steadfast pace. She seemed to have found the right way to the company. Quite soon, she raised her head and gave out her signature high-pitched whinny, which informed me that we had arrived at the familiar stud farm. We were finally home.

My colleagues at the horse keeping squad came up and carried me into my dorm. Before long, an army doctor and nurse arrived. The nurse cleaned up my wound and dressed it according to the doctor's instructions. The female cooks at the canteen prepared a noodle dish and sent it to the stud farm. As I ate the hot food, I told them in lively detail how Little Black had saved me. Many of them were moved to tears.

Two weeks later, I had recovered, but a big scar was left at the top of my thigh, close the scar left by Bandit. So my body had been scarred twice by acts of recklessness, and both accidents could have cost me my life. I certainly learned my lessons the hard way. Had it not been for Little Black, I would probably not be here to write this book.

I could now go to the cafeteria and walk around at the stud farm without any problems. So every day after dinner, I would put some fodder beans in my pocket and go to see Little Black in her stable. She was now venerated as a heroine and had a stable of her own. She was fed with good food each day, even though it wasn't a healthy lifestyle for Little Black. From my personal experience, horses were best pasture fed. So I eventually let her join her friends on the pasture.

With a pocket of fodder beans, I would walk to the railings of the stable and call Little Black by her name. She would immediately raise her head and walk to the railings before stretching out her long neck and pursed lips. I would then stuff a handful of fodder beans into her mouth. But I was not content with that limited interaction. So I would open the gate and let her out. The unbridled Little Black would then follow me like a loyal dog as I headed toward the salty land behind the stud farm.

As Little Black and I ambled in this barren area, I would occasionally feed her a handful of fodder beans and then stop to hug her neck. The fact that she could pull me out of a deep ditch at a time of peril and carry me all the way back to the stud farm made me think she was not just a horse, but rather the reincarnation of Yue, because only she would have done something like that. I kept stroking her head as she stood there upright and still, with her eyes half-closed. She was apparently enjoying the attention. By now it was completely dark. Under the bright moonlight, Little Black's silky dark hair mirrored the soft light of the moon. In the quietude of the earth, I held Little Black in my arms and our faces touched, feeling as if we had merged into one.

We walked back to the stable under the starlit sky. Since then, I formed the habit of strolling with Little Black each day after dinner. Walking with this horse on the barren land of Inner Mongolia gave me an unusual feeling of happiness, a feeling that was most approximate to love. If love was not obtainable in the human world, I would have to seek it elsewhere. That idyllic interaction between man and animal filled my heart with great joy and dispelled my solitude at the Corps.

Chapter 23

Stealing Melons

As a vet in the company, I was also required to graze the horses at night in spring, summer and autumn and to feed them in winter. One autumn night, when it was my turn to herd the horses, I came up with the idea of 'picking' – a better word than 'stealing' – a couple of melons. I was told that Little Zhao had successfully 'picked' some melons when he was herding the horses at night, but I didn't get any share of them. So I requested to herd the horses alone, claiming that I could handle twenty or so of them by myself, without any help. That way, I reasoned, the company could save labour and allow more people to rest. My true intention, however, was to get an opportunity to commit the ignominious act of theft with impunity.

Watermelons, cantaloupes and muskmelons were grown on the company farm. Cantaloupes are small in size, but are crisp and deliciously sweet. They were not available in Beijing back then. Though soldiers at the Corps got a limited share of the annual melon harvest each autumn, I never had a chance to enjoy a melon feast similar to the fish feast at the Ninth Company. So I decided to venture into the melon fields while horse herding at night. After three years in the Corps, I had become much more daring than before.

The melon fields were guarded by female soldiers from the company's propaganda team. Besides rehearsals and performances, they were also responsible for growing and guarding melons. They were all pretty girls who would easily captivate us male soldiers when they were singing and dancing on stage.

I decided to act after midnight, when the horses would be taking a nap together after a whole night's grazing. I put a halter on Little Black's head and led her towards the field, pretending to be a mere passer-by and hoping to come across the girls and then curry favour with them. If they took a liking to me, they may actually give me a melon or two to eat. If not, I would ask them for some water so they might think of giving me a melon. By then, I had a much thicker skin than before.

However, I did not see anyone when I got to the melon field. I saw a shed in the distance, which made me think the girls were holed up in there sleeping. So I went ahead in search of melons. If they emerged from the shed and came in my direction, I would then jump on Little Black and dart away.

I soon discovered a large watermelon, picked it up and smashed it with my fist. I had great strength back then. The watermelon was disappointingly unripe, so I gave it to Little Black. I tried another one, which was no good either, so once again I gave it to Little Black. She wasn't picky, but I really wanted a sweet one, so I kept searching.

Just then, I heard a high-pitched female shout. My legs began to shake as I instinctively raised my hands above my head. In front of me stood four masked women armed with steel pitchforks and clubs, their beautiful yet stern eyes flashing at me. They probably recognised me straight away, as I was quite well-known as a vet and a bookworm. I knew I would get in big trouble if this scandal got out in the company. It would be more damaging than the pig-stealing scandal because I had got caught by girls this time.

They surrounded me with their weapons, as if they had caught a major criminal. They forced me to tie the horse to a tree and set about escorting me away. I got very nervous, fearing that they might deliver me to the Company headquarters. But there was nothing I could do, nor could I see any way out. The only thing that might work was to be acquiescent. So I quietly submitted to them and did whatever they instructed, all the while hoping that they would play down the issue or even clean forget about it. I showed neither fear nor defiance and remained as calm as possible.

I tied Little Black to a tree and followed their lead. They were swishing their forks and clubs before me, as if testing my resolve, to see whether I was truly unafraid or just feigning it. But when a fork touched the back of one of my hands, I became flustered and almost fell down. I quickly stabilised myself, but my shaking legs gave me away. They must have seen my fear because I heard them laughing.

Anyway, as their captive and prize, I felt quite ashamed. I had previously thought that I came across as something of an imposing man, but now I had to bow my head and be ordered about. Luckily it happened at night, when darkness could conceal my embarrassment.

I was escorted to a pile of cantaloupes near the shed. They motioned me to sit, so I sat down before the melons. Then, the girl holding a fork walked over and shook the implement at me. She could clearly see how scared I was. So she put on a gleeful and proud air, reminding me that she was the boss of the four. She then stabbed the fork into the ground so close to my foot that it almost touched me.

Standing with arms akimbo, she began her inquisition: "Why did you steal into the melon field? Why not let us know beforehand?"

"I thought you were sleeping in the shed. I didn't feel comfortable waking you up."

"That's why you stole our melons?"

"I... I haven't drunk anything all night. I was so thirsty."

I stammered, trying hard to sound apologetic and look pitiful, so that they might forgive me. I thought they would be considerate enough to do that so long as I pleaded guilty.

"Even if you were thirsty, you shouldn't have picked the unripe melons. You knew you were wasting them by throwing them away after one or two bites."

"I gave them to my saviour, Little Black. So they did not go to waste."

"Really? Tell us how she saved you."

The change of topic made me aware that my meek approach was taking effect. I told the story with such gusto that they soon got deeply absorbed. The ice had been broken, and they were now ready to show grace.

"You can sit down and eat the ones we have already picked, as many as you want, but don't pick the unripe ones. Is that alright? We won't go easy on you if we catch you again," the boss warned.

I was totally compliant. In situations like that, I tend to sound very plausible. As the saying goes, 'A living dog is better off than a dead lion'. As if to emphasise their words, they wielded their forks and clubs before me again. In taking evasion, I stumbled and fell awkwardly on my face. They laughed and left the melon field as they set about changing shifts. I

147

was now alone with several piles of ripe melons that would be shipped to the company headquarters later in the day. My feast began as I sat there chewing to my heart's content. I didn't stop even though my belly was getting bloated. Instead, I loosened my belt, emptied my bladder and kept eating until I could hardly walk anymore. Just before I was about to leave, I looked at the golden cantaloupes again and found it impossible to leave without them. So I took off my uniform and wrapped up six cantaloupes and a watermelon, and loaded them in a big parcel on the back of Little Black and took off.

Back on the stud farm, I hid the watermelon in the veterinary dispensary and stuffed the cantaloupes into the quilts of my colleagues. When they each woke they were surprised and delighted to see a golden cantaloupe in their bed.

"Wen Bo, that's incredible," one of them said as he started eating. "How did you get these? Did you steal them?"

"How could I steal them? The girls gave them to me."

"Wow! They sure like you. You should go herding alone more."

I was touched by their compliments, but I declined to tell them the whole story, especially the most humbling part: how I got captured and was ordered to walk with them for more than a hundred metres, how I had been mocked for my awkwardness, and how pathetic and servile I had to be just to get those melons. I would rather suffer than lose face. So I began to ponder how best to get some more melons for my brethren. I decided never to steal or beg for them again.

By coincidence, the very next day a villager led to me a horse that was infected with impetigo after sustaining an injury. I cleaned the horse's wound for free. Before leaving, the villager asked me if there was anything he could do for me. I took him aside and asked in a low voice if anyone in his village could sell me a sack of cantaloupes. He said he would talk to the production team leader and see if I could get a membership discount. By noon the following day, just as I was combing Little Black's mane, the villager came over driving a donkey cart loaded with a large sack of cantaloupes. As my colleagues were all napping, I hid the melons in the veterinary pharmacy. The villager charged me seven yuan in total, which was a handsome sum at that time. During the first three years in the company, our monthly allowance was just six yuan. Although that was my fourth year at the Corps, my monthly salary was a meagre 28.5 yuan.

This sack of melons won me a lot of prestige. After I had taken the horses back to the stable, I would take six cantaloupes from the veterinary dispensary and stuff them into my colleagues' quilts. I never breathed a word about the fact that I had paid for the melons. I was particularly grateful to those female soldiers of the propaganda team who forgave me and did not tell anyone about my embarrassing encounter with them. Maybe they had forgotten about it. Even in reunion gatherings decades later, I never heard them make any mention of this episode. Maybe during that time there were countless young men who got caught stealing melons, and I did that only once. So they probably thought little of it and simply let it go.

Chapter 24

Recreational Activities

Life outside work at the Corps was dull, especially in the evenings when there was no power supply and the only source of light came from kerosene lamps. In the gloom, we spent time either reading hand-copied books or went to bed early to chat about various things. When we ran out of topics, we would tell silly ghost stories. During the day, when we had free time, some of us played the harmonica, others wrote to their family members, while I either imitated a famous broadcaster or played ping-pong.

Oradoz was my comrade-in-arms at the horse keeping squad. At first I thought his was a Mongolian name, but later found it to be Daur. China has a Daur population of more than 100,000. The original meaning of Daur was 'pioneer', which points to the resolve of this ethnic group. However, in Oradoz I saw no sign of that at all. On the contrary, he had a thin and small frame and low cheekbones. Gentle and with a light complexion, he had a pair of unfathomable eyes behind his spectacles that radiated brilliant talent. We used to sleep on the same *kang*, herd horses together and talk about life. Later, he drove the dray, worked as a secretary and finally went to college. We remained friends for the rest of our lives, and decades later, Oradoz described me like this:

> He had a set of books. He could imitate the voice of Xia Qing, the father of Chinese broadcasting. He sang in a resonant baritone, and he could tame hee-hawing donkeys and Little Black...

Oradoz was not exaggerating. I could indeed mimic Xia Qing's broadcasting style. Actually, back in high school, before I came to the

Corps, I used to enjoy fooling around with classmates who were one or two years older than me. Some of them practised singing and training their voices on an almost daily basis at school, and I joined in and unexpectedly learned the technique of diaphragmatic breathing to improve my oratory skills. The sound waves I produced were shockingly resonant, and those around me referred to it as my 'Italian utterance'. I used this special skill to imitate radio broadcasters and often won praise from my audience, which gave me a sense of pride.

On weekends, when there was little to do, I would grab a newspaper and read it aloud with my unique 'Italian utterance'. My neighbours assumed that a transistor radio had been turned on. Inspired by the acclaim of those around me, I soon got addicted to the sport. I would take every opportunity to exhibit my voice. For example, during 'daily reading' time, I would take the initiative to read *Quotations from Chairman Mao* and shock those present. But the compliments were limited to the horse-keeping squad. Despite the low profile I was trying to keep, I still had an ego, and I hoped that everyone in the company, especially the girls, would be drawn to the masculine appeal of my dynamic baritone.

Therefore, whenever I had free time after dinner, instead of staying at the stud farm as I always did, I would put on clean clothes and visit all the men's platoons. I frequented the propaganda team whose leader Daping was my high school classmate. We ended up in the same company for the same reason – politically incorrect family background.

Daping was slightly taller than me. He had a fair, oval face that featured a sparkling pair of wise eyes and a high-bridged nose. He was an intelligent man, and would often speak methodically on deep philosophical matters. I enjoyed chatting with him on all sorts of subjects, and sometimes we exchanged overheard gossip that might be relevant to our future. Another reason I enjoyed visiting the propaganda team was because I liked to take in the artistic atmosphere out there. Time after dinner was usually when they would get together and play musical instruments, sing songs or recite poems. In order to blend in with the atmosphere, I would sometimes amaze them with my 'Italian utterances', and I derived pleasure from seeing the admiration in their eyes.

I longed for more admiring eyes, especially those of girls. It was probably nothing deeper than the dormant lust lying in the deep recesses of every young man. I kept looking for opportunities, which unfortunately were often linked to political movements. It was my fourth year in the Corps, when the movement of criticising Lin Biao and Confucius spread down to our company. As it turned out, every platoon was required to select a representative to deliver a speech at the company-level criticising sessions. So I wrote a carefully crafted speech and then told Platoon Commander Zhang I wanted to deliver it on behalf of the platoon. Zhang smiled, not knowing my motivation. He probably wondered why I had suddenly taken an interest in political matters, but he honoured my request anyway.

To prepare for that day, I spent days doing push-ups in an attempt to straighten my barely visible hunchback. As a result, my chest began to bulge with muscles, and my back looked straighter. I also spent a lot of time cleaning my outfit and combing my hair as the date of the meeting drew near. When it was time for me to speak, I strode onto the stage to face the microphone and a huge audience for the first time in my life. Few of the girls had seen me before, and never in such a setting. On this rare occasion, the whole auditorium fell completely silent, and everyone was waiting for me to speak.

I took a deep breath before reading my script in a rhythmic delivery using the unique 'Italian utterances' technique. Oradoz's appraisal of my voice was no exaggeration. It did rival the voice of Xia Qing. At the first utterance of my solemn baritone, the whole auditorium reverberated with the sound of my voice, and a huge cheer erupted in the audience. My wonderful reading left a strong impression on them. I read the script with cadence and passion for a full twenty minutes. I can no longer remember what I was talking about, but the solemn voice was unforgettable because a spiritual interaction took place between me and the audience, especially among the females, thanks to my Italian utterances. I had no way of knowing whether the audience was having a good time, but I certainly enjoyed the whole experience.

Over the next few days, I received compliments from fellow comrades through different channels. Some girls began paying me attention and asking questions about me. I was told that girls on the propaganda team had even tried to have me join them. Such encouraging news made my heart ripple with joy. I began to wonder if it was actually the four melon-keepers who had recommended me. If so, their perception of me must have been transformed.

My other passion at the company was table tennis. My love for the game dates back to my teenage years, about fifty years ago, when the 26th world table tennis championship was held in Beijing. As a primary school student, I made my way into a huge crowd of adults to watch the finals of the tournament on a 14-inch black and white TV set, around which sat dozens of people. I was excited to see how the Chinese national team won the championship for the first time in history. Xu Yinsheng's smashes, Zhuang Zedong's two-front attacks and Rong Guotuan's perseverance exhilarated my young heart.

Since then, I became obsessed with ping-pong. The first bat that I bought from a department store for less than one yuan was little more than a toy. It had a layer of cork on the underside of the plywood. With bat in hand, I learned how to play ping-pong on a stone table. Later on, I spent a little more on another racket that I used until middle school. The low quality of the racket did not prevent me from going through rigorous training. When I read about Zhuang Zedong practising in front of a mirror, he became my teenage idol. Like him I practised my shots in front of a mirror, and also against a wall. The exterior wall of my grandma's newly painted house was level and perfect for practising ping-pong, and I couldn't wait for it to dry so that I could play. The marks left by the ball on the wall were imprinted forever.

Though addicted to ping-pong as a child, I was actually only a mediocre player due to a lack of formal training. The year I graduated from primary school, I saw an ad in an evening newspaper that Dongcheng district sports school was enrolling students for its summer holiday table tennis class. So I went to an admissions test together with some classmates. We joined a long line of people waiting for our turn to take part in a qualifying match. Only one coach was in attendance, watching as many as five matches at the same time. How I wished I could be selected! Unfortunately, my table happened to be located far away from the coach. So I decided I had to do something special to get noticed. I waited for the right opportunity to smash the ball with all my might, but I hit it so hard that the bat flew out of my hand. The coach took a look at me and shook his head. And that was the end of my ping-pong dream.

The First Company had many good table tennis players, several of whom had received professional training. A tall and strong young man called Shi Jun used to be a key player at Beijing No.13 middle school. Since he was young, he underwent training at sports schools in Shichahai in Dongcheng district and in Xicheng district. He had a good command of all of the basic skills. His strokes were steady and accurate, and he was a good tactician. With a stocky build, a square face and a full ophryon, which are typical signs of good fortune, he might well have been the best player in the company.

Ai Guo had a naturally solid physique. He was the champion sprinter and long jumper at the company's sports day. Quick and with explosive power, he was a handsome man with large eyes, thick eyebrows and a straight nose. His slick hair was parted to one side. Trained at Dongcheng sports school in Beijing, he was an adept tactician when it came to table tennis, using his left hand to defend and his right to attack. He would also sometimes use his left hand to smash in order to surprise his opponent. He was the second-best player in the company.

The third best player never received any formal training, but he was gifted and had a good feel for the game, and something of a healthy infatuation for it. His name was Shunzi, the young man who had willingly accompanied me when I was on duty herding the horses. Originally we were of a similar standard, but one year he returned to Beijing for a home visit and spent a full month doing nothing but practise table tennis at a gymnasium. By the time he returned to the company, he became capable of hitting perfect lobs. As a consequence, I had to swallow the bitter fruit of defeat every time I played him. I was never able to beat him again.

Toxin Shokun and Oradoz came to Shatou together, and they both lived in residential quarters belonging to Hohhot's press organisations. Although they both had Daur names, I never heard them speak the dialect. They spoke fluent Mandarin instead. Toxin Shokun used to be leader of the carters' squad. He was no taller than me, but he had a robust frame and large bones, typical of Daurs. He had smooth, glossy white cheeks and dark, penetrating eyes that glowed with charm. Toxin Shokun really enjoyed playing table tennis. We played frequently on a cement table at the stud farm. At first, we were about the same standard. But Toxin Shokun was known as a precise, hardworking man. Ever since he fell in love with the game, he devoted almost all of his spare time to practice. As a result, he became increasingly skilful and his strokes became more accomplished. All his hard work paid off, and his right forehand smash quickly became his signature stroke, and earned him entry into the company team.

Because of these four classy players, the team was able to prevail at every single competition, whether at regimental or divisional level. They became known as an invincible force throughout the Corps. Because of their prowess, I was only a peripheral figure despite my infatuation with the game. I was especially envious when I saw them go on tour. I envied them even when they were on full-time training sessions within the company, particularly when I saw them mix with the girls' team. Sometimes they would meet and play at the same table. One day, when I was passing the auditorium, I noticed two table tennis tables made by the company carpenter. I saw Zhang Juan, the shepherd girl, playing with great skill. I couldn't resist walking over and playing several points with her. Her large, beautiful eyes glistened; she hit the ball in a natural, unrestrained and graceful manner, and it came at such breathtaking speed that I had to put up a desperate counterattack to get the upper hand. But after several points, she suddenly put down her bat and said with a smile: "Why do you always try the flip shot?"

One had to be very skilled to say something like that. Obviously, Zhang Juan was highly experienced and proficient. She must have been trained at a sports school as well. By contrast, my skills were far inferior. I knew I had to be ranked fourth or better to be make the company ping-pong team. The thought of failing to get into the team inspired me to endure hardships, be patient and train hard so that I might one day beat all these higher-ranked players.

So I began to review my strategy. I knew I had to find some fresh ways and develop new tactics to beat them. Conventional ways wouldn't have got me anywhere. After much thought, I finally figured out a unique technique, which was to play with two bats, one in each hand. My thinking was that, with sufficient practice, I would be able to use this skill to beat the one-bat players. If successful, the technique may even be recorded in the history of table tennis.

Ai Guo owned a cast-iron bat designed to build up his arms. Toxin Shokun borrowed it when he was working on his basic skills. I was surprised Ai Guo gave it to me this time. The key to practising with two bats was to learn to play with the left hand first. I would toss and catch the ball on the bat with my left hand hundreds of times a day so that I would get the right feel. At night, when I left to herd the horses, I brought the iron bat with me so that I could practise my strokes and focus on left-handed attack, repeating the stroke more than a hundred times. That not only strengthened my left arm but also prepared me for using the left hand to attack. Next, I searched for a moderately good player to practise playing left handed.

Though Yuan Zhong was a member of the field platoon, he often came to the stud farm to chat with me. We enjoyed hanging out together, maybe because we had a similar disposition. He was a resilient man who loved delving into things. So we played together a lot. Yuan Zhong was a slender man with a baby face. On his well-proportioned, smiling and kindly face were a pair of clear eyes, a high-bridged, straight nose and a diamond-shaped mouth. Although my left hand was clumsy to begin with, he had the patience to practise with me. When I got better over time, I began using both hands to play, and I got bolder and more skilled. In the end, I became capable with both hands to the point of perfection. My comrades from the stud farm cheered my fine performance.

Despite my ability to use both hands, I hid this fact from my opponents and kept striving to improve my ability. During home leave, I bought two bats. One was a square Japanese bat suitable for left-hand attack, and it was covered with a circular piece of rubber bearing a plum blossom pattern. The other was designed for the shakehand grip, which was good for hitting lobs. The long rubber on the backhand side was good for slicing and hitting unconventional shots. Armed with these two bats, my skills improved significantly. But I kept waiting for the right moment. Indeed I waited almost a year, until the start of the annual company table tennis match. I enrolled in the men's singles.

The opening ceremony was quite splendid. The finals were held in the auditorium at night. Due to a power shortage, a single overhanging gas lamp lit the entire auditorium. The men's and women's platoons sat separately on folding chairs. In addition to a referee, there was a commentator nicknamed Daguai. This name, which means 'very obedient', was actually the exact opposite of his character, because Daguai wasn't obedient at all. In fact, he was downright naughty. He had a glib and blunt tongue that scared even his boss. As a commentator, however, he was perfect for the job. Of average height, he had a handsome face and a pair of round eyes that emanated wisdom. Below his upright nose was set a nimble mouth from which poured words that would cause great amusement and laughter.

In the quarter finals, I encountered Shunzi who was good at lobs and could apply tremendous spin. I maintained a steady defence. When the ball was played to the forehand on my right side, I would reply with a forehand push. If he lobbed to the backhand, I would use the long pimpled side of the bat to slice it. The slice would quickly kill the ball, and Shunzi would fail to get it back. He then lost his head and became less confident about lobbing. He tried to play short shots over the net which I returned with backspin using the long pimpled side of the bat. If the ball came to my upper left side, I would hit it abruptly and fatally with the square bat in my left hand. Shunzi was squashed and soon lost the game.

My match with Shi Jun was highly intense. Though highly skilful, Shi had never before faced a double-bat opponent. He lost the first set because he failed to adapt. Nevertheless, he was a senior player with plenty of experience, and he knew how to readjust in various ways. He kept launching lobs to my front central position, gained the upper hand and won the second set. In the deciding set, we were evenly matched, with each player taking the lead in turns until the score reached 19 all and it was Shi's turn to serve. Everyone held their breath. Shi went to attack my right forehand side, but I defended it and then he switched to my backhand. I again defended with my right hand, and he responded by again attacking my backhand, but I responded with a left-handed counterattack, striking the ball to his backhand. Shi could not respond and I won the point, and the crowd broke into thunderous applause. Now, at match point, the atmosphere was at its most intense. Shi launch another attack on my service and I kept him at bay with my backhand before I leapt in the air and wielded both rackets to exchange heated attacks to the forehand and backhand for about a dozen shots. It was a dazzling scene of furious competition. After all, two hands are better than one. In the end, a left-handed smash won me the final point and the title of champion.

Tumultuous applause and cheers reverberated through the auditorium. Immersed in the joy of victory, I was excited to see so many girls watching. They applauded and screamed my name. What an exhilarating scene! Today, forty years later, the resonance in that auditorium still rings in my ears.

Chapter 25

A Visit to my Father

It was during my third year at the Corps that I got permission to visit my family for the first time. In those days, Dad was receiving 're-education through labour' at the May Seventh cadre school in Chaling, Hunan province. On arriving there after a 48-hour train ride, I was shocked to see a stout man of just five years ago transformed into an emaciated figure. He had lost more than fifteen kilos.

He looked weak, haggard and old. His light-complexioned face was wrinkled, and his grey hair and facial stubble had merged into one. However, he was able to stay in good spirits because the May Seventh cadre school operated by the Ministry of Foreign Affairs was a relatively liberal establishment. Dad's soft eyes still gleamed with kindness, but there were also shades of humility, cowardice and gloom. He had become more diligent and agile, and was a skilled boiler stoker and model pig herder. His hypertension had disappeared and to, my surprise, he was thinner but healthier than ever before.

The next day, I went to work with Dad. Because he was still being monitored, he could not receive any special treatment on account of my visit. His job was to look after more than a hundred pigs. I saw him roll up his trousers and get serious about cleaning up the pigsty. This picture was in sharp contrast to the image I had formed of him years ago, when he would sit in a chair smoking, listening to a symphony or two, or reading nonstop. That day, however, he seemed quite absorbed in cleaning up the pigsty, which was quite an achievement for a scholarly type like him.

Having become accustomed to dirty and tiring work in the pigsty, Dad did everything without complaint. I felt a little awkward as I stood there when Chief Chen of the pig-raising squad arrived. As a former administrator with a revolutionary family background, he was able to manage and lead these 'class enemies'. He was in his fifties, and had thick, grey hair that curled upwards. With high cheekbones and a face of irregular contours that featured a pair of solemn eyes, he carried an air of inflexibility. In his presence, Dad was like a mouse before a cat.

Dad introduced me to him with a smile: "This is my son Wen Bo. He's working as a vet in the Inner Mongolia Construction Corps. He came specifically to see me."

Impressed with my profession, Chen smiled faintly and peered at me, saying: "You are a vet? Very well. Do you know how to castrate and spay pigs? We have more than forty piglets that need attention. I was having trouble finding a vet nearby."

That was exactly what I wanted to hear because I had been practising castrating and spaying skills for a long time but still couldn't find anywhere to use those skills. Now, I was finally going to be able to do so. In the process, I also might help relieve my dad of his political burdens. So I confidently nodded my head in consent. I showed Chen my scalpel, which he examined with great curiosity.

Chief Chen decided to give me all the gelding jobs at the cadre school. Chen and his subordinates drove all the piglets to be gelded, a total of more than forty, into a large pigsty. I began with the male piglets because it was a relatively simple procedure, and it was easier to achieve quick results. Chen also knew how to castrate male pigs, but he used standard western techniques. He would start off shearing the hair around the scrotum, sterilise the area with iodine, and then cut into the outer skin of the testes sac, strip away layers of sac skins, followed by tying up and removing the testicles and suturing the cut sac. He took at least twenty minutes per piglet. I adopted the Chinese approach that Vet Xiao had taught me, and was able to castrate six piglets in twenty minutes. Chen began to appreciate the difference between the professional and the amateur. In a little more than an hour, I was able to castrate all the male piglets.

Next, I went on to spay all of the twenty-plus sows by myself. My assistants grabbed the sows before passing them to me one by one. I stepped my left foot on the sow's left ear and my right foot on its right leg. The sow would then lie on her back with all four feet in the air. Holding the scalpel in my right hand, I used my left to grope for her left ilium, which was an important slit point I had discovered. Next, I cut a small incision in her left lower abdomen, poked the round head of the scalpel through the incision into its peritoneum and abdominal wall. Then, I spiralled my scalpel down so that the oviduct and ovary could be pushed out at the turn of the scalpel. With a twist and a pull and the release of my feet, the sterilisation procedure was complete without causing even a grunt from the sow. The procedure took even less time than it did with the boars. The entire process was quick and thorough, and almost perfect. Chief Chen was amazed. And my dad was certainly proud of my performance.

It took me only half a day to complete the sterilisation of all the pigs of appropriate age at the May Seventh cadre school. After lunch, Chief Chen came over and granted dad half a day off so that he could show me around Chaling county. Chen also allowed us to eat out in a restaurant, which made it possible for Dad and me to spend time together alone and talk at length after years of separation.

Dad showed me around Chaling. We got to see the Red Army memorial wall and the ancient city wall of the Southern Song dynasty (1127-1279). He told me some historical anecdotes about the relic sites that piqued my thirst for knowledge. At 24, an age when I should be graduating from college, I had actually received no more education than a first-year student at senior high school. Because I could find no books to read and since I had almost no knowledge of books, I had no experience outside horse-keeping and equine healthcare.

Dad took me hiking across Chaling county. He saw both the lack of my knowledge and my strong desire to learn. He told me things on all kinds of subjects, ranging from philosophy and Chinese history to astronomy and geography. And because I was a vet, he also discussed medical history. Though piecemeal, his briefing on all those topics served to give me a general framework of all existing knowledge and culture in the world. After being denied scientific teaching for years, the sudden access to so much knowledge made me feel like a starving man who had just received bread or a thirsty man who had found a fresh fountain.

We walked and walked as Dad kept talking. He acted as if he wanted to impart all of his knowledge in just that half day. I followed him closely and listened to him attentively not just because he was my father but also because he attracted me like a magnet. I was eager to absorb whatever flowed out of that resourceful mind.

As we started to get hungry, Dad took me to the best restaurant in the county. It had been years since we last dined out together. Born and raised in the Humble Administrator's Garden, Dad was a gourmet who had eaten at the finest restaurants in Beijing. He knew the menus well, and he knew what to order. As we sat down, he ordered some items that were so delicious that the very thought of them many years later would cause my mouth to water.

The first dish was marinated pork steamed with rice flour, a well-known Hunan dish. It is made like this: fry marinated pork (half fat, half lean) in hot oil, remove and pat dry before mixing with glutinous rice flour, starch and spices, and then wrap it up in a lotus leaf to steam. When served hot, it carries such an inviting aroma that it is impossible to resist putting it into your mouth. Indeed, it had been ages since I had eaten such delicious food.

The second dish was Chaling homestyle fish: fry a kilo of grass carp in boiling tea oil, add broth and Hunan chili sauce and serve straight away. It tasted fabulous. Dad also ordered two vegetable dishes to go with the meat and fish.

I ate three bowls of rice to go with the steamed pork and fried fish. Being able to enjoy such a big feast after prolonged deprivation of good food gave me a heavenly feeling. I ate so much that my stomach seemed to be at the point of bursting. The only other similar experience I had had at the Corps was the feast of fish at the Ninth Company and my gorging of melons at the melon shed. This feast, however, was the crowning moment of my life after a long break.

Still, Dad kept adding food to my bowl.

"Have more, you won't get this at the Corps," he said.

It was a great day, a day of wonderful memories deeply imprinted in my mind. Not only did Dad provide me with physical sustenance, he imparted wisdom and knowledge as well. The distance that previously existed between us had disappeared, and I seemed to merge with him. I was touched by his true love.

Chapter 26

Treating Constipation

Four years had passed since I joined the Corps. After working just two months in the farming platoon, I had the good fortune of being transferred to the stud farm, which freed me from the rigours and drudgery of physical labour and made it possible to have more space and time of my own. No longer did I have to bother about the reveille bugle. My job at the stud farm was to herd and graze the horses. Exhausting and time-consuming as the work was, I enjoyed interacting with the animals. Better still, after a year on the job, I was selected as the company vet. Though I had received no more than a month's professional training at the regiment headquarters, the experience opened up an official channel through which I could study and improve my expertise without being criticised. This, of course, was at a time when knowledge was regarded as worthless and potentially reactionary.

I acquired most of my veterinary knowledge through my own individual efforts. The one-month formal training that I received was actually halved because of my illness. Fortunately, the authorities also provided a book entitled *Concise Veterinary Science*. Though full of quotations from Chairman Mao, the book also contained simple methods of diagnosis and treatment for various diseases. Whenever an animal got sick, be it a horse, a cow, a pig, a sheep or a chicken, I would first look through the 'Red Brick' for simple and basic ways of treatment. If that failed, I would realise how desperately I needed to find a better veterinary science book without any 'quotations', but I was never able to, not even from second-hand bookshops.

I often felt helpless on occasions when the Red Brick failed to offer a solution. The easiest and most convenient alternative was traditional folk therapy. For instance, acute gastric dilation, a common stomach problem among horses and cattle, usually resulted from overeating after they had sneaked into a field for a hearty meal. When afflicted, the horses and cattle would moan and struggle on the floor, and they would quickly die of indigestion if not treated in time. Because the Red Brick provided no clear instructions on what to do with this illness, I had no choice but to adopt traditional folk therapy, which was to drench the sick horse with vinegar. Simple as it looked, the therapy sometimes worked.

One day, a bull ventured onto the threshing floor and took its fill of grain. After being driven away, it went to drink a lot of water, causing its belly to distend. Lying on the floor, the bull kept moaning and drooling, looking as if it could die at any time. On learning of its condition, I sent someone to the cafeteria to get some vinegar, and then took out a nose ring to grip the bull's nostrils. With the help of colleagues, we forced it onto its feet and lifted the ring higher so that its head would rise with it. I started feeding it vinegar, using a spoon made of bull's horn, removed the nose ring and let the bull lie down on the floor. In the next half hour, it kept burping, farted loudly a couple of times, and then rose to its feet, wagged its tail and discharged a large pile of dung before leaving.

Horses back then often suffered from another disease called 'intestinal obstruction' or 'ileus', which was more commonly seen in summer. In particular, working horses that sweated constantly but failed to drink sufficient water would end up dehydrated for a protracted period, resulting in congestion caused by hard and dry balls of dung in some parts of the intestines. Though its onset was slower than acute stomach dilation, ileus could prove fatal once it developed. Treatment could be very challenging and would often involve more than a pound of vinegar. At least as far as western veterinary science is concerned, remedies for ileus have low success rates and are often linked with high mortality rates so, in many cases, ileus is simply incurable.

Therapies recommended by the Red Brick were limited to the use of strong laxatives commonly seen in the west, including paraffin oil, magnesium sulphate and castor oil. But from my observation, such medicines were ineffective if not counterproductive. As a committed researcher, I began focusing on finding an effective cure for this disease that had been taking a toll on the lives of several company horses each year.

I sought advice from local vets, most of whom were traditional Chinese vets. Instead of the Red Brick, their textbook was *Anthology of Therapies for the Treatment of Horses* by Yuan Heng, a Ming dynasty veterinary masterpiece. As the veterinary counterpart of *The Yellow Emperor's Canon of Internal Medicine*, a Chinese medicine classic, the anthology is regarded as the Bible of Chinese veterinary medicine. The book explains how a vet can diagnose illnesses in horses by observing their posture. For instance, it says a horse can have 36 standing and sitting postures and 72 different symptoms. Asked about cures for 'intestinal obstruction' in horses, seasoned Chinese medicine vets were usually sceptical or even scornful of western methods, citing misdiagnosed cases of ileus that were actually cold stomach syndrome. Laxatives taken by those horse patients acted like frost added to snow and would result in a quicker death for the horses. So for cases of intestinal obstruction that are 'cold' in nature, therapies that serve to warm the tummy can provide a quick fix.

Out of deep affection for the horses, I worked diligently and gradually came up with some effective cures. Since I had little knowledge of Chinese medicine, I studied intestinal obstruction using western concepts of veterinary medicine. If intestinal obstruction was the root cause of the illness, the first step would be to ascertain whether it was a 'complete' or 'partial' obstruction. Since the illness mostly begins with the latter, without timely treatment the sick horse would moan and roll on the floor for several hours before dying in pain as a result of complete intestinal obstruction.

Usually I would not start off using laxatives to treat a horse afflicted with intestinal obstruction because they do not help discharge hard and dry faeces. On the contrary, they only serve to quicken the sick horse's bowel movement resulting in local intestinal peristalsis, or even worse, intestinal perforation. Instead, I would take a measured and conservative approach by first injecting caffeine sodium benzoate to help strengthen the heart, relieve pain and improve bowel movement. The approach is similar to stomach warming used in traditional Chinese veterinary medicine. Next, I would use soapy water to rinse the horse's intestines, stimulate certain acupoints with electro-acupuncture for twenty minutes, use a nasal tube to give the horse some saline water, and have a rider walk the horse incessantly until it farts and discharges its dung. These procedures were effective for curing mild ileus or partial obstruction but were insufficient to cure complete obstruction.

As a sentimental person, whenever I saw a horse die of ileus, I would lose my appetite and find it hard to fall asleep. I searched for an effective means of treating the condition. After reading a newspaper article that a vet called Li Liushuan had invented a new 'hammering' method for treating ileus, otherwise known as '*chui jie shu*', I began seeking an opportunity to go and learn from him in Zhengding county, Hebei province, where he was serving in a division of the Thirty-Eighth Corps. As I was just an ordinary vet in the company back then, the Corps would be very unlikely to send me there to study. However I had worked more than three years by then and was entitled to home leave. As my father was working at the May Seventh cadre school in Hunan province, I stopped by in Zhengding on my way back to Beijing from Hunan and stayed at the county guest house.

Li Liushuan was not just a vet, but also deputy chief of the army horse section. Following that news report, he became famous and was so busy I could not see him. The only other person at the vet station was a female vet whom I believed to be Li's student. So I decided to ask her about the essence of *chui jie shu*, but she only gave me a brief introduction. And without an actual sick horse to treat, I was unable to get any real practice at all, so I ended up getting just a rough idea of the new method.

Witnessing my thirst for knowledge, the female vet felt sorry for me because I was leaving the next day without having seen Li himself or practised his method. So she asked Li to give me a special lecture, though not on a one-to-one basis. When news of the lecture spread, dozens of people came over and packed into a large room. I sat in a special seat facing my idol. Vet Li, then around forty years old, was talkative, eloquent and broad and open in his thinking. In those depressing days, it was refreshing to be able to meet such a person. Apart from *chui jie shu*, he talked about many other things. He seemed to be focusing on philosophy but gave many concrete examples that made it easy for me to understand. I really enjoyed the lecture and became enamoured with the subject matter.

He began by saying that his *chui jie shu* was derived from *tao jie shu* (rectal blockage removal) in traditional Chinese medicine, which was an outstanding accomplishment in ancient Chinese veterinary science. The technique was in use prior to the publication of *Anthology of Therapies for the Treatment of Horses* by Yuan Heng. Li's invention was built on that. Simply put, the technique involves a four-step process. First, wash your hands in soap and water; second, insert a hand through the horse's anus into its rectum; third, locate the hard and dry balls of faeces and try to push them to the wall of the belly; and finally, use the other hand to bash the faeces balls until they crumble into smaller pieces. He had saved a lot of horses' lives using this method.

He told us he came up with this new treatment because he was in the habit of deep and frequent thinking. He gave two examples. A former army commander of his used to suffer from incessant hiccups. He would hiccup throughout his waking hours, and, since all treatments failed, his work performance was affected. Eventually, he was discharged from the military and sent to work as a civilian administrator. Since he was a regimental officer, he was an important individual in the county he served, and as such, he was paraded and indicted in mass criticising sessions along with all other senior officials during the Cultural Revolution.

During the later stages of the Cultural Revolution, Li Liushuan came across that veteran leader again and found him cured of his ailment. He said that he became healed without doing anything about it, adding that it might be related to those mass criticising campaigns he had endured on a daily basis. On those occasions he was forced to adopt the posture of a jet plane by bending forward with arms pulled straight back. By the time he got home, he found his hiccups had become less serious and then disappeared altogether. Based on that experience, Li Liushuan came up with a cure for intractable hiccups through physical manipulation – specifically, bending one's body forward so that it is parallel with the floor and thrusting the arms back in a way that resembled the wings of an airplane. The exercise needed to be repeated about fifty times a day. In less serious cases, the patient would feel the effect immediately; in more serious cases, however, the patient would need repeated exercise.

Here is another interesting case. One day, Li got bitten by some bedbugs while writing, and he saw one of them crawling on his desk. He dipped his finger into a bottle of cheap perfume close by and daubed a circle around the bug, whereupon it stopped moving, either because it loathed or feared the smell or simply because it had fainted. He concluded that bedbugs could be repelled by perfume. In the years to come I was able to apply what I had learned from him in my own real life. Whenever I got bitten by bedbugs, I would drive them away by spraying perfume on them. Alternatively, if any of my patients kept hiccupping, I would tell them to perform the jet plane exercise, which proved surprisingly effective.

Li Liushuan and I met only once, and the impromptu lecture he gave lasted no more than an hour. Today, forty years later, his appearance, facial expressions, the way he talked, the essence of *chui jie shu* and the vivid examples he cited are still fresh in my mind. Those deep memories show clearly how I absorbed his teaching. Back at the company, I was able to use that same technique to save dying horses, which taught me that I was going to benefit from face-to-face learning experiences for the rest of my life. And indeed, I benefited from him so much that I would become not just a good vet, but also an accomplished doctor of traditional Chinese medicine. I am so indebted to him that I have the urge to see him even now, when I am writing this book. Is he still alive and well? Where could he be?

Whenever I got absorbed in writing, I would somehow develop a feeling of being connected with heaven and earth. I do not know whether this is what the ancients referred to as 'epiphany'. During an outpatient visit the next day, I came across a former departmental chief of the Thirty-Eighth Corps who made mention of Li Liushuan. Though he did not know Li personally, he confirmed that Zhengding county, Hebei province was the headquarters of the army horse section of the 114th Division of the Thirty-Eighth Corps. He immediately called an old friend and asked about him. Before we parted, he promised to text me as soon as he got any news of him.

By noon, a text message came that said Li had later been transferred to the Henan Provincial Animal Husbandry Institute in Zhengzhou and that he had died of bile duct cancer six years previously. The text message stabbed my heart like a needle. Various images and voices flooded out of my mind. My biggest regret is not having the opportunity to treat him even though I was able to successfully treat several patients suffering from this kind of cancer. But I could at least mention his deeds and contribution to the world in this book I am writing.

His influence on my medical career was not restricted to curing horses with the method that he had invented, but more important, he had stoked my thirst for knowledge and science so that I had the confidence to try to overcome difficulties in the medical field, find cures for incurable diseases and finally become an accomplished doctor. Even though I could see him no more, I want to record his exploits in this book in the hope that his descendants will know what a great man he was. Horses and mules used to be indispensable both in war and for agricultural production, but today they have been replaced by modern technology. So, naturally, the *chui jie shu* technique created by Li Liushuan became marginalised just as he himself was marginalised after his discharge from the army. Nonetheless, his creativity and pioneering spirit enlightened and influenced me for the rest of my life.

Chapter 27

A Practising Vet

On returning to the company after a family visit, I was just in time for the wheat harvest. This was a time of year when the number of draft animals, including cattle, horses and donkeys, was quite insufficient. Indeed the need was so great that even a mare like Little Black could not be spared unless it was pregnant. It was a very distressing experience to see her drenched with sweat every time she came back, but it was the common fate for all horses back then. The sweating was a direct result of excessive labour in torrid weather. Unlike human beings who could drink water at any time, horses were given access to drinking water only after they had had finished grazing. After prolonged dehydration, horses were prone to indigestion, and that was why I became extremely busy.

After being untacked, horses would usually roll in the dirt to dry their sweat. Then, they would shake off the dirt to keep themselves clean before they were taken to their stables. Next, they would be provided with fodder, water and concentrates. These were the daily routines. The problem was, some of the horses were not being used by the horsemen on the stud farm, but were led away for temporary use by field platoon soldiers who were not familiar with horse-care procedures. So problems kept arising.

One day, after pulling a threshing stone for hours, two of the horses got exhausted and were soaked in sweat and reduced to a state of extreme dehydration. After they were done rolling, perhaps with good intentions, soldiers of the field platoon filled up the water troughs with well water for the horses to drink. Consequently, the horses filled up their bellies with cold water before eating. Quite soon, they were writhing on the ground with stomach ache. I gave each of them a shot of atropine, which, given their size, was quite ineffective.

The two horses remained curled up and rolling on the ground, looking in extreme pain. So I decided to resort to a traditional Chinese prescription. I asked my colleagues to fetch me some shallots and ginger and a large ceramic pot filled with water. When the water began to boil, I put in the chopped shallots and sliced ginger to simmer for fifteen minutes. When the soup cooled down, I poured it into two large bowls, added a small cup of liquor into each one, and then fed the mixture to the horses through a catheter. Ten minutes later, the two stricken horses managed to raise their hooves. Next, I gave each of them a shot of caffeine-sodium benzoate to strengthen their hearts, relieve their pain and enhance their bowel movement. Following that, I had two soldiers walk them continuously until they were completely free of pain. The next day, I drenched each of them with spleen-warming powder, and they were finally healed.

If the two horses were treated by a western vet, he or she might judge by their appearance and symptoms only, without looking at the cause of the illness, which would lead to a misdiagnosis of constipation. In fact, stomach cramps could be caused by drinking cold water before eating and after doing heavy physical labour or after eating too much frosted grass in autumn, even though the symptoms may seem the same as intestinal obstruction. If treated by an experienced Chinese vet, they might easily eliminate the possibility of intestinal obstruction and diagnose it as cold stomach syndrome. This would be in line with my thinking, and that was how I cured the two horses with a traditional Chinese prescription.

During the summer wheat harvest, many horses fell seriously ill due to excessive work and improper care, which meant I needed to carry out a series of tests. A few days later, I encountered a real case of intestinal obstruction. The irritable horse would lie down and get up again and again, go in circles, stretch its head and neck, and moan. It had not defecated for two days and kept looking back at its abdomen and kicking at it. At first, I tried to use traditional treatment methods: enema, surgery using an acusector and injection of caffeine-sodium benzoate, but all to no avail. It seemed that the horse was suffering from complete intestinal obstruction and a hard dung ball must be stuck somewhere in its intestines. In such cases, laxatives are counterproductive, so *chui jie shu* was the only possible option for saving this horse.

With the help of some colleagues, we put the horse in a six-column stable and tied it up by its belly to prevent it from lying down. Then, I used soapy water to administer an enema in order to clean its rectum. Next, I trimmed and smoothed the fingernails on my right hand, rolled up my sleeves and doused my whole arm in the soapy water before slowly inserting it into the horse's anus. I carefully probed its rectum into the abdominal cavity, trying to feel around through the intestines while observing its reaction. That way I would be able to locate the source of the pain and find out where the obstruction was located. I had to rely entirely on my sense of touch because it was my very first procedure. But I found nothing after groping in there for about twenty minutes, so I had to stop.

I lit a cigarette, sat on the ground and took my time puffing away, blowing plumes of smoke from my nose that slowly wafted away. On carefully observing the horse's actions, I knew it would die if I failed to find the stuck dung ball. But my patient could not of course tell me the exact location of its pain, nor could I use any optical instrument to diagnose. Therefore, I could only surmise the general location of the blockage through observation of the horse' reaction to pain. I saw it turn around and look at its lower left abdomen once in a while and kick that position with its heels. So when I inserted my hand into its rectum again, I deliberately checked its lower left abdomen and I finally got hold of a hard dung ball. When I touched the ball, I clearly felt the horse tremble and heard it groan with pain. I slowly pushed the ball to the horse's abdominal wall and fixed it there as best I could. Since I couldn't do much with the other hand, I asked Jieshi to aim at the ball and pound it with his fist as I held hard onto it. One, two, three… Jieshi gave the ball eight punches, each being followed by a tremor and a groan from the horse. I was so focused on getting the job done that I ignored how the horse was feeling, until I suddenly felt the dung in my hand getting crushed. My heart was filled with unspeakable joy. The horse was saved!

I then administered enemas until I finally heard sounds from the horse's bowel, followed by continuous farts and a discharge of fine particles of crushed dung ball and a further discharge of faeces. When I freed the horse from the six-column stable, it no longer wanted to lie down but walked effortlessly after the horseman. Obviously, the horse was now recovered.

I ran into another serious case the next day. This horse was so sick it could barely walk at all, its hooves giving great pain every time they came into contact with the ground. By now I had been a vet for two years and I already had some experience in treating such cases. After checking the horse's conjunctiva and asking the horseman a few questions, I knew it was suffering from 'saddle removal syndrome' (*jie an feng*), which is a kind of paralysis.

Jie an feng can be found in *Anthology of Therapies for the Treatment of Horses* by Yuan Heng. This acute disease is usually caused by the sudden and immediate removal of a saddle after a horse has been sweating through heavy labour or prolonged riding, when the pores in the horse's skin are opened up and cold winds penetrate its meridians and block the body's nerve conduits, thus preventing the horse from walking.

Horses suffering from *jie an feng* are usually in low spirits, have tight skin, stiff muscles and look somewhat wooden in their movement. They often fall when forced to move around. Other symptoms include a stiff tail and ears, clenched teeth, an inflexible spine and neck, and a salivating mouth, although stools and urine are normal. So, though *jie an feng* and intestinal obstruction share similar causes and both have something to do with excessive sweating after hard labour, they are actually quite different conditions. Fortunately, I have considerable confidence and quite some experience in treating this disease. I still have no idea how western vets treat this disease, but my method was rather crude.

First, I flushed the mud off the horse's four hooves with a basin of water. Next, I used a pair of flat-headed scissors to cut off a section of fur between the upper centre of the hooves, exposing the hard skin underneath.

I used a large pair of forceps to clamp a large cotton swab, dipped it in iodine and applied it to the hard skin or in the four acupoints of the horse. I then took a very thick phlebotomy needle, disinfected it with iodine and pricked four acupoints. This resulted in immediate bleeding. Since the horse could barely stand straight, it could not evade me. So I was able to insert the needle into exactly the right places. My onlooking colleagues were stunned by my swift and decisive moves. They never imagined that a bookworm like me could possess such skill under pressure. After completing the procedure, I lit a cigarette and slowly blew out rings of smoke. Next, I put on a seasoned look and instructed the horseman who came with the horse: "Now, I need you to find a large puddle and lead the horse to it. Let it soak in there for twenty minutes before leading it out again for an hour-long stroll and then it should be fine."

The horseman did as he was bid. When the horse was led over again, it started walking freely. I used the same method to treat several horses suffering from *jie an feng*, and they were all healed on the spot. Such treatment would hardly be accepted by modern western medicine because the wound after bloodletting can easily become infected, but during my career I have never come across any infection of that nature. Instead, all the victims of *jie an feng* that I encountered were cured by this treatment. Later on, I read descriptions of *jie an feng* in a book entitled *Veterinary Medicine*, which was published in the former Soviet Union. The author believed that exhausted horses can experience metabolic disorder and accumulate acids in their limbs. So, releasing blood from the horses' hooves would lead to the discharge of toxic substances from its body. That's probably why they finally got healed.

Chapter 28

Saving Little Black

Summer harvest season was the busiest time in the Corps. In the blazing sun, soldiers would scythe the wheat, bundle it, pile the bundles on the floor and then deliver them by cart to a dry and level threshing floor, where they would be spread out and crushed by stone rollers pulled by horses or cattle. For days and nights, Little Black was commissioned to do exactly that. She sweated constantly without any access to drinking water. Dehydrated for a sustained period until dusk, she would be locked up hungry and thirsty in a stable until evening grazing time. By then, however, the exhausted horse might still not be able to get enough water from the trough. If this pattern continued, Little Black would easily fall victim to awful constipation. That same season, I was kept busy treating other livestock, and during any free time I was dispatched to the fields to help with the wheat harvest. So I had no time to take care of Little Black. Eventually, she did fall ill with constipation, which made me feel guilty about the neglect and lack of proper care she received.

Little Black collapsed while working on the threshing floor. She passed out, wallowing and groaning on the floor with her eyes fixed on her belly. She fidgeted and kicked at her belly with her hind hooves. The moment soldiers of the field platoon dragged her to me, I could barely recognise her. She was much thinner, and her fur had lost its shine. Due to excessive sweating and wallowing on the ground, her entire body was covered in dirt and filth. She looked as if she had turned from a princess into a beggar.

She kept whimpering, looking so sick that only her eyes revealed a semblance of spirit and strength, and it was through the blinking of her eyes that she signalled her need for help. I was furious about how she had

175

been treated. Despite my usual good temper I couldn't help yelling at those who had abused her.

"How could you torture Little Black like this? Don't you know she's a mare? Do you really want to kill her? You guys are so cruel."

I shouted this last sentence, my eyes glaring. When the soldiers from the field platoon saw my agitated state, they got scared and let go of Little Black before slipping away.

Now I was alone with the seriously sick Little Black. She lay prostrate on the ground, groaning and whining. I knelt down, pulled up her eyelids and touched her dry tongue. Almost no saliva. I probed all parts of her abdomen with a stethoscope but hardly heard any bowel sounds at all. Her belly was severely inflated. It was an obvious case of constipation. Little Black was constantly turning around to look at the front part of the right section of her belly where her cecum was located. If she was afflicted with cecum obstruction, she would be in imminent danger. Normally, if large and hard dung balls were stuck there, even the hammering technique would not work, not to mention laxatives. It struck me that Little Black was actually going through a trial of life and death. Without a cure, she would not see out the day. Awash with sadness, it felt as if a heavy load was pressing down on my heart.

I asked Jieshi and Little Zhao to fasten Little Black to a six-column stable and started a desperate rescue mission. First I gave her an intestinal bath with soapy water, but it only yielded scanty stale excrement. Next, I closed up my five fingers to form a cone and then stuck my hand into her anus and wriggled slowly in like a snake until I reached her abdomen, whereupon I began probing for hard and solid dung balls from outside the intestines. Since I saw Little Black keep looking back at the front of her right abdomen and try to kick at the spot where the cecum was located, I went straight in that direction. Little Black began fidgeting while I finally located a large, hard mass that was the size of a baby's head. The formation of this hard ball must have taken quite some time. A solid dung ball of that size meant her dehydration must have persisted for between two and three weeks.

I took great trouble pushing the ball against the wall of her abdomen before asking Jieshi to hammer at it. He hammered his fist against the huge mass seven or eight times, but to no effect. It remained as hard as a rock. Each strike triggered a cry of pain from Little Black. I motioned with my left hand to Jieshi that he pause as I withdrew my right hand from her body. I sat by her motionless and helpless.

I lit a cigarette and puffed away as I racked my brains trying to figure out a solution. I knew if I failed to work out a truly effective countermeasure, I would have to watch Little Black die in pain.

The screams of Little Black came at me louder and louder, piercing me deep within. She was sending me a final distress signal. I lit another cigarette, stood up to pace around her and thought intensely with a keen sense of urgency. In the end, enlightenment came just in time.

I prepared two 50ml syringes, one bottle of 500ml normal saline and one bottle of 250ml liquid paraffin oil and had Little Zhao hold a tray on which rested two thick and long sterilised needles. After explaining my plan to Jieshi and Little Zhao, I clenched my fingers into a conical shape and slowly reinserted my hand into her abdomen.

Once again I pushed that huge dung ball in her cecum against her right abdominal wall. Fortunately, my arm was long enough. I used my left hand to pick up a needle from Little Zhao's tray, pointed it to the upper end of the hard dung ball and stabbed it right in. Following that, I picked up another needle, pointed it to the lower middle part of the dung ball and pushed it in there. I instructed Jieshi to take out a syringe, fill it with normal saline and inject the solution into the lump of dung in Little Black's cecum. Syringe by syringe, I injected the entire half litre of normal saline into the lump so as to soften it. Meanwhile, I asked Little Zhao to draw 250ml of paraffin oil into the syringes in order to lubricate the dung ball in the intestines.

When the saline solution and paraffin oil were injected, I was quite sure that the stubborn hard lump was now going to soften, even though it would take some time. So I set Little Black free from the six-column stable and led her onto a stretch of land behind the stud farm. She wobbled along behind me. Several times she wanted to lie down on the ground but I pulled her up by tightening the reins. It had been a long time since I last took a walk with her in the wilderness. Because it was an environment that Little Black was familiar with, she was willing to follow me regardless of the pain. She was probably thinking that she would keep staying by my side even if it meant marching towards death. By then I was convinced Little Black would be out of danger in less than an hour.

About half an hour later, I led her back into the six-column stable and tied her up with ropes. I fetched a hammer, wrapped up its head in a towel and handed it to Jieshi, reminding him this time he was supposed to use the wrapped hammer instead of his fist. That way, he would be able to hit hard without harming Little Black. By now, I was already an old hand. My right hand soon found its way into her belly and laid hold of the dung ball, which felt much softer than before. I instructed Jieshi to hammer at it. Though with each strike she still cried with pain, the volume decreased and the ball I held onto became smaller and smaller. More than a dozen strikes later, I finally felt the crushing of that huge ball of dung, and my heart was seized with excitement. I knew she was saved.

When I led her out of the stable again, she was obviously in less pain than before because she had started farting, which meant gastrointestinal decompression was taking place, as it is termed in western medicine. I went on walking her, suddenly finding myself in a light and joyful mood.

It was a perfect, star-spangled night. In the gentle and refreshing breeze, Little Black's walking became steadier until she came to a halt, raised her tail slowly and discharged a mound of squashed dung balls. I was so happy that I turned around and hugged her neck. Little Black clearly felt my sincere love for her. She knew I had saved her, just as she had saved me last time. Elated, she craned her neck and gave out a high-pitched neigh that split the night and drifted far and wide. It was loud enough for everyone in the stud farm to hear. Even though they could not see what had happened, from her loud and sweet whinny they should have been able to conclude that she was now safe and healthy.

Little Black and I had a long walk on the deserted land that night. Her gait became more energetic, and she frequently paused to defecate. Each time was a source of exhilaration for me because it meant she was one step further from death and one step closer to recovery. I roamed alone with her up until late at night. I felt relaxed and delighted. The gentle night breeze gave me a strong sense of joy. The bright moon reminded me of Yue, who had now been gone for two years. I saw no hope of her returning to this hellish place. She must be at least head nurse in a field hospital by now and might have even been promoted to a higher rank. I imagined the beautiful and heroic sight of a fully equipped Yue in army uniform carrying a gun in her arms.

Though I had the company of Little Black and for some time I saw her as the incarnation of Yue, she could of course only remind me of her. I saw Little Black as my bosom friend and confidante, or another form of Yue to accompany me. She might have been a carrier of Yue's spirit that had served as spiritual sustenance in Shatou, or a source of hope in this destitute and deserted place. I was committed to saving Little Black because I was afraid of losing her, my only bulwark of support in loneliness. In her dwelt my hope and expectations for the future. Our walk in the nocturnal light felt like a rendezvous with Yue. I began to weave my dreams and plan my future. If I were to unite with Yue, or more specifically, if I were to marry her, I would first have to get out of Shatou.

Little Black's survival meant such a lot to me. At the very least, it proved that I had made a breakthrough in curing equine constipation, even though those around me failed to appreciate it. They simply believed vets were responsible for treating various animal diseases. Those sick horses and mules all found a way to survive after my creative ways of treatment. Villagers took it for granted because things like that happened almost every day. So they saw nothing 'heroic' or 'magical' about what I was doing. In fact, in this remote and unknown village, in an average company of the Inner Mongolia Construction Corps, I had already achieved something extraordinary – at least in my own eyes – though it was known to no one else. So in that sense my talent was actually being wasted.

By rescuing Little Black that night, I not only gained unprecedented confidence, but also discovered that I possessed a rare medical gift. Given my skill as an explorative and thoughtful researcher, over time I should be able to solve any hard or complicated disease, whether curable or incurable, once I gave it due attention. I was convinced that, one day, I would be responsible for a great invention and make a significant contribution to medical science. By then, I might be a professional researcher in some medical research institute. As I charted my course, a spark of hope ignited in me, and I was immediately energised to strive for a bright future.

The night I walked with Little Black, I couldn't help showing her off like treasure to heaven and earth. Any man in my position would have indulged himself in some sort of daydreaming. I dreamed that if one day I really made it, I would raise my head, stick out my chest, straighten my back and walk proudly to Yue to ask her hand, because by then I would be qualified to marry her. With these thoughts, I became jubilant because I saw in the journey of my life a path to success that I could pave with my own hard work.

Chapter 29

Studying Cancer

Which disease should I choose to study? Now that I had cured equine constipation, there seemed to be no harder animal disease worth studying any more. So I shifted my attention to diseases affecting both animals and humans, and I wanted to challenge myself by choosing a disease where there were few effective treatments. I saw no better choice than cancer. Back then, I was twenty-four and I had only two years of clinical experience as a vet. But I made up my mind to study and conquer cancer. Why would I, at that tender age, come up with something so ambitious? Was it just a youthful passion or a whim? Not exactly, because in my clinical experience I did come across a cancer-stricken horse.

Nicknamed 'Little White', this Mongolian mare with a pure white mane was a rare, natural trotting horse. In fact, she was the only trotting horse I had seen ever since I started working at the stud farm. Trotting involves a horse whose diagonal pairs of legs move forward at the same time. Trotting horses provide a comfy ride since their speeds are no slower than the average racing horse and yet they are well suited for travelling long distances. Trained trotting horses need to be schooled by good riders so they know how to pace themselves. Such training could take months even if it was done on daily basis. If a novice rider were to take on the training process, the horses in training could get confused and forget what they had learned previously. In addition, riders capable of training trotting horses were very hard to find in the entire Corps and even among local people. I had attempted to train Little Black into a trotting horse, but failed because she was a born racer. She could never be turned into a trotting horse because her racing gait was so dissimilar to the synchronous gait of a trotting horse.

Though Little White was a natural trotting horse, she needed to acquire the correct gait. At first only Little Zhao and I knew how to ride her. Later on, when others mastered the required skills, they became capable of adopting the 'trotting horse gait', and they vied to ride her. Though I kept trying to prevent people from riding her, officers at company level all knew Little White was a born trotting horse, and they all wanted to ride her when they went on business trips. As a result of repeated riding, Little White's belly skin got scratched over and over again. Repeated rubbing, infection and prolonged injury in the same spot eventually led to the growth of a hard, bleeding lump on her belly that within months had expanded to the size of a basin.

I knew the lump was not a good sign, though I had no idea what a tumour really was. When both external and antibiotic treatment failed, I asked my colleagues at the carters' squad to send Little White to the regiment veterinary centre for treatment, but it was fruitless. During surgery conducted by Vet Li, Little White was found to be five months pregnant. When the huge tumour was being removed, she kept on bleeding until her blood had run dry. She died of malignant abdominal cancer on the operating table. Her baby foal died as well.

Little White's death pained me for several days. In the months that followed, I kept pondering over the cause of her illness as well as the entire process of diagnosis and treatment. The incidence of tumour in horses is usually very low, but I happened to encounter such a case and was able to observe the various stages of its development. And, as it turned out, it triggered my desire to study cancer. Mare, pregnancy, endocrine modification, unhealed wound… these were the terms that I wrestled with in those days. The cafeteria was just a few hundred metres from the stud farm, but I had to walk there and back three times a day. And that became my thinking time. In those days I was very slovenly, wearing dirty clothes and failing to comb my hair, looking like a typically irritable young man. I ambled along at a slow pace. While those around me might believe I was studying something, nobody knew exactly what it was about. Being preoccupied with cancer and Little White's case in particular, I cared little about how much food I was given every time I handed over my lunch box to the server in the cafeteria. Unlike my colleagues who closely monitored the ladle in the server's hand, I accepted whatever I was served.

After much research and thought, I concluded that the emergence of a tumour seemed to be related to some internal factors within the body. Specifically, it was probably an endocrine disorder that induced the tumour. During a one-month home leave in Beijing, I remained obsessed with cancer research. I visited the General Hospital of Beijing military region, Tongren Hospital and Peking University Cancer Hospital, to search for all sorts of cancer literature. I had found some blank cards from my father's drawer that I put in my bag. Whenever I came across important cancer data, I copied the main points on the cards and added the citations. When I got back from home, I had with me hundreds of cards written with notes. In those days, professional or technical books were hard to come by, and the limited number of academic journals and books could only be found in libraries attached to hospitals. I did most of my research while feeding the horses at night. The peace and quiet of the night was perfect for doing research. The one-hour interval between giving more fodder to the horses was my valuable research time. I would put the barn lantern on a clay table, take out the cards I had brought from Beijing, read them word by word and figure out the meaning behind them.

As my thoughts about cancer matured over time, I came up with a plan to write and publish them. The plan began to materialise one night when I set about writing on a stack of coarse yellow paper in the lamp-lit stable right after giving fodder to the horses. That was my first academic paper, entitled 'Exploring the mechanism of carcinogenesis'. At that time, I attributed the fundamental cause of cancer to an endocrine disorder, which was, frankly speaking, an immature view. After further research, I proposed a new hypothesis on carcinogenesis, which attributed the root cause of cancer to the 'cellular imbalance between yin and yang'. In more concrete terms, cancer is the result of long-term disorder in the promoting and inhibiting elements of local cellular secretion caused by the prolonged and repeated stimulation of various carcinogenic elements. Still later, I proposed the concept of field cancerization, or the local and internal environment in which the cell finds itself when the promoting elements are overly secreted compared with the inhibiting elements. It is within this cancerization field that cancer cells grow gradually.

I spent about two weeks writing the first draft of the paper. After much revision, I transcribed two copies of the draft, one of which was posted to President Wu Huanxing at the Cancer Hospital attached to the Chinese Academy of Medical Sciences, and the other was sent to Professor Li Mingxin, pathologist at the Cancer Institute of the Chinese Academy of Medical Sciences.

Since I did not let on what I was doing, I came across as something of a mystic. People could not make out what I was up to back then. Out of curiosity, Oradoz and another colleague decided to play a trick on me by scaring me at midnight. The two wore sheepskin coats inside out, with the fur exposed to mimic beasts. They stole quietly into the stable and stood right behind me. Immersed in writing my paper, I failed to notice their presence. I did not react right away even when they roared out loud. I merely raised my head slowly and turned around to look at them with dull eyes. In the end, it was the two friends who got scared and scampered away. The next day, probably as a result of that failed prank the night before, people began staring at me with questioning eyes. Had they detected anything abnormal about me, they would probably have put me on alert to the leadership or the health clinic.

A month later, I received a letter from President Wu Huanxing at the Cancer Hospital. I didn't reveal it to anyone even though I was beside myself with joy. Wu encouraged me by saying that my findings were reasonable and hoped I would seek opportunities for further study so that I could delve deeper into cancer research and make a contribution to medical science. Wu was the pioneer of oncology and radiotherapy research in China. The basic principles of cancer treatment that he had developed were widely applied in China's oncology community. In memory of his contribution to cancer prevention and treatment in China, a statue of him was erected in the compound of the Cancer Hospital, and a hospital named after him was built in Beijing's Chaoyang district.

That letter was the only interaction I ever had with President Wu, who was a bigger idol to me than even Li Liushuan. Returning to his home country after graduating from Cambridge University, Wu became a leading authority on cancer treatment in China. He was hardly affected by any of the political movements, and he stayed on in his job as president of both the Cancer Hospital and of the Oncology Research Institute. So he was clearly a very busy man, yet he was willing to respond to me, an unknown youth from an unknown corner of Inner Mongolia, and give me valuable encouragement. He must have taken time out of his schedule to read my paper and correspond with me. It reflected the loving care of an intellectual from an older generation for a young man with aspirations.

Needless to say, that letter changed the course of my life and directed me to a new career and a new goal. For a young man struggling on the bottom rung of society, the letter was like a cup of honey water for the hungry and thirsty. It had an enlightening effect on me at a time when I was lonely, frustrated and pessimistic.

A few days later, I also heard from Professor Li Mingxin, who affirmed the views in my paper and recognised my sound scientific judgment. In his long letter, he also suggested that I seek opportunities for further study. Such valuable advice from two senior scientists naturally stoked my passion for college education, even though most of the college students admitted then were the children of workers, peasants and PLA soldiers. College provided an opportunity to receive a systematic education. So I had a strong urge for that.

Chapter 30

Shattered College Dreams

Young workers, peasants and soldiers who were admitted to college through grassroots recommendation, and usually without taking any entrance exams, were a special category during and immediately after the Cultural Revolution. They were called 'worker, peasant or soldier students'. They had to be recommended by their employer or PLA unit and had to pass strict family background checks, which amounted to political control based on one's family background. For Corps soldiers, the review process generally involved the company issuing an official letter to the parents' employers for a background investigation. At that time, my father was under supervised labour in a May Seventh cadre school, while my mother was not yet reinstated and was preventing from wearing a full army uniform complete with cap insignia. Further weakened by the existence of foreign relatives on my mum's side, the investigation report would look so terrible that any recommendation would simply be out of the question. Even if I did get admitted, my personnel archives would undo all of my efforts. That year, there seemed to be a high quota for worker, peasant or soldier college students. The First Company that I belonged to was allotted six places. Encouragingly for me, academic examinations were now part of the process, which gave wings to my college dream that would take flight from the deserted Shatou.

I had brought some textbooks from home during a visit several years previously. During a break in my night shift, I would study those books in an adobe stable. My thirst for knowledge and the prospect of going to college filled me with joy and hope, and I felt my goal of breaking out of Shatou could be achieved earlier than I had expected. College applicants then had to go through a lengthy procedure, including discussions and voting at squad, platoon and company levels. Because girls were in a majority at the company, their votes were crucial. Although the girls did not know much about me, I had a reputation as an experienced vet who enjoyed doing research, despite the fact that I was reticent, unsociable and a little slovenly. So in their minds, people like me should go to college because it would benefit the country. As it turned out, I got enough votes to qualify as a candidate. Oradoz, who himself went to take exams at the regiment headquarters, later wrote about that experience:

> During the summer of 1973, on the eve of the exams, we all slept on the floor of the regiment auditorium. In the middle of the night, I saw Wen Bo sitting upright in his quilt and surveying his hands repeatedly as he kept saying 'left hand, right hand, left hand, right hand...' Those who witnessed him couldn't help laughing.

During the maths exam, I was so confident in myself that I spent only half of the allotted time completing the paper. At that moment, I felt like I was on the threshold of entering college. I did well enough in my exams, but anything could go wrong in those days. One day, a news article about Zhang Tiesheng's criticism against the college entrance exam system was published. At that time, each platoon had a subscription to *Inner Mongolia Daily* and each squad had a subscription to *Comrades-in-Arms Corps Press*. Because I lived in the same house as the platoon leader, I had ready access to the newspapers. After reading Zhang's piece and the editorial in *People's Daily*, my heart sank, and I had a bad feeling that a big political storm was coming. Sure enough, the test scores of that entrance exam were later voided, and political records became the crucial factor, so I knew my college dreams would be extinguished.

However, maybe because of my thirst for knowledge, I did not give up on the prospect of going to college. I hated to see the opportunity slipping away. I couldn't think what to do as I paced back and forth in the backyard of the stud farm. Early one morning, before daybreak, I brought out Little Black, put on the saddle and rode her to the regiment headquarters. On arriving in the town of Xin'an, I left Little Black at the veterinary station and went to the regiment hostel alone. Several years previously I had stayed there for a night, and the college admissions staff were now staying there as well.

They kindly checked my test scores and found that I had come top. I went on to show them my trump card – the letter from President Wu Huanxing of the Cancer Hospital attached to the Chinese Academy of Medical Sciences. The admissions staff looked shocked as they read it, and they stared at me for a long time. They couldn't imagine that anyone so far from large cities, hospitals, research institutes, libraries and labs could be so determined to study cancer and try to solve the world's medical mysteries. They felt that the country had an obligation to unearth people like me and send them to college so that China would train a large pool of talent in medical sciences and technology. However, the political winds were in flux, and they feared that I would not be able to pass the political investigation, though they promised to communicate with my company and asked me to wait for the final word.

I hung around the company headquarters every day, waiting anxiously for the decision. I carefully observed the facial expressions of each and every officer, hoping to decipher small changes that might reveal something. When I failed to see any hint of a smile, I began to lose heart. I then asked Vet Xue at the regiment headquarters to make enquiries on my behalf, and I got to know the result a day before the official announcement. I was rejected due to my foreign relatives and not directly because of my parents. My mum had five siblings in the US and one in Canada. Ten years later, they jointly financed my studies in the US to make up for my loss of college education in China. At the time, though, the spiritual blow I suffered was almost fatal.

When I learnt that my college application had failed, I walked Little Black on the salty land behind the stud farm for almost an entire night. That was probably the area I was most familiar with. Every time Little Black and I passed through it, I would forget all feelings of hardship, exhaustion, loneliness and homesickness, and instead would find relief, joy, reverie, memories of Yue and hope for the future. But that night the sky was overcast. The moon was covered, and only a few stars were visible, emitting vague, gloomy lights. I was profoundly sad. With silence all around me, the whole earth seemed dead, as if Little Black and I were the only survivors.

I tottered on, tears welling in my eyes, as Little Black followed close behind as usual. The image of toughness, tenacity and bravery that I had long tried to cultivate for myself had evaporated. Instead, my cowardice, incompetence and vulnerability were now fully exposed. I felt I was in a bottomless pit, and there seemed to be no escape. I thought I would never be able to get out of Shatou or have the chance to see Yue again. Would a life separated from her be worth living at all?

I tied Little Black to a tree before heading off to a darker horizon. I did not know what foolish move I would make next, but I was in despair and felt as if the end of the world was at hand. Just then, there came a high-pitched scream from Little Black. I shot a parting glance at her but kept stumbling forward in my despair. But the whinny grew louder and louder. She kept digging at the ground until she finally struggled free from her halter. Behind me came the galloping hooves of Little Black. I couldn't help turning back to face her, as if ready to accept my fate.

Little Black rushed straight to my chest, snorting and continuously pushing in my arms. I held onto her neck and broke down. I cried out my grief, anger and grievances, the sound reverberating in the silence of the void. Eventually, these outpourings pacified me and caused me to forsake my foolish suicidal thoughts and rekindled my courage to move on with life.

I stroked Little Black's mane and pressed my face hard against her head, rubbing her gently. She in turn rested her chin on my shoulder. We hugged each other for a long time, and this made me think of Yue. At a time of deep suffering, only love could disperse the despair; only love could rekindle the courage for me to go on; only love could help me pull myself together; and only love could empower me to move forward.

I let go of Little Black, hoping that she would start grazing. I wanted to sit down and spend that heartbreaking night with her because this would be the most difficult night of my life. However, Little Black was reluctant. She seemed to have heard the sorrow and even despair in my heart from my earth-shaking cries. She kept snorting and walking in circles around me, as if trying to prevent me from doing something unwise. She kept nudging me with her muzzle and motioned me to move back. I had no way of knowing if her strange act was the result of Yue's reincarnation or the horse's basic instinct. At any rate, I knew Little Black had realised that it would be very dangerous to leave me alone in the wasteland and that the safest policy was to have me turn back.

Contrary to her usual practice of following me closely, Little Black now lowered her head and pressed herself tight against me. She pressed her mouth against my back from time to time, as if she was escorting a lost sheep back to the fold. Conscious of her kindness, I stopped to kiss her long cheeks and climbed onto her back. Instead of sitting up, I lay prostrate on her wide back, just like when she carried me home to the stud farm after she had saved me from the ditch. I enjoyed being transported in that way, and I was happy because of her true love for me, even though she was merely an animal.

Chapter 31

The Hee-hawing Donkey

Six young people from the Corps were recommended to go to college, so they became the second tranche of educated youths who left Shatou following the exodus of military compound children into the army. I envied them immensely and wished them a successful future. Oradoz was admitted to the Sichuan Institute of Foreign Languages to study German language and literature. Also admitted to the school's English department was Zhou Yining, whom I had seen while sitting for an exam at the regiment. Though we never talked, I was able to observe her at close range. When she smiled, her face would turn pink and two dimples appeared on her snow-white, oval face. Kindness and youthful vigour were written in her eyes. I trusted she would have a very bright future.

I never made it to college despite all my efforts. I felt lost, frustrated and overwhelmingly sad, and I had to come to terms with my destiny and remain in Shatou.

A week later, I was feeling somewhat calmer, and things went on as usual. I still herded horses and served as a vet, but one thing was different: all my close friends were now gone. The 'goddess' of my heart Yue had joined the army; my friend Oradoz had gone to college; and Jieshi, who was an only child, had the good fortune of being transferred to Beijing. All my friends had left except Little Black. Now that I only had her to keep me company, I felt compelled to take good care of her, not just her health, but also her companions and offspring. Aged four, she was in the golden age for breeding.

On the subject of breeding, I should mention the hee-hawing donkey, who was given that moniker because he would yell at the top of his voice when he was sexually aroused. By the way, all hee-hawing donkeys are male. In order to breed more mules for the companies, the regiment headquarters bought a hee-hawing donkey from faraway Guanzhong in Shaanxi province and allocated it to our company.

The Guanzhong donkey is large, weighing the same as an average horse. It cost us about 800 yuan, which was a lot more than you would pay for a top horse. Because Little Black was past four years old and was ready for breeding, I had to decide who would be my next ride. The hee-hawing donkey was my first choice because it was so easy to teach him the 'trotting gait'. Donkeys are generally poor runners but brisk walkers. Although the large hee-hawing donkey was not a natural trotter, he could be easily trained to walk at a steady and fast pace. I developed a close bond with him after he became my regular ride.

The hee-hawing donkey was much taller than his peers. To ride on him was to attract a lot of attention – sometimes in a bad way. If he caught sight of female donkeys or female horses, he would become sexually aroused and would rush straight to them, all the while yelling at the top of his lungs so that all eyes would be focused on me. Forty years later, many of my contemporaries still recall the sight of me traveling between the regiment headquarters and our company on the donkey's back, carrying a medicine kit on my shoulder.

The hee-hawing donkey's head was about four times bigger than mine. Weighing about 350 kilos, he was certainly a striking sight on the deserted salty land of Inner Mongolia.

It was by no means a coincidence that I could teach the hee-hawing donkey how to trot like a horse. It all dates back to my teenage years at Beijing No. 2 Boys' Junior High School, where I had practised both long-distance running and race walking by copying a PE teacher called Jiang, a former professional athlete who often finished prominently in the city's annual spring festival cross-city races. Because I was into long-distance running, I became a great fan of him. During each spring festival, I would follow him on a bike and watch him run. Jiang ran and race walked alternately to save energy. I often mimicked his style. A prominent feature of race walking is to twist the hips so that the thighs are fully open and the legs can make larger strides. This technique makes race walking invigorating and relaxing.

At the Corps, I maintained my interest in race walking. I derived real pleasure from taking big, race walking strides on the dirt roads. One evening, while passing through a village, I came across a group of children who were intrigued by my unique way of walking. They chased me noisily as they rhythmically chanted "one, two, one", sometimes breaking into laughter. Probably because they had never seen anyone walk like that before, they initially thought I was crazy. However, on realising how fast I was, they began to wonder if that was the way some legendary heroes in ancient times might have walked.

My knowledge of the basics of race walking helped me to train donkeys and horses to trot. The trick was to have them stretch their legs as far apart as possible, have their legs on either side move in symmetry, and then ride on them with my back tilted slightly backwards, loosely controlling their heads with the bit in their mouths, so that they might trot in a natural way that resembled the twisting of a race walker. As a result, they would be able to trot at the speed of a galloping horse.

After giving the hee-hawing donkey a good training, I often rode him to the regiment veterinary station to fetch medicine or to run errands for the company in the neighbouring villages. I soon realised that riding a donkey could look just as impressive as riding a horse. Though his hee-haws were anything but elegant, there was something very masculine about the donkey. Young as I was, I knew very little about human or animal sexuality, so the donkey's strong sex drive was foreign to me. One day at noon, while passing a neighbouring company, I stopped by their stud farm to chat with some friends there. When I was about to leave, I found someone was using my donkey to mate with a mare without permission. I was livid, but the man smiled and apologised. To further appease me, he took out half a basin of black beans, cracked a few eggs into it and fed the donkey in my presence. My anger abated as I watched the animal scoff the beans, and I went on to see his true value when the mare became pregnant and gave birth to a mule the following year.

That same year, I was sent to the well-known Wangguanghe breeding centre in Balingol union for a three-day breeding training course. The centre was planning to import a thoroughbred Kabarda horse, and it was provided with refrigerated sperm for artificial fertilisation to implement a national plan to improve national horse breeding. Through formal training, I learned some basic skills of breeding and further understood the value of the hee-hawing donkey. I learned to carry out the pre-breeding exam through the rectal finger check on ovary maturity to determine optimal breeding time. The next step is to arrange mating and maximise pregnancy rates. When I saw the mediocrity of the company's stallions, I valued the hee-hawing donkey all the more. In full consideration of his outstanding build, I decided to use him as the main stud. Hence I chose four smaller or less impressive mares as his mates so that some high quality mules would be produced for the company.

So I began working closely with Little Zhao, who was born in a poor but politically correct family in a big city in Inner Mongolia. He started working at the Corps at the age of fourteen. With free food and clothing plus a small subsidy, he felt happy and at home at the Corps, and he worked with diligence and devotion. A man of below average height and with a tanned complexion – probably the result of a lack of nutrition and spending too much time in the sun as a child – he had a somewhat rough face that needed the constant and thick application of face cream, and he envied me for my naturally fine and fair complexion. He did not have much schooling, and he seldom spoke at routine political meetings. His small eyes sometimes twinkled brightly, and his saddle was always kept clean and in good shape. A skilled rider, he was an ideal person for the position of breeding assistant.

After becoming my assistant, Little Zhao would inform me whenever a mare was ready for sex. I would then lead her into a six-column stable for a gynaecological examination. If the egg developed in the ovary was found to be maturing, I would have the donkey ready for mating the following day. If the news leaked out, the stud farm would be packed with onlookers, even outnumbering the crowds that would go the cinema or outdoor theatre performances. We would then have to put up signs such as 'No admission for girls'.

The mating act began with the entrance of a mare and the hee-hawing donkey. Aware of what was going on, the sexually aroused mare got ready by opening her hind legs to urinate. On smelling her hormones in the urine, the hee-hawing donkey became aroused, his penis extending to more than a foot long. Then, he produced a roguish, ear-splitting roar and advanced towards to the mare and avidly smelt her vagina. The donkey was now overcome with sexual desire. As a breeder, part of my job was to help the donkey insert his penis correctly. The crowd could now see the root of the donkey's tail twitching up and down and the muscles of his buttocks quivering rhythmically. The adults saw what a great time the donkey was now having.

When it had ejaculated, I slowly pulled the exhausted donkey off the mare, and some men in the crowd began hooting and cheering his great performance. The scene was certainly a visual feast for all the bachelor male soldiers, and it became a favourite topic of conversation for a long time to come. Forty years later, Oradoz recalled it in the following excerpts of his memoir:

> Wen Bo put on a great 'breeding' show. Early that morning, he fed the company's hee-hawing donkey with fodder mixed with two beaten eggs before leading him to an open field at the stud farm. Rested and well-groomed, with his head held high, the donkey was in high spirits and in a joyful mood. A moment later, a villager from Shatou arrived with a frisky mare. The donkey opened his big mouth, gasped, growled and swished his tail around like crazy as he sniffed the scent of the mare from a distance. After greeting the villager, Wen Bo negotiated the terms of the deal. The breeding fees would be paid in kind, with eggs and fodder.
>
> Finally, the drama began. Seeing that the donkey was getting impatient, Wen Bo let go of the reins, and the donkey darted forth like an arrow and jumped onto the mare. In his haste, the donkey failed to find the right orifice, so Wen Bo stepped forward and grabbed the donkey by his penis and directed it into the right spot. Next, he turned around to push the donkey's behind. The whole process was quick and smooth and carried out to perfection.
>
> When the crowd was still marvelling, Wen Bo started yelling at the villager: "Pull the mare away, pull hard!" That said, Wen Bo gave the mare a hard kick on the backside to get her going

– he later explained that the kicking was delivered to make sure the sperm would sink deep into the womb. Due to Wen Bo's professionalism, that mare later gave birth to a mule, whose financial value was equivalent to that of several horses. In the end, Wen Bo became known as an 'assistant ejaculator'. Though vulgar, the nickname was effective. Villagers from around Shatou kept coming to seek his help, in the hope of producing big mules or donkeys.

Chapter 32

A Clandestine Love Affair

I strove to learn everything about breeding and actively promoted the hee-hawing donkey's breeding practice, though my ultimate focus was on Little Black, who was already four years old. As a sign of her maturity, all of her baby teeth had been replaced by permanent teeth. So she was now ready to give birth. Since horses come into oestrus only once a year, I was closely monitoring Little Black's condition.

One day, after herding the horses, Little Zhao came back with Little Black and called to me: "Wen Bo! Wen Bo! Little Black is in rut, and two of our stallions were vying to mate with her and even got into a fight, but Little Black kicked them off. She seems to have no interest in them at all."

So I led Little Black into the six-column stable. I washed my hands and arms in soapy water and administered an enema to clean her rectum. After that, I put my hands into her pelvic cavity through the anus to check her ovaries and found that her left ovary would soon mature.

"Let Little Black mate the day after tomorrow, and she will get pregnant for sure," I said to Little Zhao, confidently.

As a proficient vet and breeder, I would never let a donkey mate with Little Black because that would be the ruin of her. The next question would be where to find a stallion that could match her? I called the regiment veterinary station, hoping to get their support.

It was Vet Xue who answered the phone.

"Yes, it's time to let her mate now," Xue said. "She will definitely produce fine offspring."

"But we don't have a good stallion in our company."

"Do you remember the Wangguanghe breeding centre about ten

kilometres west of your company? It's a state-run centre to improve the local horse breeds. Last month, a thoroughbred Kabarda was brought in to provide free mating. Let them mate naturally, and Little Black will surely give birth to a superior foal."

My eyes lit up. It would be wonderful if Little Black could mate with a thoroughbred Kabarda. So I decided to take Little Black to the breeding centre the very next day.

That day, I saddled Little Black and rode her cautiously to the town of Wangguanghe. I did not let her run or gallop as usual, and I even walked with her for some time. There weren't any Corps camps in the area, but there were some settlements for educated youths. I led Little Black to Wangguanghe breeding centre, which was well known in the Balingol union. I was familiar with that place because I had been trained there for three days.

The tall and muscular Kabarda horse runs in a light-footed and graceful manner. Initially bred in the Caucasus region of the former Soviet Union, it is fast and has endurance. Most of this species live on the prairie, while a small number are mountain horses. The cavalry of the former Soviet Union were supplied with Kabarda horses.

My eyes lit up at the first sight of this purebred Kabarda with deep black hair, as if I had found a handsome gentleman to wed my beautiful daughter. A typical 'black horse prince' indeed. The only imperfection I saw that day was that he seemed to be in rather low spirits and was drooping his head.

The director of the centre, a man in his fifties, walked out to greet me respectfully.

"How are you, Mr Director?" I said. "Do you remember me? I studied here before. Little Black is a Kabarda mare. I am wondering whether she could mate with your thoroughbred Kabarda stallion."

The director narrowed his eyes and studied Little Black for quite a while. "She is a good Kabarda, but not a purebred. I reckon she is half Kabarda and half Sanhe plus Mongolian."

Deeply impressed with his discernment and experience, I seized the occasion to flatter him.

"You sure have a keen eye for horses. Her father was a thoroughbred Kabarda, and her mother was a hybrid Sanhe and Mongolian. I dare say she is one of the fastest horses in all Inner Mongolia."

The director nodded his head knowingly and touched the goatee on his chin with pride. "If she mates with my Kabarda, she will give birth to a foal of seventy-five percent Kabarda blood, who could run even faster."

The director was a little bit boastful, but his words were exactly to my liking. So I responded with excitement.

"Well said! I do believe they will create a perfect foal. Maybe a swift horse on the steppe. Would you consider letting them mate?"

"Unfortunately, you came at the wrong time. Our refrigerator broke down, and the horse's semen kept in there was all ruined."

"Can we do a natural mating then?" I asked, shocked at his response.

"There are two problems with that. First, we always do artificial insemination. We collect as much semen as possible in one go in order to maximise the number of mares who get impregnated. Second, my stallion has a high fever and is not fit for mating. So I have to say sorry this time. Come again when your horse is on heat again."

"Then we will have to wait until next year. Could you just let them mate once?" I pleaded, but the director waved his hand and walked straight inside.

There was no way around it. I had no choice but to leave the breeding station. After travelling three kilometres, however, I went back with Little Black. I hated to return to the company in such circumstances. If I missed this chance, she would have to wait a whole year, and it was very likely that she would mate with an average stallion as soon as she joined the herd. I did not want to see that happen. I felt very frustrated and anxious about Little Black. All of a sudden, an idea came to me.

"Why not let Little Black have a secret liaison with that Kabarda stallion?"

An excellent idea! But there goes my cowardice again. I had the heart of a thief but not the guts. Just thinking about such a bold move made my legs go weak. Such audacity ran counter to my basic instinct. But in those days, Little Black and I were tightly entwined. Her wellbeing, her future and the quality of her offspring were all of direct concern to me. So it was no exaggeration to say that Little Black was the very breath of my life, and so, after much hesitation, I was seized with a sudden impulse, an impulse similar to what I had felt before sneaking onto the train bound for the Corps, an impulse that I felt when urged to ride Bandit. And now it came again to help me make up my mind to do something 'extraordinary'.

I decided to act at noon, siesta time, when the entire town of Wangguanghe was quiet and deserted, and only the monotonous songs of cicadas in the trees could be heard. It was cloudy, and the sun was making only an occasional appearance. I slowly led Little Black towards the breeding centre. When I came to a big tree, I removed the saddle from her back, and led her to a high stable. I popped my head into the stable and saw the Kabarda stallion tied to a pillar. There was an iron hoop in the upper part of the pillar, through which the stallion's reins passed and then tied to another stake. Thanks to the length of the reins, the mating would not be affected.

'The Black Horse Prince' looked truly ill that day. His head was drooping, but he perked up instantly on seeing Little Black slowly approaching. He let out a long neigh and pawed at the ground with one of his front legs. I looked around to make sure no one was around and quickly led Little Black to the stallion. She wasn't shy at all. She spread her hind legs and urinated. The Prince sniffed at the urine and soon became excited, despite suffering from a high fever. He got an erection and mounted Little Black right away...

After some violent twitching, the Prince planted a precious seed in Little Black's womb.

Chapter 33

Birth of a Baby Horse

B ack at the company, I kept quiet about Little Black's adventure. I merely told my colleagues at the stud farm that it was routine artificial insemination. But everyone could tell I was now showing the utmost care for Little Black, as if it was my own wife or daughter who was pregnant. I took her temperature on a daily basis and recorded the data in a notebook. One day after taking her temperature, I couldn't help smiling broadly. It was my first such smile since failing to gain admission to college.

When Little Zhao saw me with the thermometer, he asked: "What's up? Is Little Black ill?"

"No, not at all. She's pregnant. She is going to have a foal," I said excitedly as I showed him my notebook.

"This was Little Black's temperature before she mated. This is her temperature the day after mating. It rose one degree Celsius. And these past few days her temperature has been consistently high."

"What does it mean?"

"Little Black is pregnant, that's the only explanation," I said as I gave Little Zhao a punch and returned gingerly to my room. I picked up an old army overcoat, money and rations coupons and headed towards the neighbouring Shatou village to buy some nutrients for Little Black. But what could I buy for a horse when there was no decent food even for people? The most nutritious food available was eggs.

On arriving at the village, I went from door to door for eggs, and finally found the right person, an elderly lady who raised dozens of chickens. As she came out of her house, she squinted at me and asked: "How many eggs do you want?"

"A basket," I said.

The elderly lady then came out of her inner room carefully carrying a large basket containing up to two hundred eggs.

"Do you want the whole basket?" she asked doubtfully as she narrowed her eyes to size me up again.

My eyes glowed with happiness. I was so relieved that Little Black's nutrition problem was now solved.

"Yes, I want all of them! How much?"

"Thirty yuan," called out her husband before his wife had a chance to reply.

Obviously, the husband wanted to get the most from what was a rare business opportunity. Thirty yuan was a lot of money in those days, so he must have been trying to take advantage of me. But my mind was so full of Little Black that I didn't consider haggling. I emptied my pockets and produced a bundle of one-yuan and two-yuan notes, even notes of ten cents or twenty cents, but they were not enough to cover the eggs, so I gave them some rations coupons too. The elderly couple looked at the coupons again and again without making a decision. "The money and coupons are only enough for half of the eggs," the husband finally said.

The elderly lady stooped to pick out some eggs. I stopped her before taking off my overcoat and passing it to her husband. The couple immediately consented.

Holding the basket in my arms, I went back briskly, humming some tunes all the way. As I came close to the stud farm, I decided to hide the eggs in the veterinary pharmacy for safekeeping, just like what I had previously done with the cantaloupes. I was sure that this was the safest place to lock them because I alone had the key.

Afterwards, I would unlock the veterinary dispensary at regular intervals to take four eggs, which I would then break and mix into a small basin of feed. After pouring the feed into the manger, I would call Little Black over to eat. As she started munching greedily, I would watch her and imagine rich nutrients being absorbed by her body and then transferred to the new, rapidly growing living entity within her. I fancied that, inside Little Black, a swift 'prince' was already developing and growing.

As the days passed, Little Black's belly kept growing, until it seemed to be unusually large. I began to worry that the 'princeling' would grow into an oversized foal that might cause an obstructed labour. To prevent that, I decided to cut back on her normal fodder and give her a more nutritious daily diet of eggs, black beans, carrots and alfalfa. In addition, I resumed our three-hour walks every day after dinner.

I led Little Black onto that familiar dirt road. Though her black coat still had a healthy lustre, she was no longer as slim as before. Her belly was round and protruding. According to experienced horsemen, that meant the foal would be a colt. I was secretly happy.

Because of the pregnancy, Little Black's gait was no longer as light as before. She walked unsteadily sometimes, so I had to slow down and be extra careful. Looking back on Little Black's secret mating session, despite my nervousness and fear, I did find the whole process to be very interesting. For better or worse, the stolen seed was already in Little Black's womb and was growing into a noble 'prince'. The thought of this filled me joy and excitement, and I looked forward to the delivery day.

Early one morning, at dawn, I was woken up from a deep slumber by Little Zhao who was on night shift. He rushed into my room and shouted: "Wen Bo! Wen Bo! Get up! Little Black is giving birth. She's having a hard time. Get up and help!"

I immediately realised my biggest concern was now coming true. Little Black was again confronted with a life-and-death test. I jumped out of bed, and put on my clothes.

"Quick! Get me my medicine kit," I shouted. "And go fetch a bucket of water."

I dashed off after Little Zhao through the open field to the stud farm where Little Black was delivering. As I ran, I was filled with anxious thoughts. If anything bad happened to Little Black, would not all the good things and dreams evaporate? I began to regret having forced her into being impregnated with such a large foal. I also regretted having given her so much nutrition. The eggs must be partly responsible, I thought. Thus over time, the foetus grew bigger and bigger, so much so that I recently noticed her panting as I walked with her.

I ran faster and faster. Finally, in the open field about one and a half kilometres from the stud farm, I saw Little Black lying on the ground, groaning with pain. She seemed to regard me as a saviour. I saw that familiar look for help, a look that only she and I could understand.

During the past few years of our companionship, we had saved each other on a couple of occasions. Whenever I saw the imploring look in her eyes, I rushed to her rescue at whatever cost. Even so, this was going to be a completely different situation in which I would have to race against time to save two lives at once. Little Zhao soon arrived with a bucket of water. I put about twenty millilitres of disinfectant in it, and the water immediately turned milky white. After washing my hands and arms in it, I gently probed Little Black's vagina and touched the head and two forelegs of the colt. The baby was in the correct position, but its sheer size made delivery difficult.

Little by little, I moved the head and forelegs of the baby foal out of Little Black's vagina, and in the rhythm of the uterine contraction, pulled out the foal by degrees. Little Black was working hard too, knowing that I was helping her. By now, my co-workers had arrived on the scene, and I asked one of the bigger guys to hold my waist from behind, and the others followed his lead so that a human chain was formed to do the pulling. Though I had never received any professional delivery training, I kept in mind the key points of delivery that I had learned from the Red Brick. The pulling had to be done in tandem with the contraction, and there had to be a steady use of force when pulling the foal out little by little. With our combined efforts, we finally pulled it out completely. We all fell on the floor, and our hands and faces were all smeared with mud. With sweat on our foreheads and bright smiles on our faces, we all looked happy because we knew Little Black and her baby were both safe. We celebrated the birth of a new life.

Little Black looked relieved as she rose from the floor to lick the newborn colt. Looking a natural parent, she bit off the umbilical cord that was connected to the placenta and licked away the mucus covering the foal. Then, the foal with jet-black fur stood up before our eyes. It was almost twice the size of an average foal, though it couldn't stand firm and was looking sleepy.

"It's a colt," Little Zhao shouted.

About an hour later, I gently carried the sleepy colt to her mum and directed his mouth to Little Black's swollen nipples, and he started sucking right away. The colostrum he imbibed contained antibodies to protect him against disease. News of the hybrid colt's birth quickly spread, and he became an instant hit in the company. Almost everyone came over to take a close look at the newborn prince.

While grazing on the pasture, Little Black and her colt stood out in the herd. The black prince was so adorable that whoever saw him wanted to touch him. Simple and good-tempered, he would never refuse to be touched or stroked, although Little Black prevented strangers from approaching him.

However, I soon came to notice that, unlike other colts, the black prince looked listless most of the time. Though tall and slim, he could never run fast, nor would he do much jumping. He had none of the vitality and wildness that his mother had on arriving at the stud farm. I'm not keen on placid horses. What I wanted was a wild pony, alive and kicking. But the black colt was just the opposite – a meek and quiet weakling.

Hence, I couldn't help reappraising what I had done, and I began to doubt the wisdom of my actions.

One day, finally, I couldn't help asking Little Zhao: "Why does the black colt look so feeble? Why is he so slow?"

"It looks like the colt of a foreign horse is large in size but not useful. A good horse is either exceedingly dynamic or naturally impetuous. The black colt is a typical sloth who will end up being an incompetent horse."

Each of Little Zhao's words stabbed me in the heart. Doubt turned into disappointment, and disappointment turned into intolerance. Before Little Black gave birth, I had often dreamed of her producing a beautiful and sturdy black horse that would suck milk by itself right after being born and would soon run wild on the pasture. These dreams helped me endure that depressing and forlorn year in the Corps. Now that the dreams were broken, my life was no longer quite the same.

How rapturous and ecstatic I was when the black colt was first born. I felt as if it was my own baby. And yet all of that joy would be gone by the time the black colt's true self – its cowardice, underdevelopment and indecisive personality – was revealed.

But now I had to face reality and acknowledge the fact that the black colt had a docile disposition. Based on years of experience in horse keeping, I knew good horses would have impulsive personalities, and swift horses all start out with fiery tempers. Little Black was known to be petulant, and I suffered considerably because of that. But her offspring was just the opposite. Though taller than his mother, the colt was slow and docile, with no vitality or strength. In the words of the locals, a fat colt always ends up turning into a fat horse.

I felt frustrated and annoyed. I had to admit I had made a big mistake in being entranced by that princely black Kabarda horse's beauty and ignored the key fact that the stallion was running a fever at the time. Anyone with medical knowledge would know that a fever can affect the quality of the semen. Despite the successful secret mating, the end result was a lousy fat horse. So I had to see that adventure as a failure.

In retrospect, the director of Wangguanghe breeding centre was right in not letting Little Black mate with the Kabarda. As a breeding expert, he made the correct decision. The outcome resulted from my misplaced passion and the rash decision to let Little Black mate with a stallion running a high fever. My other mistake was overfeeding Little Black during her pregnancy, which almost led to delivery dystocia. Even so, Little Black did give birth to a colt and her clandestine love affair helped pull me through that hard year. Even though that secret happiness eventually ended in nothing, it dispelled feelings of loneliness and despair that came from my failure to attend college. It gave me something to look forward to so that I did not have to keep crying in a life of hardship. It gave me something positive and beautiful in my heart that would keep me going and give me the courage to live on in Shatou.

In an imperfect world, we cannot expect perfection. So we learn to come to terms with life and yield to the hurdles we cannot cross and bow to the difficulties we have no power to overcome. Still, 'a living dog is better off than a dead lion'. In times of adversity, the only option is often just to wait – wait for the turn of time and fortune, wait for changes in the world and wait for future opportunities. That was the only positive attitude I could hold onto after years of struggle in adversity.

Planning for the colt was much like the planning parents go through for their child's future. If the child turns out to be a genius, the parents would fund his or her study at primary school, middle school, high school, college and even foreign study. If the child was not academically gifted or even had a congenital disability, they would need to face reality and find another route. They may want their child to acquire a basic working skill, get a technical qualification and find a suitable job. The parents may further help their child find a thrifty and diligent spouse, virtuous but not necessarily beautiful, to establish a new family, have children and lead an ordinary life.

After a whole night's discussion, Little Zhao and I came up with a practical plan for the colt. He would be in charge of implementation. The plan was for the colt to be raised with the herd of donkeys after passing the lactating period of about two months. Several months later, the colt began to feel at home with the donkeys. As a tall and slim black horse, he stood out among the donkeys.

Over the next year, Little Black had fewer and fewer opportunities to see her foal. The Black Prince gradually lost his equine identity after being herded with donkeys by Little Zhao. That's why he looked nonchalant on seeing his mother. He clearly did not think of himself as a horse any more. He was later trained as a special breeding horse for female donkeys and his immersion with them gradually earned him the nickname 'Donkey Prince', which spread far and wide. Living with donkeys that were a lot smaller than himself, the prince became quite arrogant. The jealous female donkeys often had to fight to get a chance to flirt with him. This separation from other horses made him a real prince among the donkeys. He was very content with his life. I thought it was a very pragmatic way of handling the colt. If he was not going to be a swift horse, he might as well be a down-to-earth prince among donkeys. If he raised valuable mules for society, our investment in him would have been worthwhile.

Chapter 34

Failed Audition in Yinchuan

L ittle Black's successful delivery released a major burden in my heart. With little else in my life, I began to feel bored, lonely and melancholic. I could no longer bear staying in Shatou. One day, as I stood behind an old adobe brick wall of the stud farm looking into the distance, I saw nothing but a barren stretch of salty land. The desolate view filled me with an unutterable pain. Was my youth going to end here? Would I have to stay in Shatou forever, and even die here?

Five years had passed since I first arrived here. Life at the Corps wasn't exactly intolerable. The sad thing was that we educated youths were toiling in this remote land in an era when we should have been at school, absorbing knowledge and building up skills.

Fortunately, things have a way of working out. Without any warning, news emerged of the impending disbandment of the Corps. As a first step, military personnel would be withdrawn. Next, the Corps would be transferred to the local authorities, which meant most of the educated youths would have to leave and be relocated.

Various theories for the break-up were put forward. One was that the Corps was an expensive operation to run. Flour in those days cost more than 10 Chinese cents per 500 grams, while the production cost of flour at the Corps was 1.8 yuan per 500 grams. In other words, the Corps was uneconomic despite all our best efforts and suffering in the harsh environment. There were insufficient funds in the national defence budget to pay for the Corps. As a result, the state and the army couldn't take it anymore, and the Corps had to dissolve in order to save resources for national defence. In other words, the Corps was disintegrating.

Another theory was that the formation and disbandment of the Corps was a political necessity. The original purpose of the Corps was to fight 'Soviet revisionists'. The former Soviet Union had assembled up to a million troops on the Sino-Soviet border, something that was pushing the two countries to the brink of war. So, hundreds of thousands of educated youths under the leadership of the PLA, along with demobilised PLA troops, were deployed in the vast Inner Mongolia frontier region to build a 'Great Wall' of people. However, five years later, the Soviet troops withdrew, and the prospect of war between the two countries receded. So the Corps lost its raison d'etre, and its dissolution became inevitable.

Whatever the real reason, when we heard that PLA troops were soon withdrawing and the Corps was to be administered by local authorities, we were all shocked. Everyone began looking for employment. The Corps now had no intention of keeping anyone. We would get permission to leave as soon as we found a unit that would accept us. Those with *guanxi* easily found an exit.

Zhang Wei, my high school classmate and a student platoon leader, was transferred to Luoyang, Henan province. He was a handsome man with a wide and healthy face featuring large eyes, thick eyebrows and a high-bridged nose. His handsome features and capability made it very easy for him to find a good wife and a decent job in Luoyang. Zhou Jun, the horseman with whom I was well-acquainted, was the owner of Xiaojunma. His parents were both factory workers, and he was happy to join them there after being recruited. Yuan Fang, a beautiful girl from Hangzhou, got transferred to a local railway bureau through a convoluted family network. She had curly black hair, two lovely eyes under slender eyebrows, and her long eyelashes that matched her high-bridged nose gave her a kind of foreign appearance, but her cherry lips and small dimples were the features of a typical southern Chinese beauty. Her departure broke the hearts of many male comrades, some of whom would never be able to forget her. Altogether, there was a surge of people leaving Shatou. Where they ended up depended largely on their individual capabilities and family networks.

I certainly had the urge to leave, too, but could not think of any opportunities or *guanxi* to exploit. Nor did I have any skills to earn a living from except as a vet. That was until I realised I might try broadcasting.

My standard Mandarin and 'Italian utterances' might be put to good use in a local radio station. I wrote to an aunt, who was an editor at Ningxia Publishing House in Yinchuan, about the idea and got her endorsement. She said that she knew someone who worked at Ningxia Radio Station who could possibly recommend me. She also invited me to stay with her in Yinchuan for a couple of days during the spring festival.

It might be a possible way out of Shatou. After some difficulties, I got a week off work during the spring festival. I set off with nothing but a shoulder bag. At a ticket window in Urat Front banner railway station, I learnt that the twenty yuan in my pocket would only be enough to get me a one-way ticket to Yinchuan. After much hesitation, I decided to spend less than two yuan on a ticket that would get me onto the train so I could keep the rest of the money for the return journey.

I might reasonably borrow some money from my aunt once I got there, but I didn't want to do that unless absolutely necessary because I was already going to put her to the trouble of eating and staying in her house for several days.

It was 3am when I boarded the train at Urat Front banner railway station. Since most passengers were asleep, only a few wall lamps were on in the carriage. Reclining in my seat, I recalled my previous train journey to the Corps from Beijing several years ago and, of course, I thought of Yue. There were no educated youths this time and not many young people at all. They were mostly average people, men and women, old and young. Loaded with bags of varying size, they were on their way either to reunite with their families or visit relatives during the holidays. I too was going to visit a relative, but I only had a shoulder bag that contained nothing more than two bottles of linseed oil.

Before long, the train arrived at Linhe station, where the third division of the Inner Mongolia Corps was based. According to the ticket I had bought, this was to be the station where I should get off. But I did not. Only a couple of people and a few Corps soldiers like me alighted. The train sounded a long whistle and then pulled away again. In two hours, at about 6am, it arrived at Wuhai city railway station, where many people got on and off, and almost all the seats were taken. There were only a very small number of vacant seats scattered here and there. The noise coming from the newly

210

boarded passengers soon woke me up, and routine ticket-inspection began. I was in the ninth of twelve carriages.

I took out a pack of cigarettes from my chest pocket and offered one to an older passenger seated in front of me. He accepted it with a smile, and immediately struck a match to light mine before lighting his own. As wisps of smoke issued from my mouth, I began to figure out ways to evade paying the full fare. When the conductor came over to our carriage, all of the passengers held out their tickets, ready for inspection. I took out my ticket to Linhe, put it between my lips, threw my bag on my shoulder, and with cup in hand, walked hurriedly but casually towards the conductor pretending that I was going for some water. I nodded and smiled to her when she shot a look at me. Then, I swished the ticket around to let her know I had a ticket and was busy getting some water. In doing so, I successfully bypassed two conductors and walked until I came to the third carriage, where I saw a vacant seat next to the window. I sat down quickly, spread out my arms on the small table in front of me and rested my head on it to sleep. I slept until noon, when the train at last reached Yinchuan, the final destination. Passengers vied with one another to get off the train before coming to a halt at the exit to wait for the final ticket check. Rubbing my eyes, I stood up, threw the bag on my shoulder and began to wonder what to do next. When I saw a middle-aged man walk out through a side gate, I realised it could be a staff exit, so I went that way too and soon found myself out on the streets of Yinchuan. I had succeeded as a fare dodger.

I stayed several days in my aunt's house. My young cousins were curious about this person from Inner Mongolia. They probably marvelled at my unkempt appearance, dishevelled hair and good appetite. They also heard me read the newspaper using my 'Italian utterances', which made them laugh behind the door. I was actually preparing for a broadcasting exam, which my aunt had been able to fix because of her *guanxi*. The exam took the form of a face-to-face interview and was scheduled to take place on the day right after the spring festival. The only requirements of the test were to read an editorial and sing a song. The reading part was easy for me, but the singing was more challenging because I had no talent for it.

As a child, I attended Huiwen primary school, a western-style private school in Beijing. My music teacher had studied abroad, so she had a unique western approach to teaching. During one of her classes, she taught us a song that contained only four lines of lyrics.

Instead of teaching us line by line, she played the piano to lead us. After practising the song a couple of times, she encouraged us to perform solo on the platform. She closed her eyes, as if in meditation, but her fingers kept tapping on the piano keys. I was the last one to go on stage to sing the song. To my surprise, as I finished the last line, the piano accompaniment suddenly stopped. This gave me an ominous feeling, as if something embarrassing was going to happen. Sure enough, the teacher stood up slowly, crossed her hands in front of her chest and pointed at me.

"How do you like his singing?" she asked the whole class.

A female classmate raised her hand and stood up. "He is actually talking," she said.

"Correct. What is it called? It's called being tone-deaf. Tone-deafness can be complete or incomplete. Complete tone-deafness, which means zero sense of music, is caused by congenital mental deficiency. He belongs to the former category, which can be gradually improved through training, but is very difficult."

My aunt soon discovered my problem and became worried about me. She asked her husband to teach me a complete song entitled *I Love This Blue Sea*. He must have been very disappointed with me and might have regarded me as a hopeless case because I was constantly out of tune. Knowing what was most important in the exam, my uncle went out of his way to find me a tutor in a suburban county seat of Yinchuan. The tutor spent an hour teaching me the basics of broadcasting.

The exam took place in the broadcasting studio of a radio station. The walls were in the shape of a glass dome. Because of the good insulation, I could hear nothing from outside. In front of me sat two rows of leaders, including the director, assistant directors and division chiefs of each department, who were there to judge my performance and decide then and there whether or not to hire me. So I was rather nervous. Fortunately, some of these people were friends of my aunt and uncle and had been told to judge in my favour, which gave me a strong sense of security.

I was asked to read a paragraph from an editorial and felt good about it because I saw people nodding outside the glass dome. The singing part was a little different. They probably wanted to get a better understanding of my tone, volume and range. So I sang at the top of my voice. But I soon sensed something wrong when the judges started rocking with laughter. I was out of tune and off key. The exam ended in disaster, and so was my entire trip to Yinchuan.

Chapter 35

Decision

By the time I returned to Shatou from Yinchuan, another group of comrades who had *guanxi* had left. Some PLA soldiers were packing and were also ready to leave. Everyone was in a hurry, as if any delay would somehow spell doom. This made me panic, and I started to become anxious. By now, my mum had regained her job at the General Hospital of Beijing military region, where she provided nutritional care to hospitalised high-ranking officials. Therefore, she came into contact with some senior officers of the Corps, including division-level officers, guesthouse managers and even a deputy commander-in-chief. I didn't use these contacts before because I did not want to be redeployed within the Corps.

I wanted to get out. Specifically, I wanted to go to school or find a job in Beijing. But so far, all my efforts in that direction had failed and I could not even leave Shatou. What made me especially anxious was that, once the PLA soldiers were gone, my mum's contacts would no longer be of much help. Fearing the prospect of being stuck in Shatou forever, I wrote to my mum about my fears. She sent back a letter saying she knew a kind-hearted couple with wide social connections. The husband Wan was a guesthouse manager and his wife worked in the clinic of the Corps. Mum urged me to contact them as quickly as possible because they were set to leave the Corps soon. She suggested that I ask them to at least help me move close to Hohhot or Beijing.

I found Mum's words very reasonable. One cannot always expect to accomplish everything in one go. A step-by-step approach similar to the plan I had developed for Little Black might work better. Following the Chinese saying that 'frequent transplantation is deadly for trees but beneficial for men', I resolved to stop all daydreaming by leaving Shatou and seeking opportunities elsewhere. In other words, I would grab whatever came along.

In those sleepless days, I spent every spare second thinking of ways to leave Shatou and where to go from there. Because I had recently taken time off to go to Yinchuan, I had to wait another two weeks before I could ask for leave again. That fortnight was almost unbearable because every minute of waiting meant a lost opportunity. It was like torture. Fortunately, I still had some days of home leave to use, so I set about preparing for my departure. At the headquarters hostel of the Corps in Hohhot, I contacted the warm-hearted Manager Wan who had a broad, whiskered face and a sonorous voice. He put me up at the hostel and said something that was very reassuring.

"Make yourself at home here. We'll take care of your food and lodging and help you find a way out. Before you leave the Corps, we'll make sure you get a good placement."

The three-week paid home leave came as a great relief. Manager Wan struck me as someone I could trust, and I just wished I had known him earlier. Those weeks were a real pleasure. After breakfast at the hostel, I took a stroll along the streets of Hohhot, trying to get familiar with the city since I might one day live there. Around lunch time, Manager Wan came to see me at the hostel and told me the best option was to place me at the Corps' chemical fibre factory in Hohhot. The factory, which was directly affiliated with the Corps, would soon be taken over by the local government. All Corps soldiers placed there would become state employees, with a good income and benefits. Unfortunately, the factory's personnel director was away on business, so we had to wait. A week later, he came back with bad news. The factory wasn't hiring anymore because all positions had already been filled.

Once again, I was seized with panic, scared that I might be forced to return to Shatou at any time. Manager Wan then came up with a suggestion that made me recoil even though I was open to almost anything. But he said that was the only way out, and he asked his wife to talk me into it.

I was twenty-six, and while I was lean, I was also tall, strong and handsome. The plan was to have me marry a Corps girl who worked at the factory. As the spouse of a working-class woman, I would be able to be transferred to the factory directly. But I had to marry her before the PLA soldiers withdrew.

It seemed that I had only two choices: either return to Shatou and take root there or be chosen by one of the female factory workers. The latter meant that I would be transferred from a backwater village to Hohhot, the capital of Inner Mongolia. If I got chosen by one of the female workers and was sent a transfer order, I would have to commit to living with her for the rest of my life. At a time when the Corps was dissolving, I seemed to have no other alternative. Also, I didn't feel comfortable turning down a kind offer that would solve the problem of employment and consummate marriage at the same time.

A week later, at noon on Saturday, Manager Wan invited me over to his home for lunch and told me his wife was waiting to see me. I was pleased a girl had chosen me, and I hoped she wouldn't be too ugly. To my surprise, only two middle-aged women were there to dine with me: Mrs Wan and another lady who was introduced to me as Xiaohong's mother. There was no young woman at all. During dinner, I bowed my head in silence and ate slowly, trying to look as refined as possible. While serving me food, the two women started asking questions about my family. I was worried that they would ask about my uncle on my mother's side or any other relatives abroad, which had become such a difficult topic for me. In those days, people were segregated by family background. Those from a 'red five' category were not supposed to marry someone from a 'black five' category. A red-black marriage ran the risk of being rejected by the authorities.

Family origin played such a pivotal role that those from politically incorrect families were not only barred from joining the army or going to school, they were actually looked down upon even in romantic relationships. Being jobless in a remote rural area, I had nothing to offer but a tall and strong physique. So I was in no position to be choosy. I simply had to wait to be picked by any female factory worker. So I looked down at my bowl and played with the remaining food with my chopsticks.

Seeing the embarrassment in my flushed face and neck, the sophisticated women stopped asking me questions and started talking about Xiaohong, my potential fiancée. I listened quietly, never raising my head. From their glowing words, I fancied that Xiaohong would be a tall, comely and capable girl with a strong personality. She was also a platoon sergeant at the factory. So she could reasonably be my type.

Xionghong's mum seemed to be quite happy about me too. I realised I might have been overly concerned about my family background.

People were starting to become more pragmatic and less political in their marital considerations. What they cared more about was the actual person, whether he or she was honest, skilled and promising. They even began to prefer marrying those from intellectual families. Xiaohong's mum probably liked my personality. With my bashfulness and honesty, she may have thought her daughter would easily exercise control over me. Despite my silence at lunch, Xiaohong's mum was happy to invite me to her house for dinner that night.

Xiaohong's home and Manager Wan's home were only three units apart. There were many similar housing blocks in this compound, which were inhabited by a total of around eighty households. Each row had ten households, and each compound contained eight rows. Well-known as the 'Corps compound', these were the homes of Corps officials.

Back then, they were commonly regarded as high-end residences, but to those like me who had been living in adobe brick buildings, they looked more like luxury mansions. The residences were standardised, each containing two rooms, a kitchenette and a courtyard, but there was neither a toilet nor tap water. At the end of each of the eight rows of houses were two public toilets. In the middle of each row of houses was a huge basin built of cement bricks about ten metres long, fed by a row of taps. This was where residents would gather to do their laundry and fetch water in buckets for daily use.

After lunch, Xiaohong's mum walked me out, showed me where her house was, and reminded me again and again to go to her home for supper at 6pm sharp. I thanked her without giving any affirmative reply before taking off for a stroll downtown. I found myself in a park. Every time I had a big a decision to make, I would try to find a place to walk so that I could ponder my future path. If I were in Shatou, I would walk with Little Black, but in Hohhot, I had to walk alone.

In the context of those twisted times, most people had limited vision.

217

They had little independence or freedom. They could only seek to change their life course by taking advantage of subtle social changes. The transfer of ownership of the Corps was one of those subtle changes that I could exploit. Only a fool would give up the opportunity to get transferred to Hohhot from a remote village. On the other hand, if I married someone I disliked or didn't love, given my inclination to compromise, I would definitely make do with that marriage, especially if it yielded a baby. In that case, I would have to accept my lot and never return to Beijing.

I still had high hopes for the future and believed that big changes would take place in society one day, and with those would come various opportunities. If I was back in Beijing by then, opportunities might arise to go to college. Therefore an expedient marriage would only drag me down. Besides, I could never forget Yue, whose image was reflected in Little Black and kept me company for five years. Though I had not heard from her over the years, I might try to find her in Beijing and rekindle that short but touching love affair.

As I walked along a lakeside path in the park, I found myself in a dilemma. Finally, I decided that I should not barter away my youth so casually and that marriage was a serious matter. I was at a loss what to do next, but one thing was for sure: I had no desire to return to Shatou, although I did want to see what Xiaohong looked like. So, at around 5.30pm, I stole back into the Corps compound, where I hid in a corner to observe what was going on in Xiaohong's house.

About ten minutes later, a young woman carrying a large bucket came out. She was apparently going to fetch some water. Standing 1.65 metres tall, she had wide shoulders and a strong, athletic build. Greeting the neighbours and chatting with them casually, she carried the bucket to the tap. Suddenly, amused at something, she was so carried away laughing that she did not notice the water in her bucket was spilling over. She turned off the tap, lifted the bucket and carried it home deftly. I knew right away she was a cheerful, domineering and capable girl. Though I did not see her face clearly, I could see her beautiful frame and her unique demeanour. What impressed me most was her strong physique. If we were to live under the same roof, her personality would surely overwhelm me. Her uncompromising air definitely suited her position as a platoon sergeant.

Deep within, I rather liked girls of this type, probably because their strength and capability could compensate for my lack of masculinity. So I did have an inclination to go over to her. But I knew if I followed her into her home, I might never be able to leave. I would become her captive for life, maybe even a prize for her to show off in front of her female friends. Probably because I felt subconsciously that I had the possibility of securing a better future and a better match, I was sober enough to overcome the temptation.

I stood behind a tree, my legs seemingly pinned to the ground, unable to move a step forward. I began to play in my mind what it would be like to live with Xiaohong. If I stepped into her apartment, I would end up marrying her, and I would live in that house after being transferred from Shatou to Hohhot. In that scenario, I would be the one lifting that bucket of water and carrying it into the house. I would no doubt be the one spilling water on my trousers and shoes. Xiaohong would then scold me for my clumsiness, maybe even give me a kick. On Sundays, she would order me to do all kinds of chores, such as doing the laundry or going grocery shopping. She would walk proudly ahead of me with her head held high and greet every acquaintance and chat with them along the way, while I would tail behind like a servant following his master.

I would not mind such a life even if people scorned me, because as a cowardly bookworm I could hardly escape such a fate whomever I were to marry. It seemed inevitable that I would end up as a hen-pecked husband. But that wouldn't be so intolerable. My priority then was my career. I had to repeatedly ask myself: what could I do at the chemical fibre factory? Xiaohong was already a platoon sergeant, and her next promotion would be workshop manager. So I would end up going to work with an imposing workshop manager every morning. All the female textile workers would greet her while ignoring me. Plus, I might even have to carry her purse around. Yet I believed I had a sufficiently thick skin to stand all of this and could even derive some pride from all the respect paid to her.

But what could I possibly do at the factory? Most likely I would be repairing machines. With hundreds of textile machines running every day, there would be no shortage of maintenance and repair jobs. The job wouldn't be a demanding one involving three shifts. Repairs were needed only when machines broke down. With such a leisurely and respectable job and Xiaohong as my spouse, I would be making decent money, raising children and enjoying life in a cosy home in a big city. And that's exactly the kind of dream many people were pursuing in China back then.

I would have readily accepted this job five years ago, but now I could not let go of veterinary medicine. As a vet, I had already made impressive achievements in treating difficult horse diseases, including equine constipation. Meanwhile, my interest in medicine had expanded to the study of cancer, and I had spent countless hours studying the disease. If I continued to study, I would definitely stand a good chance of success, maybe even one day make an extraordinary contribution to medical science.

A man's career is a serious matter and I decided it should be my top priority. I walked quietly past Xiaohong's house and peered inside. She and her mum were busy preparing a big meal, trying to show the best hospitality to a possible marriage candidate. I felt very bad about it, but I refrained from going inside.

The appointed dinner time had passed but I was drawn back to Xiaohong's home by the alluring smell from her kitchen. While my stomach was grumbling, a sweet home was opening its door to me, and a beautiful, robust and passionate girl was welcoming me with outstretched arms. As a twenty-six-year-old, my thirst for romantic love had come to a point where I could hardly control myself. I felt like running into her house and thrusting myself into Xiaohong's open arms and committing myself to her for the rest of my life. But I didn't because my vision for the future overcame immediate lust.

Back on the street, I dared not return to the hostel for dinner for fear that Manager Wan might see me and force me into Xiaohong's house. To fill my empty belly, I went to the famous Qingcheng restaurant in Hohhot, where I ordered lamb. Early the next morning, Manager Wan pulled me out of bed and asked me why I failed to show up for the appointment, and he told me of the girl's disappointment. I lowered my head, not daring to say a word. Manager Wan was a warm and dogged person. He kept pressing me for an explanation. After some prevarication, I finally told him I had a girlfriend who was in the army. The dubious Wan touched his head and expressed his deep regret.

With only one week left in Hohhot, I found myself no further forward. Manager Wan, scratching his head and pacing up and down in my room, seemed to be at the end of his tether.

"In a suburb of Hohhot, dozens of miles from downtown, there is a livestock farm," he said finally. "They need people because it's new and still developing. It will be relatively easy for you because not many people want to go there."

Much to Wan's surprise, I agreed without hesitation. Here is what I was thinking. A suburb of Hohhot was much better than Shatou. First, the people there lived in houses built with bricks and tiles instead of mud. Second, though located in the suburbs, the farm was only a little more than an hour's drive to the city centre. Third, my veterinarian skills could be put to good use on the farm, enabling me to continue my medical research into various difficult diseases. More important, I didn't have to marry anyone to get there, and I could continue to pursue true love.

Because the animal farm still belonged to the Forty-Second Regiment, I needed the approval of a Corps-level officer, which reminded me of Deputy Commander-in-Chief Kang whom my mum had mentioned in her letter. She had taken very good care of him when he was hospitalised in Beijing. Kang knew I was working in the Corps, and he told her before being released that she could seek his help if needed. Hence, Manager Wan took me to Kang's office. What I saw was a rather stout man in his sixties with a kindly, wrinkled face. He sat squarely in his chair as Wan explained who my mum was and the purpose of our visit.

Raising his head, Kang looked me in the eye, nodded and asked me doubtfully: "Do you really want to go to the Forty-Second Regiment?"

"I heard it will soon become a livestock farm. I previously worked as a vet, so I think the job suits me."

"Your name?"

"Wen Bo"

Kang tore off a sheet from a table calendar and wrote on the back: "Transfer Comrade Wen Bo to the Forty-Second Regiment."

After signing and dating it, he handed the note to Wan. We thanked him again and again before heading off to the personnel department of the Corps headquarters. In the office, a clerk took a look at the note, filled out a letter of transfer, stamped it and handed it back to me.

I took the priceless letter in my hand with deference and walked excitedly back to the hostel. Inside my room, I read it over and over. This was the sweet fruit of much thought and effort. With Wan's help, I had finally secured a suitable position that put me in a place about a thousand kilometres closer to Beijing, a place where I would enjoy ample space of manoeuvre. I was finally out of Shatou.

I owed my success to Wan and Deputy Commander-in-Chief Kang. Now that they have passed away, I want to pay great tribute to them here for their help.

Chapter 36

Farewell to Little Black

The procedure for getting approval to be transferred from the Corps headquarters to a company was usually very long. It could take several months. But in that period before the Corps was to be disbanded, everything seemed to happen quickly and easily. After I had submitted all the necessary paperwork, my company gave prompt approval for my departure. It was now time to say goodbye to my comrades-in-arms.

A few days later, a farewell feast was held in my honour in a large room of an adobe brick house on the stud farm. It was actually no more than a simple meal around a brick table covered in newspapers in the centre of the room. My colleagues at the horse-keeping squad were all there. The dishes set around us included stewed chicken, scrambled eggs with tomato and braised Chinese cabbage with vinegar, and there was a cup of alcohol in front of everyone. It took me several days just to prepare for such a simple meal. I first sorted out all of my old clothes, then went to Shatou village nearby to trade them for eggs, live chickens and linseed oil, and finally went to a small grocery store to buy two bottles of spirits. Several good cooks among us offered to help. Since the time Corps soldiers started leaving Shatou one by one, several parties of this nature had been held. Before long, all of the soldiers would be gone from Shatou. It was just a matter of time. Many of my comrades-in-arms were able to go to their chosen destinations such as Beijing, Hangzhou, Tianjin or Hohhot, without any hassle. Being able to settle down in a suburb of Hohhot was no big deal because I was still part of the Corps. So in other people's eyes, my departure did not merit ostentatious celebration. We were merely finding an excuse to eat and drink.

I had lived in Shatou for six years, in what should have been the best years of my life, and I was fed up with the place. This is a time for school and learning and for building up skills, but I spent them toiling in the salty fields and on the desolate steppe. Now, on the threshold of my departure, the hardest part about leaving Shatou would be parting from Little Black.

When the meal was over, I walked over to Little Black, combed her hair and placed a beautiful saddle on her back. Still tipsy, I put on my boots and led the horse around the stud farm before jumping on her back. Within seconds, she was galloping in the endless wilderness, kicking up clouds of dust.

After covering about four kilometres, we came to a town called Pangsan that we used to visit. On arriving there, I dismounted and threw the reins on her saddle, whereupon she followed me silently to a small restaurant. I tethered Little Black, went into the restaurant to buy a kilogram of Chinese pancakes and moved her to a stone trough nearby, where I took off her bit, unfastened her belly band, tore up the pancakes and spread them out in the trough. Little Black sniffed at the food and took a questioning look before diving in. It had been quite a while since she last travelled with me and had such delicious food. She did not know this would be the last time we had an excursion together and the last good meal I would give her.

I stood beside Little Black and watched her greedily munching the pancakes. Tears fell onto my clothes, as well as on the pancakes and Little Black's nose. She was always sensitive to my tears because she understood my frailty. Always a good reader of my feelings, she sensed something troubling must have happened every time I cried. She looked stunned as she raised her head. Alert, she tried to touch my face with her mouth. After sniffing me, she stuck out her tongue and licked away the tears on my face. I put my arms around her neck and wept uncontrollably…

The four-kilometre dirt road from Shatou to Pangsan was quite flat. A homebound horse needs no whipping. I had no way of knowing whether Little Black had sensed my imminent departure from Shatou, perhaps never to return to the region. But she let me ride her for as long as I wished. Maybe she wanted to provide a memory. Quite soon, she shot forth like an arrow, galloping for all her worth.

I arched my back slightly and pushed out my rear. My booted feet set firmly in the stirrups, I balanced in time with the tempo of her movement. The way she accelerated gave me the sense that she was determined that I should remember her racing potential through this last ride. She leapt several metres in the air as her belly brushed against the grass tips. Her tread was steady and firm, and the sound of her hooves reverberated between heaven and earth. I could feel the wind against my ears. Obviously, Little Black wanted to give me a stimulating time. She wanted me to bear in mind that she was a real swift horse on the steppe.

Back at the stud farm, Little Black was sweating all over. In order to mark our farewell, she had run a desperate race, which made me feel guilty. I used a stiff bristle brush to comb her repeatedly until her wet coat glistened. Early the next morning, I would leave Shatou.

I decided to have a last stroll with her on the salty land, on what would be our last night together.

I took off the bridle to let her follow me like a dog. The night was lit by the moon and the stars, and a cooling wind dispelled my sadness and gloom. Little Black raised her head and kept neighing, her melodious whinnies spreading far and wide, as if she were singing a song for me to remember forever.

I recalled all the ups and downs I had experienced with Little Black over the years. Without her companionship, it would have been so hard to exist in that desolate village where she had been both my companion and spiritual pillar. The kind of love and friendship that existed between us might be hard to fathom for the average person. In an age when there was an absence of human love, this special love filled the void in my heart and made it possible for me to endure hardships. When Yue left me, it was Little Black who kept me from falling apart. I even saw her as the embodiment of Yue, my first love. It was she who saved me when I fell into that deep pit. It was she who had delivered me from suicidal thoughts after I had failed in the national college entrance exam. For my part, I had saved Little Black when she was almost dying of constipation and when she was in a critical condition because of her obstructed labour.

But now, the hour of parting had arrived. In the silent night, I once again hugged Little Black's neck and burst into tears. She began to fidget and give out loud whinnies that blended with my cries, resonated in the wilderness and shook heaven and earth. They sounded like invocations for blessings from above at a time of parting.

A horse like Little Black, so sensitive to human emotions, must have perceived our imminent separation because she suddenly got in front of me and blocked my way back, in an obvious attempt to spend more time with me. She stood still before me without her halter on, as if she wanted me to ride on her bare back. She started ambling in a steady fashion. Silence reigned again, the only sound being the rustling of leaves in the gentle breeze. As winter was approaching, the broad and boundless grassland had lost its verdancy. At that moment, a sad song sprung from my heart, rang in my ears and rippled out to the grassland of late autumn.

> I took Little Black to the endless grassland,
> I recalled how our days turned into months, seasons and years.
> She dispelled my loneliness and bitterness,
> She accompanied me through the trials of life,
> She helped me pull through the traumas of youth,
> She taught me true love of this world.

> Little Black, you are my dark beauty!
> Your long black hair is so shiny.
> You are the moon in the sky,
> You are the running stream on the ground,
> You are the swift one on the grassland,
> You are the goddess of my heart.

> I rode Little Black out in the wilderness,
> Recalling the wonderful time we spent together.
> My heart is filled with grief and sadness.
> I am all tears at this sad hour,
> When indelible memories flood my heart.

> Little Black, you are my dark beauty!
> Your long black hair is so shiny.
> You are the moon in the sky,

You are a living stream on the ground,
You are the swift one on the grassland,
You are the goddess of my heart.

Epilogue

My life was transformed after I left Shatou and Little Black. Thanks to help from friends, the Forty-Second Regiment did indeed become a springboard from which I returned to Beijing in less than a year. In 1977, when I was waiting for a job assignment from the neighbourhood committee, I was just in time to sit the national college entrance exam. I passed and got admitted to the Beijing University of Chinese Medicine. Two years after graduation, I went to graduate school in the US. I then returned to China and established my own cancer research centre, setting the stage for research into a nontoxic approach to cancer treatment. So in a sense, I am quite established in my career.

I married a beautiful, capable and kind-hearted woman. The way we met and the experiences we went through could be the subject of another book, so I won't go into detail here. I must thank my wife for giving birth to our daughter who grew up to be a film actress and who resembles a movie star whom I used to adore. However glamorous my life and career may seem today, I can never forget the hardships I suffered in those times, nor the love between me and Little Black that was no different in many ways to the love between humans. I missed Little Black in all my quiet moments. Memories of her were so strong that I felt compelled to return to Inner Mongolia with my family thirty years later in order to find out the whereabouts and ultimate fate of Little Black.

My daughter loved horses when she was a child. Horses were quite rare in central Beijing but near my home in Deshengmenwai was a garden where people liked to feed birds that provided a temporary home for two tiny ponies that were about my daughter's height. My daughter quickly became attached to them and they got on well. She busied herself pulling up weeds for them to eat and she would often play with them for hours on end. From then on, she begged me to take her to the bird garden every day, to see the ponies rather than the birds. Eventually though, the ponies were taken away, and she failed to see any sign of them on two consecutive occasions. She lost interest in the garden and missed the ponies so badly that she looked as if she were lovesick.

Because I had so much close contact with horses, I could easily understand my daughter's sense of loss. So I drove dozens of kilometres to a suburban riders' club in Beijing to look for horses. The club offered a range of recreational activities, including swimming, table tennis and bowling. But my daughter's sole interest was horses. And the way she endeared herself to them was quite similar to how I befriended Little Black. She kept hand-feeding the horses with weeds pulled up from the ground. Tired and hungry after being ridden by visitors all day, these horses were now being treated with greens. So, much to my daughter's amusement, they were eager to please her. I soon found in my daughter a faithful listener to my stories about Little Black. She was so captivated that she wanted to see horses in Inner Mongolia during a summer holiday. That suited me because I always wanted to know how Little Black had fared after I left. That was ten years ago, when the Corps was celebrating its thirty-fifth anniversary. It was also the thirtieth year after I had parted from Little Black. That year, many educated youths were paying nostalgic visits to their former places of work in the countryside, and we joined them on the journey. We left as a family without bothering to secure sleeping-berth train tickets.

On a sultry summer day, we pushed onto an overcrowded train full of vendors, peddlers and migrant workers. The air in the carriage was very poor, reminding me of that epic journey over thirty years ago when, as soon as the train pulled into the station, passengers getting on and off the train crammed together at the gates and on the platforms. I found an open window to push my luggage through before clambering up and throwing myself in. By the time the train started moving, I had already found a seat. This gave me a sense of superiority over those who had failed to get on board.

We found a Mongolian yurt dozens of kilometres from Hohhot and fulfilled our great desire to ride horses. The vast grassland and fresh air reminded me of my youth and my six years' companionship with horses. I began to miss Little Black as a surge of sentimentality overtook me. What had happened to her after I left the Corps? That was thirty years ago, when Little Black was five. She would be thirty-five now if she was still alive.

Would she have survived human cruelty and pragmatism when she became old and no longer useful?

Where could Little Black be now? Was she still alive? How many offspring did she have? I was certain Little Black would have had more than one foal. She could have many descendants by now. I had seen for myself how a mare that had given birth to eight ponies was able to get pregnant again. What I really wanted to know was whether Little Black had given birth to a truly swift horse.

In Urat Front banner, Inner Mongolia, we found Xue Wenhe, known as Vet Xue, who used to work at the regimental veterinarian centre. He was an official at the banner's Bureau of Animal Husbandry before retiring and was now working as a vet again. After I told him the purpose of my visit, he personally took us to Wuliangsu lake in the hope of finding some herds of horses, but we saw no sign of any.

"Nowadays, people are very pragmatic," he said. "Horses are not as fast as motorcycles but cost a lot more. So modern means of transport have replaced carriages and riding horses. Horses are very hard to come by now."

I was anxious to know what happened to all those horses that my company was keeping and especially where Little Black was.

Don't go there," Xue said with a deep sigh. "It was a tumultuous time when the Corps was disbanded. Some people took advantage of the situation to try to make a fortune. They brought in a bunch of horse dealers from nowhere who bought almost all of the horses at bargain prices. They were sent to the inner provinces by train and got slaughtered for meat that was shipped and sold in Japan. The poorer quality meat was minced and sold locally in China."

I could sit still no more. I felt spasms of pain in my heart and the bulging of the veins on my face. Could Little Black have...?

Seeing the change of expression on my face, Xue quickly changed the topic of conversation. "But Little Black was much luckier. A cavalry regiment stationed about a hundred kilometres from here sent people over to buy Kabarda horses from us, and they were particularly interested in younger mares. Little Black must have been chosen. She will have joined the cavalry."

I heaved a deep sigh of relief and my heart was set at ease.

"As an army horse," Xue continued, "Little Black's main duty would be to breed. If she gave birth to a pony a year, she would have bred more than ten ponies by now. I hear the place where she was taken is no longer a cavalry base. The horses there are now used for shooting films."

These words gave me comfort. It was such a relief to know Little Black had found a good home. I firmly believe that her amazing racing genes must have been passed on down the generations. I decided to pay close attention to movies produced in China that featured running horses. All those that resembled Little Black could be her descendants.

A horse's average life expectancy is between thirty and thirty-five years. Only a few horses can live past sixty. Since it's been forty years since I left Little Black, she would be forty-five now if she were still alive. Could she indeed be alive? It's very unlikely. In fact, I have given up all hope, but I still miss Little Black from time to time, especially during the year of the horse. Apart from dedicating this book to her, I would sometimes fantasise about riding her again in my blue jeans across wide expanse.

My wife knows how much I love Little Black. She created a fantastic electronic picture of me on Little Black. I had it enlarged and printed and framed two copies of it. One is on my desk at home, and the other on the office desk in my clinic. I want it to accompany me when I write and treat patients. Little Black accompanied me during the hardest times of my life, and she gave me strength, courage, true love and good luck. I want her to continue to be there for the rest of my life.